"Doc is truly an American icon. *There and Back Again: Stories from a Combat Navy Corpsman* chronicles his legacy and impact on our country, which will live on for generations to come. He is a man for others in the purest form, which is shown through these stories."

—JUSTIN SPEIER, USMC Veteran and Former MLB Player

"Doc Jacobs' memoir, *There and Back Again: Stories from a Combat Navy Corpsman*, of his tumultuous upbringing, reasons for joining the world's greatest navy, his time serving as a Fleet Marine Force corpsman, and his life since departing the uniformed service of this great nation is a book for everyone. You will find no self-pity here, nor is Doc looking for any. What you will read in these pages is success, failure, overcoming challenges, perseverance under the most extreme of circumstances, and a never-quit attitude regardless of what life throws at you. Everyone can take something away from this book in order to apply it to their own life . . . and you will be a better person for it."

—JUSTIN D. LEHEW, SgtMaj. USMC (Ret)

"*There and Back Again: Stories From a Combat Navy Corpsman* is a magnificent and engaging read . . . about the horrors of war, overcoming physical disabilities and still performing as a corpsman, insights into our military's command and control, and the blessings of friends, family, and life."

—BRUCE BAILEY COLONEL, USAFR, (Ret.) and Past President/CEO of Mt. Soledad National Veterans Memorial

"Doc Jacobs is an inspiration and a true American hero. His memoir, *There and Back Again,* depicts his relentless drive to conquer any obstacle in his path. His determination to succeed is superseded only by his dedication to service for others. Simply put, Doc represents the best among us."

—TOM SANTI, Former NFL Tight End and Founder of Dry Creek Partners

"*There and Back Again* chronicles the courageous journey of an American hero in his attempt to recover and rebuild from serious wounds received in combat. Doc Jacobs shares his compelling story of stubborn perseverance while navigating bureaucracy after bureaucracy with grace and humility. Doc's indomitable spirit shines through this mosaic containing a little something for everyone, including leadership lessons, lots of friendly advice, and insight into the things that really matter. This brave story is a must read for anyone leading warriors before, during, or after combat."

—TWAYNE HICKMAN, Former USMC Infantry Company Commander

"Navy Corpsman Doc Jacobs has experienced more in a few decades than most do in a whole lifetime. In his memoir, *There and Back Again,* Jacobs demonstrates his ability to persevere through incredible struggles and injustices. It's a journey that's been honored by a Bronze Star of Valor and Purple Heart. You'll never forget this story of how a hero is forged."

—CAROL VAN DEN HENDE, Award-Winning Author of *Goodbye, Orchid*

There and Back Again:
Stories from a Combat Navy Corpsman

by Doc Jacobs

ISBN 978-1-64663-127-8

Published by

 köehlerbooks™

3705 Shore Drive
Virginia Beach, VA 23455
800-435-4811
www.koehlerbooks.com

THERE AND BACK AGAIN

STORIES FROM A
COMBAT NAVY CORPSMAN

DOC JACOBS

VIRGINIA BEACH
CAPE CHARLES

DEDICATION

This book is dedicated to Adam and Aubrielle. You two are my core and my world and I love you both to the edge of the universe and back. This book is also dedicated to my 3/7 family. This book is dedicated to Van, Z, Miho, Timmy, Bob, Dr. Maz and your wonderful families. I wouldn't be who I am without you all and my love for you and our nation's heroes will never cease.

PREFACE

B efore I get into the nitty-gritty details of my time in service to the people of these United States and my short stint of service helping the people of Iraq, I would like to share some personal stories that laid my foundation of eternal strength and resiliency. My childhood is one that seems normal to some and completely messed up to others. All I know is it's in the past and has helped create who I am today.

I was born at Oak Noll Naval Hospital in Oakland, California. On a September Sunday, I became a Navy brat. Although I don't recall anything of our time in the Bay Area, I hear stories of our family of four struggling to make ends meet. My dad would collect cans and copper to turn in for recycling when he wasn't busy being a Quartermaster in the Navy. My mother stayed home with my brother and me. I've been told that I was a colicky baby and cried a ton and couldn't sleep much.

We lived in Vallejo, California, when I was born and stayed there for six months until we moved to Long Beach, California, for thirteen months. My dad was soon transferred back to the Bay Area, Alameda, for another eighteen months.

I don't recall too much before my sister was born, since I was only four years and nine months old. I recall being at the hospital when the doctors took my mom back for a C-section, or cesarean section. My memories started to become clearer as my sister grew up a bit. My brother and I used to be your typical terrors. Mom still to this day wouldn't believe it, but my brother was the leader of our shenanigans. When we would get in trouble, when we weren't spanked or paddled, we were sent to our beds. The worst was when a confession was needed for us to get out of trouble, and even though my brother was the guilty party, he would wait it out until I couldn't take the waiting any longer and confess to something I didn't do. Don't get me wrong, I would get into my fair share of trouble, but I would typically own it and take my punishment so we could move on.

When all three of us kids shared a room, my brother and I had the bunk bed and our sister had the separate bed. When we would get in trouble and were sent to our beds, I had the top bunk, and my brother would lay there and tell me how he did it and I should confess if I wanted to go back to playing. He seriously told me, at least once every couple of minutes, what he did and how I should go confess. I started to pick up on his game and waited him out to see how he liked it. This didn't work too well because he was—still is—a bookworm and loved to just lay and read for hours on end. I was the kid that wanted to get out and play, and I hated being stuck in bed, either being punished or waiting for the adults to wake up.

When we lived in town, we lived in a small apartment complex with wide and barely used streets to ride bikes on. There was a canal nearby as well. This allowed for many things to do as kids. I remember one of the neighbor kids, Ty, and I used to ride our bikes around the nearby blocks and enjoy our childhood years.

While in that apartment complex, I did some growing up and realized that I needed to be a protector of my mother and siblings. Mom was dating a guy who was verbally abusive to her, and when they fought, we were sent to our rooms. During one fight, I heard stuff being thrown around, and I went to check it out. I saw this guy throwing porcelain cookie jars at my mother. I didn't hesitate to go back to my room and sneak out the window. I ran to the local Texaco to dial 911. The officer that responded came and took me back to our apartment. He took the guy away, and life was better for a while.

I have one other memory in that apartment, and it took my brother about two decades to finally admit his wrongdoing. We were playing, and I was swinging my toy baseball bat. I had the sudden urge to poop and barely tossed the bat as I ran to the bathroom. I heard a loud crash on my way out but figured that I didn't do anything wrong. I handled my business, and Mom came flying in and ripped me off the toilet and started spanking my ass. I had no idea what was going on, but my brother told Mom that I threw the bat at the ceiling lamp and broke it. It was my word against his, and I lost that battle. In my twenties, my brother told me that he did it and felt bad that I got in trouble.

Life in the other apartment in the complex wasn't all that to write home about. Mom was with my now stepfather. I recall a few things from that apartment. We would watch *Tales from the Crypt,* and we had a little pool in the back where my brother tortured my sister and me in. I tried coffee for the first time, I tried beer for the first time, and I even encountered Child Protective Services (commonly known as CPS) for the first time. They came to the apartment more than once. I recall there being a stun gun and being threatened with it. We even got beaten with a paddle, one my dad made on a ship that said my name on one side and my brother's on the other. I remember that paddle was engraved and burned with our names. When our sister got the paddle, it seemed like she was not exempt from one side or the other. It didn't matter what we were hit with: wooden spoon, paddle, belt, wooden back scratcher, flyswatter . . . etc.

When CPS was to show up, we were told that we were to be on our best behavior and to not tell them certain things "or else." We never wanted to find out what the "or else" meant. So we were dressed up like we were going to the finest church and Jesus was set to be the guest speaker.

Speaking of church, we'd go to church on Sunday mornings, and we weren't allowed to go into Sunday school, for the most part. We were told to sit still and keep quiet throughout the hour service. Of course, everyone appeared to be the most perfect humans on the planet while at church. Then we'd get home, and the trash talk and F-bombs started. I loved going to church because I heard about how to "love thy neighbor" and "do unto others," basic moral compass guidelines. I also hated going to church because it felt like we were being judged by others, and then when church was over, it was back to the hate-filled house.

We lived in town until shortly after my maternal grandmother passed away in a car accident. Soon after, we moved up in the hills in a cabin near the family. This cabin was small and only had one bedroom and one bathroom. My brother, sister, and I slept in the bedroom, and our mother and stepfather stayed out in the main area. We ate TV tray dinners and played outside a lot. I began to venture out and hike around the mountains to escape the tight living quarters and the abuse. Two memories that I have from that place are my stepfather going to jail and receiving calls from the county jail. I can't recall why he went to jail, but I do remember the collect calls coming in and going to see him in the county jail.

This cabin, a temporary home for us, sat across the road from our family's many acres of land that reside in the high desert about an hour east of Bakersfield. Our family's land was literally at the end of the blacktop. The property was all dirt road and could be a pain throughout the many seasons. In the summer months, the roads would be just as hard as the blacktop roads, and the winters brought the slippery mud. It was either fast fun for bikes or slam on your brakes and skid for as long as you could without crashing.

We used to have one of those red wagons with the handle that steered at the front. After watching the movie *Cool Runnings*, we would run and ride in the wagon down whatever hill we could. Only we would put our sister in the front so when we crashed into the bush, she was the one that went flying into the bushes.

You may be asking where my dad was during all of this. He was out to sea and was granted thirty days and every other Christmas for his custody of my brother and me. This was the time that I counted down for. This was my escape from Mom and that environment. I felt a ton of guilt because my brother and I would be leaving for thirty days and would be leaving our sister behind and really unsure of what she would encounter. All I could really think about was how that made her feel to see us leave and then how she felt when we came back. I never really thought that she'd harbor any resentment toward us because she always seemed happy to see us, but it may have been more of a comforting excitement.

Again, I was told that I had better not spout off about home life. Or else. We were driven to Los Angeles International Airport (more commonly referred to as LAX) to meet Dad. That drive seemed to drag on. We'd then fly to Ohio for our thirty days with Dad's side of the family. This was a completely different environment. I was allowed to be up early and able to play and even work on my grandparents' small farm in the mornings. This was an environment of love and nurturing. Granted, my grandmother (I referred to her as G-Ma), my grandfather, or Dad wouldn't hesitate to discipline when needed, but it was evenly distributed. When we would call Mom, I hated talking on the phone and disrupting my time with Dad and his side of the family. My brother would report every single move I made, and I would get into trouble in Ohio and when I would get back to Mom.

I would spend my days in Ohio with freedom and fear. I dreaded the days we'd return to Mom's because I knew I would be in trouble for something, and I even lived in fear of the "or else." These fears were valid when someone you lived with pulled a gun on your grandfather or told you how he "knows how to make people disappear." These fears were not just for me but for other family members.

While with Mom, I was never allowed to talk to Dad on the phone alone. I had to sit at the table on the phone with the cord while either my stepfather or Mom listened in on the other line. This was either another intimidation factor or another way to strip me of freedoms. Any letter that I sent out had to be in an envelope that wasn't sealed so it could be read before being mailed. All the while, there was constant trash talk about Dad and his part in my parents divorcing. I knew early on that parents shouldn't be talking about the other in a negative light to, or in front of, their children. This always annoyed me because I loved my dad and knew that he was working hard to provide for my brother and me. When we were with Dad, he never spoke an ill word of our mother. He would always say things like, "I am just grateful for you boys, and I love your mother for giving me healthy and smart boys."

I wish I had more time with my father while growing up, but I knew that he was always out to sea doing his job as Quartermaster (or ship's navigator) in the Navy. Out of twenty years in the Navy, he spent thirteen years of it out to sea. So when my mother, or anyone else, would talk trash about him never being around, I remind anyone of this fact. Obviously, it is hard for people to understand that my father wished every day to be with us, but he was trying to provide for my brother and me.

I would try to sneak letters to Dad to let him know what was really going on so he could act and fight for us. I asked him later on in life why he never came to fight for us, and he looked at me with a puzzled face. I told him about the letters, but he told me that he never received them. He was torn up when I told him a lot of what happened growing up. I told him that it didn't matter now because it was all in the past and it was a building block for my life's foundation.

Throughout my years of growing up, my mom and stepfather fought a lot. I can't tell you how many times I glued the phone back together or how many times I played Nintendo with my sister just to be in her room to protect her. As I got older, I stepped between my mom and stepfather. I was then choked with the phone cord. Apparently, that was enough for Mom. The next day, we took our time getting home, and I knew something wasn't right. When we got home, he wasn't there. My mother then explained why.

After my stepfather was transferred to a prison, for the duration of his sentencing, we would travel out through the desert and down to the prison in Norco. In all honesty, I felt bad that he was in there and was with hardened criminals, but what was in the past should stay there. My mother stuck by his side, and he was released into a halfway house in Bakersfield. During those few years, we felt at ease around the house. Mom worked crazy hours to make ends meet, and she did a damn fine job at making things happen.

My stepfather soon landed a great job and was doing really well with his second chance that he had. Mom soon worked less and seemed less stressed as well. My stepfather was working his ass off and making good money, all the while making a name for himself in the construction business. He had a company truck and a company card and was traveling all over the country as a foreman on various job sites. The company liked him so much that they would fly my mom to him for long weekends. Those were the best times. We felt like a regular family, and things were looking up.

That all changed just a few short years later, around my sixteenth birthday. I am unsure of what happened or why it happened, but my stepfather worked less and less and had to return the company truck and card. Things soon returned back to the way they were before, but they seemed worse. I am sure it seemed worse because my knowledge of life was expanding and I would hear people talk.

I was in high school and was being severely bullied but not by anyone at school. I was being bullied by those within my own home. I was constantly told that I was stupid and that I'd never amount to anything in life. I shrugged this off as much as I could to show that they couldn't get to me. I did my chores and tried to keep my same scowled face around my family. That didn't really do much except cause more trouble. The constant verbal and mental beatings continued for years.

I had one instance in middle school where I got bad grades and tested my mom. She told me that she'd hold me back a grade. I called her bluff, and sure enough, I found myself repeating the sixth grade. That didn't hurt as bad as what my father had to say.

I have always taken my father's word as gold and may value it way more than the worth of gold. Needless to say, when I was called to the table to speak to him on the phone, after proudly boasting my bad grades and not caring because "I was going in the military," I was very nervous. I was more nervous about the situation because of the look on my mother's face, which seemed to have this evil tick to it. Normally, she was never excited about talking to my father or having us speak to him. This day was different.

I lifted the phone off the receiver and was shocked to hear Dad on the other end. This wasn't a long or pleasant conversation. I was expecting to hear him say something along the lines of, "I heard you got bad grades, and I am going to blister your ass when I see you again." I would have welcomed that over what I heard next.

He said in a soft and ever-so-sincere voice, "Son, I will tell you right now that the Navy doesn't want stupid people. They only want the smart people, so pick up your grades and you'll be one of those smart people." This was a conversation that changed my whole world. I was bawling when we said our goodbyes, but I promised him I'd be one of those smart people.

The second go-around in the sixth grade was a better one. I seemed to make friends fairly quickly and realized that I had a new selection of girls to be "boyfriend-girlfriend" with. Although it seemed to help ease the shame of being held back, it didn't do much for watching my "old" friends as they advanced and I had to start anew.

I had my issues with home life and tried to not let it interfere with my school and social life. I say this, but looking back, it really did, and I am glad that my social life as an adult wasn't hindered by my social disadvantages growing up.

I was hardly ever allowed to go hang out with friends or do anything fun like any other kid was doing growing up. I was always grounded for one thing or another. It seemed like I would be grounded for having a "look on my face" or a "tone in my voice." Eventually, I would stop asking to do things or go anywhere. It came to the point where it felt like I was isolated with school privileges.

After my grandmother's passing, my grandfather moved into a new place on the family's property, and we moved into his old place. This adjustment was an easy one, seeing as it was fairly close. We moved in and began a life on the side of a mountain in the southern Sierra Nevada Mountain Range. This allowed for me, and my isolation, to set my mind at ease, and I did much thinking and dreaming while hiking around. I would spend my days running mountainous trails, climbing rocks, or just hiking.

I am not here to air out dirty laundry and call people out, even though some may see it as that, but I am sharing my story and am sharing parts that are important to show how I have never had it easy and how I have dealt with it my whole life. Having said that, I have never had the luxury of not having my dirty laundry aired out and for everyone to know about it. I have made mistakes in my life, but we all make mistakes and screw up. I regret any pain or hurt that I have brought to folks throughout my time on this earth, but we have processed them and have since moved past. Even in doing so, I still live with the guilt and will take it to my grave.

Growing up and having your medical business put on blast and to be laughed at for it is not okay by any means. I was shamed for having a condition that my mother didn't believe was possible. In her disbelief, she shared it with everyone, and I was laughed at for it, and she blamed it on my father.

One day, I was asked why the toilet was always so dirty. I told my mother that it's because I pee in "V" shape and I thought I had two pee holes. She went hysterical with laughter and told me that it was impossible. This was something I couldn't just show to her but asked her to trust me and take me to the doctor. She absolutely refused and instead went and told just about everyone we knew. The laughter lasted years. This ended after I went to see a urologist in the Navy, and they said it was completely possible and fixed the problem. What had happened was when I was forming as a human, I had an extra piece of tissue that split my urethra and, in short, caused a "V" shape when I excreted urine.

Another incident happened one day when I was a teenager and out hiking the hills and came back for supper before dark. I did a quick shakedown for bugs, especially ticks. I apparently didn't do that great of a job and had one that had latched on my left pectoral muscle. I didn't realize it had latched until later that night. At this point, the tick was already burrowed in, and I had to get tweezers to pull it out. My goodness did it cause some pain. It was pain like I was punched in the chest during a sparring match with a boxer.

I didn't think anything of it until I noticed a yellowish ring around the bite site. I went and talked to a teacher, and they sent me home. My aunt Charity took me to the pediatrician. This infuriated my mother and stepfather and caused a ruckus between them and my aunt, but I know my aunt was doing what was best for me. This was another cause for my medical business to be put out for everyone to laugh at me some more. We would be sitting around, and all I would hear was, "Hey, Mr. Lyme Disease! Get me a soda." Then everyone would laugh. I would hear, out in public, mind you, "Mr. Lyme Disease, go to aisle six and get some candy bars."

Those two instances had nothing on one key instance that almost altered my whole life. I was seventeen years old, and I acquired a nasty ingrown toenail on my right big toe. I told Mom, "I think it's bad, and I need to go to the doctor and have them do it."

I was immediately yelled at by my stepfather. "That's a f-ing stupid idea. Here, I can take it out myself with a knife and some needle-nose plyers."

I told him, "No, this hurts, and I think it's already infected, and I need to go to the doctor."

He said, "If you don't let me take it out, you sure as hell ain't going to no doctor."

I said, "Fine! I'll f-ing live with it until my whole f-ing foot rots off from infection."

Months later, I moved in with my aunt Sheila and uncle Tim—that caused a huge fight, and we will get into that momentarily—and my aunt took me to the doctor at the nearest Naval Base, Port Hueneme. It had gotten so bad that my toe was constantly oozing blood and puss. When I would take off my shoe and sock, the room immediately smelled.

The doctor at the Naval Clinic, who cared for me, was astonished and pissed all at the same time. He put me on some antibiotics to help with the infection and swelling. He told me to leave my sock off as much I could to help air it out and not let the infection have a warm, moist environment to grow in. He also took some x-rays to ensure it wasn't down to the bone.

The doctor came back into the exam room and pulled up the x-ray. He said, "It looks like the infection hasn't spread to the bone, but I can't be too sure. I would have to wait for the radiologist's report, and even then, only a surgery can ensure that with one hundred percent certainty."

I asked, "What would surgery entail? What would happen if there is an infection in the bone?"

He responded, with a semi-puzzled face, "There are a few outcomes, and the most severe two are that we have to shave down some bone or even amputate the toe."

My immediate response was, "Can I still join the military with only nine toes?"

With a solemn face, he simply said, "No. You need all digits to pass the physical."

This was some seriously tough news for me to handle, but I knew that things would be all right and I would live my life to the fullest, regardless of this outcome. That mindset didn't help my feelings toward my mom, my stepfather, or the hell I was still living.

Let's backtrack to before I moved in with Aunt Sheila and Uncle Tim and visit some memories of why they had decided to help me move and to give me a second chance at life.

As you now know, it seemed like I was always being grounded or never allowed to do anything. I was constantly belittled and verbally beaten down. As I grew older, it seemed like my time with my father grew shorter. I was sixteen, not yet seventeen, and my brother had moved out. My grandmother bought a plane ticket for me to go to Ohio to spend the summer with her and my father. I knew deep down that I would not be "allowed" to go without my brother to be there to watch my every move. I told my great-grandfather and my grandfather about this plane ticket and expressed my concerns. They both reassured me that my mother would be fine and to just be honest with her.

I brought the email confirmation with the flight itinerary. She took it from me and told me, "No! What the hell are you thinking? That you're going to just leave and never come back?"

Although leaving and never returning crossed my mind many times per day, I knew that Dad and my grandmother would get into trouble, and I'd never put them in such a situation. I responded, "No, but my dad does still have custody rights, and I have every right to go see him."

She took the paper and said, "I will take care of this!"

I never did get on the plane to see Dad. Between my brother's high school graduation and my high school graduation, I never really was allowed to speak to my father, let alone able to see him. I spoke to my grandmother years later, and she said she never received any sort of refund for the "cancelled" tickets. We may never know where that money ever ended up, but the principle of it wasn't good. One thing that I do know is that, if I was to not be on a flight back to Mom when scheduled, she would have notified local authorities and charged Dad with kidnapping, as she said she would have many times.

This incident landed me on "restriction" until "further notice." I knew what that meant: I was to basically finish out my time as a youth being grounded. Sure enough, that was what happened. The only fun I was to have was chores and errands.

Prior to my grandfather's sixtieth birthday, he was diagnosed with esophageal cancer. This news brought many more family members to celebrate his sixtieth and what would be his last birthday with us. His birthday was mid-June 2003. I was not yet eighteen and entering my senior year of high school. I was on "restriction" and was not allowed to do anything but the aforementioned chores and errands.

Of the big group of family members that attended my grandpa's sixtieth birthday celebrate were Uncle Tim, Aunt Sheila, their three kids, and Uncle Mike. They fully enjoyed their dirt bikes, and when they brought them up, I did as well. The chances of them bringing the dirt bikes up was fairly great because of the time of year and the amount of time to ride.

The birthday celebration arrived, and we all went over to Grandpa's house to be with him and show him our love and to celebrate his sixty years of life. When we arrived and everyone else was there, it was well known that I was grounded and to not have any fun. This really ate me up because even in celebration, my business was put on blast, and no matter what the circumstance, I was to be within eye or ear shot of Mom. I was seventeen and about to turn eighteen, literally counting down the days until my day of freedom, and I was treated like a prisoner in a low-security facility.

My cousins were half-heartedly bugging Mom to let it slide and to let me have some fun for the day. She kept telling them no and wouldn't budge. I was embarrassed to be in the situation and just hung my head in shame. I can't remember the exact reason why I was grounded, as it could have been many. I wasn't perfect and rebelled a bit against my mom and my stepfather, especially after the whole incident with not being able to see my dad and grandmother. I called phone sex lines, I stashed porn in the air vents in the house, and I just did little things that I knew would get under their skins. Looking back, I figured I did it to get any sort of reaction and as a way of saying, "You want to break the rules? I will, too, and we can either live in cooperation and peace or I can play your games!"

After the umpteenth time of one of my cousins asking my mom to let me play, she snapped! By snapped, I mean snapped! She lost it and started screaming and making a scene. This embarrassed me even further. I couldn't believe that was happening, even though it could be my grandpa's last birthday with us. She stormed off, and everyone slowly went back to what they were doing and murmured as they did. Aunt Sheila and Uncle Tim walked up to me and said, "Do you want out?"

I thought they were making light of the situation and trying to make me feel better by asking me a rhetorical question. "Of course I want out," I half-jokingly said, thinking whatever could be followed up on their end could be too good to be true.

To my surprise, they said, "We can help you out and can develop a plan."

I was seriously taken aback by the offer but super excited and was already eager to hear the plan.

There are one hundred seven days between my grandfather's birthday and mine. Their plan gave us around three-and-a-half months to plan. I was even more shocked by how fast they wanted to set the plan into motion. They said, "At least one of us will be coming up a few times before your birthday. Each time we come up, we will take a bag of yours down with us. Go get a bag now and we will start today."

While everyone was at the party, I ran home and packed a bag and threw it in their truck before anyone saw what I was doing. The rest of the party was uneventful, but my excitement level was through the ceiling. I knew I had to contain the excitement and keep up my same old routine; otherwise, they'd be on to me. To help conceal my excitement, I would do extra chores or would do hundreds of push-ups and sit-ups in my room. I would go for long runs to burn off the energy and to pass time.

Every time my aunt or one of my uncles came up, I would sneak a bag into their vehicles. One of the most difficult parts of planning my escape was when I started school. I started my senior year at one high school knowing damn well that I was not going to finish the year there. I felt so sad about leaving. I had friends there that took me in when I was held back in the sixth grade that I had been friends with since. That tore me up as bad as leaving my sister behind. I knew I had to leave in order to better myself. If it wasn't for the opportunity of leaving on my eighteenth birthday, I was going to leave for the military as soon as I graduated, anyway.

Every day that I went to school, I was packing an extra pair of clothes and anything else I could to make it not seem too suspicious. My locker soon filled up, and some of my good friends let me put some stuff in their lockers. I knew they were sad about knowing I'd soon be leaving, but they knew I needed to get out to be a better version of me. I am forever grateful for their help, and I hope they read this and know how much I appreciate them.

Throughout the summer, I almost got caught. Well, I did, but it was followed by threats and being grounded. I wrote a letter to my aunt thanking her for the opportunity and for helping me out. It was intercepted, like every letter was. When the threats were being hurled, I brushed them off and stood there shaking my head while being told, "You aren't going anywhere! You're keeping your ass right here until you graduate."

That confirmed all of my suspicions that my dad and grandma never received any letters the years prior. The various threats, bargaining, intimidation, and rationalizing just fueled my fire to leave. While all these things were being said, shouted, and pleaded, I was in deep thought. I was thinking, *Why would I stay? I have an infected ingrown toenail and am being denied medical care. My medical business is put on display for their amusement. I've been accused of doing drugs, and my room is periodically torn apart because they swear I am a druggie, even though I am never out of their sight. My stepfather does projects at two o'clock in the morning while I am in the middle of finals. I am abused. I am always told that I'm stupid and will never amount to anything in life. Why? Why stay and knowingly subject myself to more of that? Why stay when I have an incredible chance to go somewhere and start fresh and be the best version of me?*

The day of my eighteenth birthday finally arrived. I went about my morning like I normally would, and I remember that the car ride seemed to take forever. I sat in the backseat and let my sister ride in the front while I took in the sights one last time. I would occasionally look in the rearview mirror and look at my eyes, and I could finally see peace and happiness in them. I felt like a big dark cloud was being lifted off of me, and I could finally see true freedom and peace within.

I remember Mom dropping us off, and she said a quick happy birthday. I acknowledged it and began to head in. I pretended like I was heading to class to not give my hand away. I walked to the bathroom, and then, when I saw the coast was clear, I went into my counselor's office and requested a meeting. I told her, "I want to sign myself out of school." When I saw her puzzled face, I said, "I want to unenroll. I am leaving the valley and will be going to another school." She was shocked by this news and advised me that I may not get into another school so easy and may not even graduate on time. I thanked her for her concern, but I was done.

She handed me the paperwork, and we signed the documents. She said that she wasn't going to lie to my mom if she asked. I told her to not worry and that I would take care of it. Once the paperwork was done and I was officially unenrolled, I went to my friends' lockers; they were sad to see me going but helped me out to my waiting Uncle Mike. He was a bit anxious about hanging out for too long. I hurried up, and we headed out of the valley without turning back.

When we were about an hour away from the house, Uncle Mike handed me his cell phone and told me I needed to call my mom and tell her. I was a bit nervous about it but knew it needed to be done, especially before she went to pick me up and I wasn't there. I dialed and anxiously awaited the answer with every ring. She answered, and I told her, "Don't worry about picking me up from school." When she angrily questioned why, I told her, "I won't be there. Today or any other day. I moved out."

At this point, she was pissed and said, "I knew you and your dad had this worked out all along!"

As much as I would have loved that, it wasn't the case, and I responded, "My dad? No, I am moving in with Uncle Tim, Aunt Sheila, and Uncle Mike."

She screamed in the phone so loud that Uncle Mike heard what she said very clearly: "Happy fucking birthday, you little bastard!"

I wasn't surprised by that response, but everyone else was, and this solidified any doubts they had for helping me out.

It took a few days to get into the new high school, and their standards were higher than my previous school. That meant taking six classes and an elective. I knew it would be tough, but I knew I could get it done and graduate on time with my new classmates.

Soon after being enrolled and starting out fresh, in the middle of my senior year, I had to get my toe fixed as well. It seemed like I had a lot of work ahead of me, but I knew it would be worth it in the long run. My main goal was to work hard, help out around the house, and stay out of trouble. That was all easy to do because I was taken in and treated right. I had no need to rebel or feel fear. Granted, I was not a kid and never got a chance to be a kid, but I wasn't going to ruin my one shot, and I wanted to show my family how grateful I was for them giving me a chance.

I enjoyed doing chores because I got to happily do them in good company. We would have weekend *Halo* parties, and I was able to ride dirt bikes on our trips with freedom. I was able to be me and not feel judged or to feel afraid of anything. I was happy, and it showed.

One time, we all went to visit my grandfather in the hospital before his passing. My mom and stepfather were there, and I could feel the evil glares from across the room. I heard my stepfather ask me, "Why do you look like that? You don't have a scowl on your face. Why?" I just got up and left the waiting room and went to sit in the truck. I was upset that I knew my grandfather's time was extremely short, and this was how I had to spend it with him. I didn't want to stir the pot or be treated badly for the decision that I made to better myself. I did get some quality time with my grandfather before his passing and will always be grateful for that.

I learned so much from living with Uncle Tim, Aunt Sheila, their kids, and Uncle Mike. I learned the value of hard work, attention to detail, not half-assing anything, giving others a chance, understanding things from another's perspective, and appreciating the value of family. Uncle Tim congratulated me when I graduated from high school by saying, "Congratulations. Now, get a job and pay rent or get out of my house." I was soon off to Ohio to sit down with a Navy recruiter and my dad.

Once back in Ohio, I started speaking with a recruiter while I was finishing up a task that my grandma gave me. She told me I wasn't allowed to run off and join the Navy without sending out my thank-you cards from my graduation first. During this time, I had begun the process of enlistment. It's a fairly lengthy process but not too bad. Just a lot of waiting around.

I did the whole DEP (Delayed Entry Program) qualification book in two weeks and was granted E-2 right out of boot camp. My dad, however, being a former Navy recruiter, sat down with this recruiter and made sure I wasn't about to do something I'd regret for the next some-odd years. We all shook hands and enjoyed a few laughs over some coffee, and he assured us all that I would get what I wanted.

Little did I know that, once you sign the actual contract at MEPS (Military Entrance Processing Station), the recruiter has no say in what jobs are available, what the needs of the Navy are, or if you are going to get that job. So once it came to pick my desired job, they told me Corpsman wasn't available but, because I scored high in electronics, I could be an aviation electrician or, seeing as I scored high in mechanics, I could go off and be an aviation mechanic. I looked at that person and said, "Can I make a phone call?"

He said, "Yes."

I called Dad, and he gave me some advice. When I hung up, I looked at the Navy personnel guy, then at the computer, then at the door, and said, "If I don't get HM (the Navy's rate for Corpsman) with FMF (Fleet Marine Force) and a sign-on bonus guaranteed in writing, then I am going out that door to join the Army to be a medic." He nodded and said he'd take a look in the computer. Wouldn't ya know, a spot just opened up with guaranteed green side and a $5,000.00 bonus. *Poof*, like freaking magic. I was off to boot camp two short weeks after.

Recruit Training Command (RTC) is commonly known as Navy boot camp. RTC is located in Great Lakes, Illinois. I, as well as many others, arrived there on August 10, 2004. For the majority of us, we arrived into Chicago's O'Hare International Airport. Upon our arrival, we had to check into the USO Lounge. Once all of us checked in, we were told to break into formations and file off into the buses. We all did so without speaking, other than the few motivators shouting off, "Aye, aye," which is a Navy and Marine Corps common response for acknowledging a command or order.

For those of us who knew little about the military, we were shocked and frightened to see these monstrous military guys in their black trench coats and dark covers that revealed no facial expressions standing in the rain motionlessly, awaiting our arrival. When the doors opened, they came onto the bus, yelling for us to get off their bus. We high-tailed it into the reception area to make our quick phone calls to our families to let them know we arrived safely, we loved them, and we'd talk to them in a few weeks.

The whole night was full of processing into boot camp—the whole first week, in fact. That night, however, we were stripped of our civilian attire, and we sent it all back home. We all had fresh new haircuts, military physical fitness attire to wear around, sewing kits issued . . . etc. The Navy's physical fitness attire from when I went through boot camp in 2004 was what we called the blue berries. They were cotton sweatpants, sweatshirts, standard white cotton shirts with the Navy logo, and blue shorts to wear underneath. We were issued those to start out with while we waited for the day to get our other uniforms tailored and issued.

The whole first week was worse than the rest of boot camp. This time was known as the processing week, or P-Days. It could last more than a week depending on how long it took to form up and get everyone processed and ready for training. P-Days included things such as tailoring uniforms, issuing uniforms, getting vaccinations (this took a great deal of time due to the amount of vaccines required in the military, and you couldn't receive them all at once for a variety of medical reasons), enduring medical exams, dental exams, drug tests . . . etc. The waiting around while we all got our stuff prepared for training was the worst. I just wanted to get into training and start my naval career already, although technically I started on my arrival day.

Once we formed our divisions, we headed to our ships (barracks), and upon our arrival, we'd soon start our training. Personally, I enjoyed boot camp and didn't find it to be all that challenging. I say this because I ran track and played baseball in school, so I knew how to work as part of a team, and I was in good shape. Another reason was because my dad and some other Salt Dogs—guys who had been there and done that—told me about their boot camp along with various other military stories, so I had mentally planned for it to be like that.

Granted, I did get an upper respiratory infection and refused to go to medical until my Recruit Division Commander, or RDC, a Navy Corpsman, noticed me coughing up blood on the track during

PT (physical training). She told me that if I didn't go to medical, she would destroy me, and a URI would be the least of my worries.

During Navy boot camp, they teach you the ropes, literally and figuratively. They teach you military drill, uniform and personal appearance, marksmanship, shipboard firefighting, and a whole bunch of other good stuff. I really enjoyed my time and soaked up a bunch of knowledge, but I was getting anxious to start the next portion of training as Hospital Corpsman.

In early October 2004, I reported to Naval Hospital Corps School (NHCS) Great Lakes. Basic Corps School is an "A" school for naval training purposes. Other branches commonly refer to this phase of training as "MOS," or Military Occupational Specialty, School. Once you graduate from boot camp, you then report to, and complete, your "A," or MOS, school. From there, you can go to the fleet or to your job if it doesn't require additional training. For the majority of us docs, we go on to "C" schools. These are advanced schools for your trade. My "C" school was Field Medical Service School (FMSS) which is now called Field Medical Training Battalion (FMTB).

Once you complete your "C" school, you are given a new NEC, or Naval Enlisted Code, and are then assigned to a duty station so you may work within your new NEC. For instance, upon completion of Basic Corps School, you are assigned the NEC of 0000, or quad zero, and this is the basic rating for corpsmen. For most docs who aren't assigned a "C" school, they are then sent to a Military Treatment Facility (MTF) or clinic so they can begin their naval careers. There are a majority of us who either had Field Med guaranteed or volunteered because of the Global War on Terror. Upon completion of Field Med, we were granted our new NEC of 8404 (Field Medical Service Tech) or, as we like to call it, Green Side. Yes, by going and completing Basic Corps School and Field Med, we hold both NECs, 0000/8404.

I didn't class up on my arrival to Corps School, so I spent my days with the other PSIs (Pre-School Indoctrination) raking leaves in the cold windy days on the shores of Lake Michigan, constantly field daying (cleaning) the barracks or keeping up with our fitness by PTing. Needless to say, we were all excited to class up and think that we'd be done with those days. Nothing changed except adding a ton of classroom and studying time while taking away the minor busy work. Field day continued on, as it did throughout the Navy, as well as PT.

Corps School was some good times. I made friends with some excellent Devil Squids, and our friendships have since grown past a decade. Although the time I spent at Corps School with my buddies was great, I was again chomping at the bit to push into the next phase of training.

I was getting anxious because I would always grab the latest issue of the *Navy Times* and the *Marine Corps Times* and read about what was going on overseas on the frontlines. During my first month in Basic Corps School, one of the Marine Corps' biggest modern-day battles took place. November 7, 2004, was the beginning of the second battle for Fallujah, commonly known as Operation Phantom Fury.

As I sat in the Basic Corps School classroom and read the *Navy Times* and the *Marine Corps Times*, I was getting anxious, in a good way, about finishing up my training and getting to whatever Marine Corps unit I was to be assigned to so I could be of use in helping bring back my Marines and fellow docs. Although I knew I was going through training so I could join the ranks on the frontlines, I still felt like I was useless. The more I read, the more I wanted to be out there.

I graduated Basic Corps School in March 2005, and was placed on another grad hold for a couple of weeks while awaiting orders. This really tore at me because I had just finished "A" school only to be held back for another chunk of time. I would have been all right if I wasn't assigned to the Medical Records Department. I have nothing against that department. I was just a fresh moto boot who wanted to as much as I could to help out, and there I was . . . in the Medical Records Department.

I have a funny memory from my four weeks in that department. Share a laugh with me, won't you? First, I will have to explain one of our old working uniforms called the working blues, commonly known within the Navy ranks as "the Johnny Cashes." These uniforms were black pants that weren't loose and comfy like a pair of office slacks, a tight, long-sleeve black shirt (not your usual casual Friday Hawaiian shirt), and a necktie that had to be nice and tight according to the uniform regulations. So basically a tight black suit with no breathing room, especially in the neck.

In March 2005, I was assigned to the Medical Records Department at Great Lakes Naval Hospital. I had my Caduceus (the common symbol for medical or healing) and was now a Hospitalman Apprentice, the fancy term for a boot corpsman. After a short time of being in the records department, I answered a call at the front desk, and it was a retired Sergeant Major. He was calling about his medical record's whereabouts. I told him I would take a message and personally look for it myself and get back to him. He told me that he'd been getting that same bullcrap response for the past few months while his record had been maintained at Great Lakes Naval Hospital.

I informed him again that I would personally look for it and that I would get back to him the moment I found it. I gave him my name and rank and told him he had my word that I would find this record. I got off the phone with Sergeant Major and began my search. I knew this search would be a lengthy one seeing as it wasn't in the recently used or filed records, and the staff said he'd been calling for months now and they hadn't found it, either.

One day, I was going through the records on the lower shelves. As I searched through them one by one, I was beginning to feel lightheaded. I stood up and walked around for a bit then drank some water and got back at it. As I was kneeling there filing through these records, on my mission to honor my word to Sergeant Major, I flopped on the ground, *poof*, out cold. I had accidently choked myself out with my working blues shirt and tie. I couldn't believe that I was so fixated on the mission that I hadn't really noticed I was strangling myself.

I came too pretty quick with an HM3 helping me out and saying,

"Damn, killer! They're just medical records. You don't have to kill yourself over them."

I was sent to the emergency room to make sure I was okay. It turned out that I was super dehydrated because I was strictly drinking coffee to stay warm and awake during the wintertime in Great Lakes. I was given two IV bags and sent to the barracks for the rest of the day as SIQ (Sick in Quarters).

The next day, I returned fully hydrated and bound to find Sergeant Major's record. I didn't find it that next day or the next thirteen. I was hellbent on honoring my word and finding Sergeant Major's record that it took me about two weeks of looking through every single record in the department before finally locating it. His record jacket was wedged between two bigger records, making it look like it was part of one of the others.

When I found it, I double verified that it was his record before I even approached the front desk to make the call that I had envisioned since my promise to him. I didn't walk to the phone. No. I tucked his record jacket like a running back getting the hand-off at the goal line about to get that game-winning touchdown during the last seconds of a playoff game. I tucked and ran from the aisle of records I was in, cut left, and bolted for that endzone dance.

I excitedly dialed Sergeant Major's number. It occurred to me that I had no way of providing evidence to him without him coming in to physically sign out his record. He answered the phone, and I greeted him with, "Good morning, Sergeant Major. This is Hospitalman Apprentice Daniel Jacobs at the Great Lakes Naval Hospital's Records Department. We spoke a few weeks ago, and I promised you that I'd find your medical record."

He said, "Well, did you find it or are you wasting my time?"

"Sergeant Major, I have your record in my hand, as I promised," I replied.

"I am on my way! Don't move! Don't let any of those fucktards touch my record. You hear me?" he said.

"Aye-aye, Sergeant Major!" was all that I could muster.

Sure enough, he arrived faster than I would have expected. He walked in and locked his eyes on my nametag and then his record. He had a mix of emotions on his face. I could see the excitement, the anger, the relief, and the frustration. He looked me dead in the eyes and said, "Where the hell was my record?"

I pointed to the aisle where I found it and told him it was wedged between two records. I told him that I went from the very beginning aisle and pulled every record and, in doing so, I organized and did other work as I went down the rows looking for his. He came back behind the counter and went to grab the HM1 to bring him out to me. Sergeant Major brought HM1 out to the front desk and said, "This! This is one helluva Corpsman! You tell your lazy piles of shit to be more like Jacobs here. He is the definition of dedication, honor, and hard work."

HM1 was extremely grateful that I found Sergeant Major's record and acknowledged that in front of him. Sergeant Major then shook my hand and said, "You're going to be a great doc one of these days. Any Marine battalion will be lucky to have you as a doc amongst them." That concluded my mission for Sergeant Major and my first encounter with a Marine.

On February 25, 2006, I was struck by an Improvised Explosive Device (IED for short and also known as a roadside bomb). At that moment in time, I was on my first tour and had been on deployment for about one hundred seventy days. A few weeks prior to my arrival into Ar Ramadi, Iraq, I had checked into 3rd Battalion, 7th Marine Regiment (or 3/7 for short). 3/7 is an Infantry Battalion that is based out of 29 Palms, California, and is a detachment of 1st Marine Division (1st MarDiv). There were a good chunk of us corpsmen, or docs, that were assigned to 3/7 as IAs (commonly known as Individual Augmentees, basically a bunch of individuals pulled from other commands to fill the needs of a deploying unit). When we checked into 3/7, the main body had just completed their pre-deployment training, and they were heading out on pre-deployment leave. So we were given two options: go on pre-deployment leave or go to this two-week course and then try to get a week of pre-deployment leave. The majority of us took the two-week course, which at the time was a volunteer course. In today's military, however, Combat Trauma Management (CTM) is mandated for all division corpsmen going overseas. A good portion of us had completed Field Medical Service School, or Field Med or FMSS, just a few weeks prior to being assigned to 3/7. We learned a lot during our training at Field Med but knew we needed as much training and knowledge as we could get before actually stepping foot into a combat zone.

CTM was a two-week intense course that mentally and physically prepared us for just about any injuries that anyone could encounter over in a combat zone. The instructors of CTM had all been tested in combat and had proven worthy to instruct those who were to be sent over. It was an awesome concept, and it was way better than having someone with no proven combat life-saving experience teaching from a book or through someone else's stories . . . or, worse, through PowerPoint. I thank God every single day for that training. Not only did it save my life, but it helped in saving many others, and I attribute that to the course and its instructors.

After the CTM course, we began our whole week of pre-deployment leave. I knew that I had to cherish this leave time because my first "senior" Corpsman was injured in the same city we were about to deploy to. All he said to me when I told him about my deployment orders was, "Hahahahahahahaha! Good luck with that one!"

I kind of frowned and just said, "Aye, HM3."

My whole week of leave was a good one. My dad and grandma had flown in from Ohio to spend that week in Southern California with me. We spent the majority of the time in the Bakersfield, California, area. My mom's side of the family lives out in California, and seeing I was stationed in the state, it made sense to stay there.

During this week, I made a promise to Mom that I would attend her first chemotherapy appointment with her as she began her battle with breast cancer.

Just two months prior, Mom had told me, while I was in Field Med, that she had been diagnosed with breast cancer. It was pretty rough to know that I was about to deploy into one of the most dangerous cities in the world and my mom was going to be battling breast cancer. Throughout the time of her telling me the news and my pre-deployment leave, we had discussed me transferring to a unit closer to her so I could be there and help out as much as I could.

A little background on my relationship with my mom. At the time and the years leading up to my deployment, it wasn't the greatest of relationships. I remember Mom telling me, "I will be fine, because I have my husband, your brother, your sister, and your aunts to help me out." She told me that this was my dream and had been since I was twelve years old, which was true.

I remember one day while studying for my US history class telling my brother that I was going to go in the military and would go off to fight in Iraq. My brother, being fourteen and in advanced history classes in high school, told me that was impossible, because we hadn't been at war with Iraq since the early 1990s. Honestly, I am no history buff, but I just had this gut feeling that I was going to be the one to carry on the family tradition and go forth into battle to sweat and bleed for this great nation.

In all honesty, I wanted to be an Army Ranger just like my papa (my maternal great-grandfather). He fought in many battles during WWII and had also shed blood for our freedom. I had many uncles that had served in the various branches, and whether they shed blood or not, I am damn sure they would have sacrificed if their country needed them.

I went and followed the footsteps of one of the greatest men I have ever known, and I am blessed to call him family and a fellow Doc. Some of the main reasons I raised my right hand to take the oath and begin my walk down such a blessed and sacred path were because of listening to Uncle Tim talk about how us docs bond (on and off the battlefield) with our Marines and the stupid shit we do with our Marines. Most important was the fact that I knew deep down inside that I had what it would take to be the one called "Doc," the one Marines would call out for in their time of need, whether it be for back up in bar fight or to be there in their darkest hours.

Back to my pre-deployment time with my family. I kept my promise and was there for my mom's first treatment. Before the treatment really hit her, we had all decided to go to a local pizza joint that had an amazing variety of pizza with an all-you-can-eat buffet and a good-sized arcade. It was a great turnout from the family. I knew deep down inside that those moments could have been my last with my family, and in that moment, I decided to lie to them and say, "I will be fine; I probably won't even go outside the wire into combat. I am a medical person and will be protected by working in the base hospital." I told them all of that to ease their minds and hearts, knowing that in the weeks prior, I had volunteered for a Line Corpsman position, which would take me outside the wire, or secured zone on base, and into combat with his Marines.

After a few days in the Bakersfield area with my mom, we then headed down and stayed down at my aunt's house in Ventura County. I had a little farewell gig with family and friends down there as well. During our stay with my aunt, I kept having this reoccurring dream, and I knew it was because I had the deployment on my mind and that, by keeping my combat job a secret from my family, it weighed heavier on me. There was one family member that I had always been able to talk to and vice versa. So right before I loaded up and headed back out to 29 Palms, I decided to tell Aunt Sheila's oldest daughter that I kept having this dream of being shot in the leg by a sniper. She told me to shut up and not to worry because I would be fine since I was going to be working in the base hospital. I told her that what I told the family was partially true, but I still had this gut feeling that

I was going to come home wounded but alive. She cried and told me to shut up again and not to worry. I left it at that but felt a little better letting someone know that this could seriously be a possibility.

Soon after our brief stint in the Ventura County region, my dad and grandma took me back out to 29 Palms. I had to be back a few days prior for our official waiting period to complete all of the standard pre-deployment stuff. This consisted of all the last-minute admin, logistics, pay, briefings, and medical work-ups. So I said my farewells to G-Ma and Dad. During this waiting period, I headed over to the podiatry clinic at the 29 Palms Naval Hospital to get some custom graphite insoles for my combat boots. Little did I know how much these insoles would help me throughout the next seven months.

One of the worst parts about the whole waiting period was trying to acclimatize to the horrible August heat in 29 Palms. It was great for the long-term plan, seeing as we were going from 29 Palms to Ramadi, Iraq, and the temperature difference was about a ten- to fifteen-degree jump. August average temperatures for 29 Palms is one hundred one degrees opposed to one hundred eleven degrees in Ramadi. So getting acclimated to the dry heat was a rough stretch for me, seeing as I was in hot and muggy North Carolina just weeks prior. Heat shingles developed on my back and made the acclimation phase a very unpleasant one, but the training had to continue on, and there was no time to bitch about it.

Before I knew it, the day arrived. It started with dropping our gear off into a big neat pile to be loaded up, and then we were off to draw our weapons from the armory. After those long, drawn-out hours of processing everything for our departure, we loaded up. The families said their "I love yous," "see you soons," "be safes," and "write me when you cans," and we pushed out to a secured location to start the next hurry-up-and-wait phase. This phase wasn't too bad because I had my phone, phone charger, and all the cookies I could eat from the lovely USO folks. This allowed for some quality talk time with the family and time to work on my deployment journal. After a few hours, we began another working party to shift our gear from the staged location into the cargo/luggage hold of the McDonnell Douglas DC-10 aircraft that would be taking us to Kuwait. Soon after, we shut off our phones and said our farewells again. About five hours later, we landed at the Baltimore/Washington International Airport to gather some fuel before heading off on the next portion of the trip to Frankfurt, Germany.

I wanted to add this portion of the story because of the irony behind it. As we were taking off from Baltimore, I was thinking to myself, *Oh my God, this is real! I am on my way to war, and this may be a one-way destination for me.* Although I never said those words aloud, I sure as hell let my mind dawdle on those facts for a bit. It wasn't a one-way ticket, but the irony was I came back the same route and just the same way I told my cousin how I would come back.

Now, before we begin, I would like to let y'all know that I get off track sometimes and ramble a bit. For that, I apologize in advance, and I will limit my random sidetrack ramblings, even though I just get excited and want to share as much as I can with you guys without knowing how to appropriately put this all in a timeline. Thank you again for reading, and let's begin.

1.

INITIAL TREATMENT

I refuse to go into too many details with what happened the day I was injured because that isn't what this book is about. I will tell you about the initial treatment I received, well, what I can remember, and also say a special thank you to those who helped treat me along the way during my initial care.

I was hit in late February 2006, and I was medically evacuated (medivac) fairly quickly. I was hit in the afternoon, and one of my initial thoughts was, *Fuck! I hope we get some badass Marine helicopter pilots to come get us out of here! Otherwise, we will be here until nightfall!*

We pulled up to Charlie Med, the medical station on Camp Ramadi, and they offloaded us into Charlie Med to be triaged and prepared for surgery or the medivac. I was assessed, and during that time, I took my little notebook with my family's contact information out and handed it to my fellow 3/7 Doc and told him to call my mom and tell her I loved her in case I didn't make it home. He didn't want to take it and kept assuring me I'd be fine, but I kept insisting. After being assessed, I was carried out on a stretcher to the flight line. Sure enough, I saw a CH-46 coming in with two Cobras on her sides. I swore I was looking at angels, and it was beautiful! I was loaded up into the 46 and secured in.

The flight to Balad Surgical seemed like it took forever and not because I was in pain; I couldn't feel a damn thing. Once we arrived at Balad Surgical, we were offloaded and triaged again. I told the medical staff that I wanted to wait to go into surgery because I couldn't feel anything, and I wanted to make sure everyone else was taken care of. I'm unsure if that had anything to do with me being the last one to go back into surgery or not, but I was the last one to go back. As I was being wheeled around the corner into the operating room, I felt the medications taking effect, and I was out for some time after that.

I woke up in the Intensive Care Unit (ICU) of National Naval Medical Center Bethesda in early March 2006. I remember waking up and knowing exactly where I was and how I arrived there, even though no one told me. One of the main things that I can initially account for is being pretty pissed that I had a breathing tube down my throat. After some time, I began to chew on the breathing tube as my way of communicating to the medical staff that I wanted them to remove it to see if I was able to breathe on my own again. Yeah, that didn't work out too well. I couldn't breathe on my own when they took it out, and I remember going to sleep right away and then waking up with another damn breathing tube in. That pissed me off more than the first time I woke up.

I knew I was in good hands, though. My best friend Curt, a fellow Corpsman but an ICU Doc, had been taking care of my Marines that were coming home injured for my whole deployment. I knew from the success stories that my Marines and Curt had told me throughout the length of my time overseas that the whole ICU staff was probably the best to be in the care of if need be, and I am blessed to have had them take care of me and our troops that have unfortunately passed through those doors.

So when I awoke and he was right there by my side, I knew everything was going to be okay. He went way out of his way to get me a TV and placed it on a bedside tray so I could watch ESPN and anything sports related. He had to place it close enough for me to compensate without my recently destroyed glasses. I felt so bad for Curt, though. When I had the breathing tube out for the final time, I was always feeling discomfort from the Foley catheter, so I always asked him to take a look and make sure it wasn't moving.

For those who haven't had the joys of a Foley catheter, as a male, I will give a brief description of the severe discomfort. It is a sterile tube that is inserted into your bladder and flows into a sterile bag to drain urine. It is used for critically injured or ill persons who need a constant surveillance of fluids entering and leaving the body. Foleys can be used for a variety of purposes; you can have one that is used for a one-time usage, such as in an operating room setting when the medical staff needs to just do a quick release of your bladder fluids if the surgery is lasting for a certain length, or for a prolonged usage, like a lengthy hospital stay or for the elderly that may lack control of their bladder. I had the pleasure of a long-term usage Foley catheter. I can't begin to explain the extreme discomfort it is to have one of these in place.

So, to me, I thought the catheter was tugging. I would always call in Curt to check on it, and the poor guy finally got tired of seeing his best friend's private business, so he fixed the situation for good. He grabbed a good chunk of tape and gave the Foley a bit of slack and then taped that bad boy down.

Another major reason that I knew everything was going to be okay was when I first opened my eyes and my dad was right there by my bedside. I found out a bit after I had woken up and transferred to the surgery ward what kind of battle Dad had been dealing with behind the scenes and all on top of being a father, sitting waiting for his son to wake up and start recovering. I will go into those battles momentarily. My pops got me a little radio and put it on a country music station to help ease my mind. I know there wasn't much that he could do on his part in order to help me, but just hearing country music, watching sports, and knowing I had my dad and best friend with me was all I really needed at the time.

Before I go into the onset of the two-and-a-half-month battle my dad had been fighting, I would like to back brief you on something I'd say to my dad when I ended our conversations, letters, or emails. I would tell him, "Everything I do, I do for you." He would always say something along the lines of, "No, kid, everything you do, you do for your Marines and yourself." I think he did it to avoid any emotional conversation.

So when I had the breathing tube taken out, I wanted to ensure that my first statement was to my dad, and I told him, "Everything I did, I did for you." I never once saw a tear in Dad's eyes until that moment in my life, and it was indescribable. I forgot what he said after that, but I do remember that being my first sentence when I could speak again.

A very emotional and rough part of my long ICU experience was not having my mom there right away. I know she would have been there when I arrived at NNMC Bethesda like my dad was if she could have gotten the time off work soon enough. The family kept her and my siblings up to speed while they were unable to be at the hospital. At the time, I wasn't able to use my hands or arms due to the injuries I had sustained. So I had asked Dad to call Mom and place the phone against my ear. The phone rang just a few times, and Mom answered. With my raspy voice from having the breathing tubes, I told her that I was alive and awake and that I loved her. I remember hearing her pull off the road really fast, and she told me that she loved me, too, and she would get to Bethesda as soon as she could. I think I told her not to rush because I would be there for a while, just me making light of the situation. That moment was a major turning point in the broken relationship with my mom.

Within a few days of my arrival to NNMC Bethesda, my mom had arrived with my brother and sister. I am not a momma's boy by any means, but when one goes through an extreme, near-death situation, having your mom around immediately after is a comforting feeling that not too many folks in this world can explain. So when Mom walked into my room, I encountered that unexplained comfort. It was like Momma Bear was here to protect her cub and nobody and nothing could harm me.

One night after visiting hours were over, I laid there in my room listening to country music on my radio and watching the snowfall drift past the window to my left. When I would turn to the right, I could see the nurse's station, and above the nurse's station was a digital clock with big and bright red numbers that I could easily see without my glasses. I dozed off for a short time and woke up shortly after one in the morning to some commercials on the radio that were louder than the songs. To try and make myself sleepy again, I turned my eyes to the left to see the slowly drifting snowflakes fall by the window outside. As I lay there watching the snow fall, wondering how my vehicle commander and turret gunner were doing—they were in nearby ICU rooms—I said a prayer then and there, as well as many others, asking the Lord God to watch over my Marines, both in the ICU and the ones that remained in combat.

At one point in my prayers, I told God that I was ready to come home if it meant that one of my Marines who was there in the hospital with me may live and that I would be glad to take their pain and let them live on with their loved ones. At the time, I was a whole twenty years old and just wanted to be deployed with my Marines still. The knowledge that I had, I knew that my chances of being back on the frontlines and being the first line of medical treatment for US and coalition forces was not in my favor. This was very upsetting and depressing because I had a huge passion for being a combat trauma specialist, and I loved doing it. It was something I envisioned myself doing for a good portion of my life, well until I advanced in the corpsman rate and then forced to grow into a different job within the rate.

There were two major things that edged me to decide to tell God that I was ready to go in place of another Marine. One was because I was already feeling guilty about being a survivor of the incident, and I would have rather it been me to go than any one of my Marines. Second was not knowing what direction to head in now that the only training I had experience in, and a massive passion for, was combat trauma, and that wouldn't transfer into a whole lot on the outside. My original plans for when I returned home from deployment, well, before Mr. IED had to go altering my plans, were to become a firefighter paramedic while doing my reserve time because I was National Call to Service, or NCS. Being a combat trauma specialist, I was pretty damn sure a Marine Reserve Unit would have loved to have me as their doc, so this seemed like a legit plan. All of this required a great need for healthy and strong legs.

During this whole thought process, I began thinking of all of the jobs that I would like to do that had a requirement of being on your feet a lot and/or overall good health of the lower extremities. This was an issue that I would have to work on in time and gradually overcome the depression, which I hardly ever showed to anybody. One thing about laying in a hospital bed is you have *a lot* of time to think about shit and do research on this thinking, and sometimes doing all that puts a huge damper on life plans. At the time, I really let it get to me, too.

So after looking at the time and realizing that I needed to try to go back to sleep, I turned to the window to watch the snowflakes trickle down. After a short time, I turned toward the door again to see the time. This was one of those long nights where I just laid there watching the snow fall while listening to the country station. Nights like these seemed to drag on and on, and I couldn't wait until the visiting hours approached so I would have some company.

My dad had been dealing with a lot of crazy, behind-the-scenes shit, and it went back to before my arrival at NNMC Bethesda. I had arrived into the States with all of my limbs, minus two fingers on the left hand, which was my fault, and I will explain about how my fingers were partially amputated and how I didn't return with them. So I arrived with my legs being considered "limb salvages" and my arms being thought of as a very hopeful recovery. My injuries were pretty bad, orthopedically speaking. My left leg was pretty shattered and banged up, but the biggest issue was the chronic neurogenic pain that I had. I will later explain my battles with that. As for my right leg, my foot was so damaged I had shattered and missing bones. So naturally the Army Orthopedic Trauma Surgeon had told my dad that he had to amputate both of my legs. Dad's immediate rebuttal was, "He made it all the way here with both of his legs. So somewhere along the way, a surgeon or team of surgeons didn't amputate his legs for a reason. So I will not be responsible for taking his leg or legs. That will be his decision when he wakes up and/or in his own time." This was the beginning of a two-and-a-half-month battle with the Orthopedic Surgery Department, well, not so much of a battle but more a bargaining with the Plastic Surgery Department, to save my right leg.

The day I left the ICU and headed to the surgery ward, located on the fifth floor in the East Wing, felt like a day of freedom. I felt that if I was able to transfer out of the ICU, where I required around-the-clock care, then things were going fairly well for me. Five East was in a different wing of the hospital and required different elevators to reach the fifth floor. The transfer in a hospital bed was not an easy one by any means.

Right before I was wheeled up to Five East, I was given some pain medication through my IV to ease the pain of moving throughout the hospital and getting settled into a new room. The trek began by two corpsmen wheeling me from my ICU room to my room on Five East. Let me say that this trip would have been an easy one if we didn't have to encounter those small bumps in the hallways that cover cords and/or divots in the doorways, plus the bumps going in and out of the elevators. So these two corpsmen began wheeling me over the bumps in the hallway. The first time, I just grimaced and thought I could tough through it. Then the second time I asked them to slow down. Well, their idea of slowing down over the bumps still wasn't helping my case at all. By this time, I realized I had no idea how long the remainder of this trip to the surgery ward was because I hadn't been out of the ICU since I had been there.

I had them stop for a second, and then I asked them to go over the bumps slowly but then as fast as needed in between to hurry the process. By the time I arrived at my room on Five East, I was in extreme pain. Mind you, the medical team at Bethesda had kept me fairly comfortable for my injuries, and this was a new test of my pain threshold, at least in my mind. At the time, I didn't understand why I was in so much pain, but now that I remember that my whole body was in pain from absorbing the blast of an IED.

I don't remember too much when I first arrived on Five East. This was due to the medications that I was on and being in surgery every other day. Most of the time was spent in the operating room to perform irrigation and debridement to the wounds, especially those that couldn't be closed. For instance, one of the wounds that wouldn't close was the top portion of my foot. This part was blown off and was a huge hole in my foot. They had to keep this part cleaned out and wrapped until they could devise a plan to close it up. All of my other wounds still had drains and wound vacs in them.

One of the things that I do remember upon my initial arrival to Five East was my pain level. I did argue with the medical staff regarding my pain that I had encountered on my transfer from ICU. When the Corpsman came in to take my vital signs upon my arrival to Five East, I informed him of my pain level and asked him to notify someone. So the Corpsman went and informed the nurse of my pain control issue. The nurse came in and told me that it wasn't possible to get more pain medication because I had received some prior to my departure from the ICU and it was too soon for another dose. I tried to plead my case with the nurse, but after a quick argument, I asked if she could just get the orthopedic surgeon to come up and I could explain to him. Once the doctor arrived, he agreed with the nurse.

I had told some of the staff some terrible things, and I can't remember exactly what I said, but it went along the lines of this: "Well, maybe if you didn't hide here in the States in a hospital and actually go do some war fighting, you might understand what it is like to be in my shoes. So don't sit here and tell me you 'understand' or can 'sympathize with me' when you have no idea what it is like to have your whole body in pain from the simple move from one portion of the hospital to another." I probably shouldn't have said those things to a naval officer. Soon after the battle was said and done, he approved the medication and the nurse came in to push them through the IV.

Don't get me wrong, I understand from a medical standpoint why I wasn't authorized the medications at the time. There are side effects of taking too much painkillers within a short amount of time, but holy shit, man, was I was hurting! It was eventually sorted out, I was comfortable and grateful that it was all said and done, and then I was finally getting settled into my new temporary location.

2.

BETTER PLACE

Due to the amount and strength of the medications and the surgeries every other day, I don't recall too much of the first few weeks of my time on Five East. There are some things that stuck in my memory and for a reason. I am about to tell you of the memories that I have, both good and bad.

One of my first memories, besides arriving on Five East, was one night when I felt the urge to make a boom-boom. That is my official term for a bowel movement. I pressed the call bell button, and a few moments later, the evening Corpsman came into the room. I explained that I was feeling the stomach cramps that occur in the moments leading up to a bowel movement, and he left the room and brought the nurse in. After briefly explaining to the nurse that I had to go, she stated that wasn't possible. I pleaded my case with the nurse, and she reassured me that it wasn't possible because I hadn't eaten anything since the day I was injured, the apple I grabbed from the chow hall on my way to the trucks before leaving on patrol. I told her, "I am a human and have had bowel movements for twenty years now, and I know what that feeling is." Again, she stated it wasn't possible and let me be.

I let them leave the room, and within a few moments, I just released my bowels and did it without any remorse. As soon as I knew I was done, I pressed the call bell button once more. As the Corpsman entered the room, I said, "Take a big whiff and tell me again it isn't possible." He ran out of the room and brought back the nurse. Soon, the whole night crew had to come in my room and roll me over to clean me. They then had to transfer me to the adjacent bed and take the other one out. At this moment in my recovery, I couldn't utilize any portion of my body, other than lifting my left arm to bring it down gently on my right arm, where the NNMC Five East crew had taped a call bell button onto the cast/splint on my right arm. As I lay there with no ability to help, I just smiled as they had to take care of my shit and clean me up. If someone tells you they have to shit, freaking listen and let them shit. It's not a difficult concept. They could have placed a bed pan under me and it would have been less time and work.

For the first weeks, I was in and out of the OR every other day doing irrigation and debridement, or I&D, surgeries as well as various orthopedic corrective surgeries in order to save my legs. This seemed like a lengthy, drawn-out process. Some days, I honestly didn't know whether I was coming or going. I was happy as could be, though, once that crazy schedule of surgeries every other day wore off.

One day before I was to head out for a surgery, in walked some of the Miss USA contestants from their respective states. I can't recall which ones walked in as I was being wheeled out for surgery. The medical staff informed them that I was heading out for surgery, and to my surprise, they agreed to put on the goofy-looking yellow protective garments, which were to protect me from anything that could cause me harm, such as bacteria. They were pretty awesome and hung out with me while the staff prepared me to head out for surgery.

This next part that I remember about my early phase on Five East is a very emotional part for me to speak about, and very few people have *ever* heard this. Naturally, the medical personnel that I spoke to about this put it in my medical record as a "hallucination." I will scan a copy of the note that they put in the system as a "hallucination" so you can see the timeline for yourself. You can take it for what it is, but I know what I saw and heard. The evidence of my dad's arrival into my room the next day proves this to be right.

It was an evening in early March, and it was soon to be time for visiting hours end, so my dad and grandma called it a night, and in doing so, they ensured that I was set up for the night. I couldn't do a whole lot in regards to moving about but had a little luck with moving my arms, well enough to lift one onto the other to ring the call bell, and being able to slightly move my head, as much as a cervical collar (also known as a c-collar) would allow. So as I lay there trying to bore myself to sleep, I'd watch whatever sports I could find on TV. In early March there were, and still are, some good sports on the air, but not too many that I would be overly excited about. I mean, there was college softball . . . but having a Foley catheter in, it was and wasn't something I desired to watch based on the serious levels of pain and discomfort. I will save that pain and discomfort story for later.

I must have been asleep for a good while before I awoke, because when I did wake, my door was only slightly opened. Therefore, one of the staff members must have come in to grab my vitals or some blood. I liked my door all the way open, as a comfort thing, just the thought of knowing that if a nurse or corpsman walked by, they could see into the room and know I was okay. So I admit I was a little nervous that something was up. In my nervousness, I started to pray and then thought to myself, *Maybe there is a new staff member on the night crew, seeing as they rotate every so often, who does things differently than what the other staff members do, or maybe someone forgot I liked the door open.* In all honesty, laying in a hospital bed in a dark room all by myself (especially that close to the initial injury and coding at least once up to that point), I was a bit freaked out. I mean, there was an odd eeriness to it all. So as I lay there, I got my

Jesus on, my term for praying. During this prayer, as well as hundreds of thousands of others, I asked that all of the pain and fear that was within my Marines to be placed on me so they could be pain free and at peace. I, again, asked that if it be his will that I would be glad to go instead of one of my brothers. I soon finished up my prayers and started staring back at the TV to zone out and get back to sleep.

I was in a two-person room, and I was in the bed closest to the window, maybe a few feet between the bed and the window. The TV came over the edge of the bed and was placed right over the bedside tray. The window was fairly large and allowed for an awesome amount of ambient light throughout the daylight hours and large enough to watch the snowflakes peacefully and gracefully fall. My bed faced the center of the hospital, toward the nurses' station.

On this night, as well as many other nights (shit, let's be real, I still do), I left the TV going and watched the snow drift by my window. Although it wasn't much snow, it was peaceful to watch and very relaxing. As I was watching the snow and the reruns on ESPN, I was in and out of sleep. A quick side note, I would like to inform you of why guys like me, someone who has been through a tragic event, leaves the TV on or has music or some other noise playing softly in the background. It is because we need that noise to drown out the constant ringing in our ears, if we were exposed to excessively loud noises, and/or to keep our minds from wandering into where we don't want them to wander . . . to the tragic event that we lived through. As for me, it's for both, but that background noise just dulls my mind when I need it to, then *poof,* out cold. Let's get back on topic here. So on this particular night I just had this odd feeling about me and couldn't quite grasp what it was, but I'd soon find out why.

I woke up after being in a short sleep and realized that I woke up to the door being closed. I figured once again it must have been the medical staff doing their nightly duties. So I turned back to the window to watch the snowfall again, and I saw a figure standing in the window. No, the one in the window wasn't outside the window looking in, but from within the hospital . . . right there in my room! My glasses were damaged in the blast, so I didn't have that great of vision, and initially, it was difficult to identify the person with me.

In a panic, I tried to move to see if it was real or just somebody being in my room and not actually "being there." I turned as much as I could, and sure enough, no physical person was there. I looked back toward the window, and the figure was closer. I may have been freaking out pretty bad by this point. I was unsure what to do or who this was! So I shifted back to my right to see if the person magically would appear. No such luck on that round of battling this identity crisis. I turned back to my left to look at the reflection, and sure enough, this person was coming even closer, and quite fast.

For the sake of trying, I looked to my right again. No luck on the identity revelation. I turned back to my left, and at that moment, I then knew *exactly* what was going on! I felt like someone had punched me through my chest, then they had grabbed my spine and speared my heart with it . . . then gave it to Edward Scissorhands. It was honestly one of the most devastating moments in my life.

It was one of my Marine brothers that was in my room with me. He must have felt my thoughts, emotions, and prayers that I had been sending his way. He didn't say much to me, but what he did say to me is something I will never forget. He said, "Doc, don't worry anymore. I am in a better place now." Other than tearing up, okay . . . actually crying, I couldn't think of anything to say, and to be honest, I still don't know what to say.

There is a lot from early to mid-March that I don't recall. This loss of memory was due to the constant need for surgeries, just about every other day, and the need for around-the-clock medications. I do recall not being able to move my body other than my arms to push the call button taped to my cast. This proved to be difficult because I would have to lift my left arm and bring it to the top of my right arm in order to ring the call bell. I was able to slightly maneuver my head a little bit, but it required a great deal of strength. I had to lift my head off the pillow by utilizing my core to turn from side to side.

Here is a little breakdown of my early immobilization situation. You can see the pictures for a better visualization as well. (Caution: they are graphic.) Early on, I was in surgical splints for both my arms and legs. They had to do the surgical splints early on because of the constant need for further surgeries. Once the need for ongoing surgeries decreased, they placed casts or hard splints on me. I had a collar around my neck due to an avulsed ligament in my neck.

I do remember when Aunt Sheila, Uncle Tim, and their kids came out to see me. My cousins, the middle and youngest of my aunt's children, used to fight over who was going to feed me when it came time. It was actually pretty amusing. I do recall one of those oh-so-healthy hospital meals came in for my daily lunch. It was a sandwich, and it was accompanied with some yogurt. They fought over who was to help feed me the sandwich and who would feed me the yogurt. After I had had enough of the argument, I interrupted their debacle and said, "I appreciate your guys' love and willingness to help me out, but the longer you guys argue, the longer I lay here hungry as shit." They soon agreed to cut the sandwich in half then share the duties.

During their trip out, I can't remember a date or exact timeframe, but I was hoisted out of the hospital bed and transferred to a reclining chair. During the time on the machine hoisting me out of bed, I was officially weighed, and it was severely disturbing. I weighed a whole one hundred forty-four pounds.

This means that during my few weeks of being injured, I had lost nearly sixty pounds. Before we left Camp Ramadi for Blue Diamond, I weighed myself at a lean two hundred five pounds. Then, I felt that I was the healthiest I had ever been in my life! So when I was weighed at a thin one hundred forty-four pounds, I was not too pleased with the thought of losing all of that amazing work I had put into my body and the thought that I may never have that again.

Oh, man! I do remember one issue I had in the hospital, and this is a two-part story. Back when I was in the ICU, I wrote about how uncomfortable the Foley catheter was. I am going to inform you of how bad this sucked! For those who have been deployed for months on end, then became injured and had a Foley catheter in for a while, you should understand what I am speaking of.

My Foley catheter sorrows did not end right after my stint in the ICU was over. In fact, they had just begun. When you are deployed for six-and-a-half months, especially into combat, you are hardly ever around a female. When you are around females overseas, you are around the fellow deployed females, which is not allowed in any way. Yes, I am speaking of that. Even being around the females of the locals in the village/town/city, for that matter, is also a *giant* "NOT ALLOWED." All I am saying is when you are away from the opposite gender for months on end, it isn't good by any means, and then to throw in a Foley catheter in a guy for a few weeks . . . I'm mean, that's as bad, if not worse than some injuries. Okay, enough of that garbage talk.

In early March 2006, the amazing Admiral of National Naval Medical Center Bethesda awarded me my Purple Heart while in the hospital. It was a very emotional moment in my life. I am the second person in my family to be awarded the Purple Heart. I am not too sure how many of us fought in combat, though. My maternal great-grandpa was awarded the Bronze Star and a Purple Heart from his time in World War II. He was also missing in action during World War II. I felt in that moment that I was bringing more pride to the family military heritage.

During the few weeks leading up to March 20, 2006, I was consistently in and out of the operating room for various orthopedic issues to my lower limbs. During that time, the Plastic Surgery Department was seeing me. They were planning a major surgical procedure to keep my right leg. A back brief on why the Plastic Surgery Department was involved was due to a portion of my right foot being blown off. So they had to plan this procedure for me to keep my right leg.

I promised the plastic surgeon that I would do everything within my power to keep my leg. So on the morning of March 20th, I was wheeled into the surgical preparing area. I was down there well before it was even light outside. After the lengthy surgery, I was readmitted into the ICU for around-the-clock supervision and wound care.

I am unsure of the exact timeline of events, but all I know is when I lay in the ICU after surgery, I was asked if I would like to take my FMF (Fleet Marine Force) Board so I could earn my FMF pin. It was either then or a later time. I agreed to do the board while in the ICU, so I wouldn't have to worry about it later.

3.

SHARKS

The previous things that you read about were some of the personal issues I had to deal with for the first month or so while I was in Bethesda. Now I am going to discuss my initial battle after my injury. This is one of many, and it is disturbing how things went down. Please note that what I am about to say is the truth about how I was treated, and I am sure it happened to many others as well.

Since I arrived at National Naval Medical Center in Bethesda, Maryland, the orthopedic trauma team wanted to amputate both of my legs. I had lucked out with this battle because Dad and G-Ma had arrived at Bethesda before me and were there by my bedside day in and day out throughout my three-month stay. Well, they were there for the majority of the time. When my mom and the other family members would come into town, they would use that time as a break. It was a good thing that I had somebody with me to sign the consent forms. I am glad that somebody was there because the first month or so is still kind of a blur for me. If I didn't have somebody there with me, I would have signed the forms while having my mind altered by medications.

When I first arrived at Bethesda, I was in a medically induced coma. So having Dad and G-Ma there from the start was more than needed. Let's just say they were my voice when I didn't have one. So while I was lying in a hospital bed and on a breathing machine, the doctor kept telling my dad that he needed to amputate both of my legs. My pops refused to sign any consent form that had anything to do with amputation. He said he didn't want to be the one responsible for amputating my legs, and it would be a decision I would have to make on my own, in my own time.

I remember one incident while lying in the ICU. When Dad and G-Ma were out, the trauma team came in and asked me if I wanted to amputate. I was still on the ventilator at this time, and I just glared up at the doctor. He then told me to move my eyes side to side for a "no" and up and down for a "yes." I just glared more and wouldn't even move my eyes at all because I knew how ridiculous this was.

My dad told me his theory for why he didn't give in and sign the consent form. He told me that I made it to Bethesda with both of my legs for a reason. Somehow along the way a doctor had some sort of hope of me keeping my legs. This is true, though. If I made it from Charlie Med in Ramadi to Bethesda with both of my legs, then there must be some hope. I respect my dad's decision to not amputate and let that be my choice, anyway. I wouldn't have resented him for it if he had to make the choice to amputate, but I am glad that he saw things the way he did.

My battles with the orthopedic team didn't end when I left the ICU. Every day, the group of orthopedic surgeons would do their rounds. During their rounds, they would discuss the current situation and what the options were to make the situation better. Every single morning, they would try and throw in amputation as an option. After so long of hearing the same thing, I was growing tired of hearing it. I voiced my anger to Dad and G-Ma about the pressure I was constantly under to amputate.

Dad and G-Ma would come into my room before the team would arrive for their rounds. The doctors knew my dad's answer and knew he didn't want their pressure on me to make that decision. So the orthopedics' answer to Dad and G-Ma coming in earlier was for his team to also show up earlier. This battle of who got to my room first continued for quite some time. Finally, when the ortho docs had me alone, they told me it would be easier on me and would save the government time and money if they amputated both of my legs and sent me on my way. I then repeated what my dad had told me about how there must be some hope because I'd made it this far with my legs so why not keep trying? Their rebuttal to that was to have some amputees come by and talk to me about amputation. I told them they could have some folks come on by, but it would be an educated decision that I would have to make, and I would be the only one influencing that decision. That seemed to hold the circling sharks off for a while, but they were soon back at their antics shortly after.

I was scheduled for a late morning/early afternoon surgery. I thought the consent form was already signed by my dad, and off to the surgery holding area I went. Right as I was being wheeled into the operating room, someone said, "Is the consent form signed?" and I thought it was, so I said yes. The nurse came over and looked in my chart, and sure enough, it wasn't signed. I was asked to hurry up and sign it so we could keep the OR schedule. I began to read it over and then realized what was going on, and I refused to sign. Although I don't recall what the form contained, I just know I made them call/ page my dad. After a brief attempt to get a hold of my dad, they told me he wasn't around to sign the form so I had to hurry up and sign so we could get into surgery. Again, I refused to sign. I don't remember how long it took for them to get my dad to come down. I just know I was lying there for a good amount of time while waiting.

There were some amputees that came through my room, and I discussed the predicament that I was in and what the ortho surgeons were saying. Every single one of them told me that it was a decision that I would have to come to in my own time. I should take all the information in and make a decision based on how I felt about everything and what my needs were, definitely not what made someone else's life easier. That's how I make decisions, anyway. I take in all the knowledge and apply it to my needs.

During this time, I had already considered amputation and tried to discuss it with my brother. When I brought it up to him, he started to tear up, so I told him I was just considering it. Then I realized that I would have to make this decision on my own. Others would be too emotional, and some wouldn't think rationally about it. So I decided to deal with the severe nerve pain and shattered heel.

I'm not going to lie, though; being told I would never be able to walk again on my own two legs wasn't depressing at all. It gave me a challenge and something to look forward to achieving. It was a rare kind of excitement for me. I know that sounds absurd, but learning to walk again would be my challenge. I wouldn't look at it as being something depressing. This is one of many of these kinds of stories I will discuss with you. It just doesn't seem like reason enough for me to give up and quit. I will later tell you how this story panned out.

There is another main concern I have about being a combat-wounded service member: visitors. Having to go in and out of surgery every other day wears one out. Some of these surgeries are minor and some are major, which requires a lot of rest time. People who have had surgery before know how much it wears you out. Then you need time to recover. So when someone is in and out of surgery a few times a week, the number of outside visitors should be severely limited! I mean, people going to see the troops to get their picture in the paper just so they can say that they support the troops for their own personal benefit . . . seriously? Come on, now, that shit needs to stop. America's heroes should not be put on public display for someone else's benefit. If someone really supports the troops, contact your congressman and get the troops better pay, benefits, or even gear for training/deployment. Or how about support them for recreational events for later on in their care?

I am not speaking about anyone in particular. I am not saying that everyone who travels through to visit the troops has ill intent. There are many folks out there that have amazing intentions and are appreciative of what we have done. I am beyond grateful for those fine Americans. I just think there should be an easier way to show support. I say this because I have pictures with some people and I don't even remember them. In that timeframe, I was just out of surgery and still medicated. I know I would have appreciated spending time with those gracious folks over a weekend of bass fishing, playing golf, or just shooting the shit at a baseball game. Or just simply when I wasn't highly medicated.

My time at Bethesda wasn't all that bad, though. There were plenty of good times as well. Let's just say that I spent a lot of time down at the vending machines and the RedBox during the evening hours. I used to annoy the shit out of the nurses, though, by hitting my cast constantly with my hand, well, until my dad created a device that I could hit my cast with without having to nearly break my hand. Well, that and wheelchair jousting! Haha, that didn't last long.

Let's get back to the hitting the cast real quick, though. I had a nerve pain issue, and I was taking the maximum dose for it, but it was still occurring, and the only thing that seemed to help was to hit my cast at a certain spot so it would temporally numb the nerve. This would allow just a few brief moments of relief. Well, my pops asked for a rubber mallet, and the hospital told him they didn't have one. So my dear old dad decided to go get a hammer and masking tape for me to utilize like a soft mallet. It worked extremely well. Good job, Pops.

Quick funny story about that mallet, though. One day, G-Ma was asking questions, and I didn't feel like being bothered by her questions. G-Ma didn't like the fact that I wasn't responding and that I was being disrespectful to her. So she took the masking tape off the hammer and rolled it into a ball then proceeded to roll it around in my hair until I answered her questions. Haha, some serious interrogation tactics that woman possessed! That was only the beginning; apparently, I didn't learn from my first mistake.

One of the greatest things was the liberty I was allotted. I would use that to go to Nationals games, the Mall, and the on-base exchange. My first trip out, I remember how amazing it was when I first felt the sunlight on me. I was told to go to the exchange and buy some really nice clothes. I did as ordered, and I wouldn't have guessed it, but shortly after, I was sitting at the commandant's house. After sitting downstairs in complete awe of his awesome house, down walked the commandant and President George W. Bush. You can have whatever beliefs about President Bush you want, but know this: he cared about his troops. He came around to every wounded warrior and was genuinely concerned about our health and well-being. He asked if we needed anything as he handed me a coin, and I answered, "Yes, sir." He looked down at me as he stood over my right shoulder and answered briefly. I said, "Is it okay if my dad has a coin as well?" He chuckled and said, "Of course, son," and shook my dad's hand as he gave him a presidential coin, too.

4.

NMCSD

The sixth of May in 2006 was my transfer date to Naval Medical Center San Diego (Balboa). The weeks leading up to this transfer were a political battle, honestly the very onset of said political barrage. I wanted to be in Southern California, but I was being told it wasn't possible due to no program set in place to care for someone with my injuries. The options laid out for me were Walter Reed Army Medical Center, Brooke Army Medical Center (BAMC), or Palo Alto. I would have accepted Palo Alto, but it was the brain injury center, and I knew my dome piece was rattled around a bit with minor damage, so I didn't feel like wasting a spot. So I held out for a few weeks until I got the answer I wanted, Balboa.

I was in luck due to Balboa building a center for wounded warriors called the Comprehensive Combat Casualty Care Center, or C-5. This center was initially known as the Amputee Center or Amputee Clinic. A dear friend of mine that trained and deployed with me and I were the pioneers of this new program. So after weeks of debating and arguing my point that I shouldn't go to BAMC, the burn center, or to Palo Alto, I claimed victory on my first political fiasco.

On May 6th, I was wheeled out of National Naval Medical Center Bethesda, into a bus, and on my way to the aircraft that was set to take a group of us to various locations around the nation. I thought this trip was going to be a quick process. Haha, I know, I know! That was horrible for me to assume that. All in all, though, the trip wasn't all that bad. We ended up in Palo Alto for the night, and Pops and I ordered Domino's for some grub and just relaxed in the cool spring air. The next day, we continued on with the adventure to Balboa via Miramar. Shortly after we arrived at Miramar, we were escorted off the flight line into the patient transport bus. It was a short ride to Balboa, probably shorter than the time it took for the staff to come to a decision on what to do with us. I was immediately transferred to the surgery ward.

A handful of doctors who were overseeing my specialties then greeted me. I had to stay the night, which really sucked because I had heard of this amazing thing called "con leave," or convalescent leave. Due to my need to still be non-weightbearing, it would be difficult to ride in a vehicle for a few hours while traveling to Ventura County to spend my con leave with some family.

The next day when I was allowed to check out on con leave, in walked Aunt Sheila and her friend with the gurney from their ambulance. They had company permission to come down and take me home in an ambulance. It was pretty cool because the hospital staff looked so confused when she said, "I am here to get Daniel Jacobs." So once all the paperwork was set to go, I was loaded into the back of an ambulance (for the first time in my life), and away we went. I arrived in Fillmore to some friends waiting at the house with the family. It was good to arrive home with some familiar faces (and that weren't the ones I would irritate in Bethesda . . . by accident and some on purpose).

I thought this part of the transition was going to be a good portion and I would finally get to sleep for more than two to four hours without someone coming in to take vitals or draw blood. This was far much worse than what I had mentally prepared for. It's funny, because after a short time, I was begging to go back into the hospital as an inpatient.

Once I was settled into the house in Fillmore, I was finally able to get set into a routine. It was a fairly nice routine as well; the kids were at school during the day, and the adults were working. Well, Aunt Sheila worked twenty-four-hour shifts as a paramedic, so she was home periodically. It was nice to go run errands and stuff with her because it was refreshing to be out and about. Plus, I would wheel myself around in my chair, and it was good exercise.

Just a short while into my con leave, I was called and told I had to attend mandatory appointments with physical therapy, mental health, and occupational therapy. Both occupational therapy and physical therapy were at the house, but mental health was a different story. I had to go out in town to a Tricare provider. I had to schedule those appointments around the family's work schedule. The in-house appointments went well, for the most part, minus the intense pain during physical therapy. That was mainly due to the physical therapist just doing his job. On my left leg, I had some intense pain due to a shattered heel and chronic nerve pain throughout the whole bottom portion of my foot. The pain was so bad that I had to take pain medication in order to put a sock on my foot and put it in the walking boot, which was ironic because I wasn't allowed to walk. The pain in my foot didn't allow for washing the bottom of it, so instead I would just soak in some warm soapy water and then let it air dry.

The downstairs bathroom doorframe wasn't wide enough for me to get my wheelchair in, and this caused more work for the family. I felt bad about them having to help me out with things that I could normally do, plus I felt like I wasn't independent like I used to be. So I contacted the orthopedic team at Balboa, and they submitted a consult for me to get a bedside toilet. Well, this made life on me easier but not too much on the family. I was able to use the toilet whenever, but I was still limited due to the family's school and work schedules. So to get around that, I would just slide on my butt from my room into the bathroom when I had to go when nobody was around. When shower time rolled around for me, I would have to sit in my room on the shower chair and be carried into the shower. I would then strip down, shower, and be ready to be carried back out. It wasn't a bad system, just a tedious one.

After a few weeks of being settled in with the family, I was finally getting into a routine. I was sleeping better and feeling more self-reliant. During the hours that the family was gone during the day, I had a lot of time to think about a lot of things. One of them was the challenge that the ortho doctor in Bethesda gave me; I would never be able to walk again on my own two legs. Well, I am about to tell you how I accepted that challenge and battled to win as well.

One day when the family was out at school and work, I decided to use the walker to assist myself around the house. I would normally put my left leg up on the seat part and use my right to push off with. I decided that I was able to use my right foot to bear some weight on it, well enough to push myself around. I was thinking that the walking boot could be used as a cushion to prevent some of the pain. Surprisingly enough, the walking boot cushioned the blow on my right foot. During those first weeks of having this walker around the house, I would gain some confidence.

One day when everyone was up and gone to work, I decided to go about my normal morning routine to prevent anyone from coming back in and catching me up and walking against doctor's orders. So I used my walker and gained some confidence but without the boot on my right foot. It felt a little odd, but it was a good, relieving feeling that I hadn't felt until that moment. I maneuvered to the cereal and gathered all of the appropriate items for a delicious massive bowl of Frosted Flakes to take to the couch region. I sat and caught up on the morning news and the latest on the Travel Channel. Then it was on to the rest of the day.

I waited just a little while longer until I put on the walking boot for the right side. I don't exactly remember why I waited, but I know I must have done it for a reason. So I put on the boot in my room at the end of the bed then got back on my walker. I went out into the den area, which was the biggest room on the ground floor, and stood up from my walker. I then pushed my walker as far away as I could, thus allowing a three- to four-foot perimeter of open space around me. I did this to force myself to walk without any assistance, other than the walking boots. I knew I didn't have much time before the pain would start to become overwhelming. I figured walking again would be like riding a bike, with the muscle memory. So I led with the left foot and just took the necessary steps to make it to the couch. I felt the adrenaline pumping through my veins, the feel of victory.

That adrenaline high I was feeling inspired me to walk some more. I went from the couch back to my walker. Though I was on this adrenaline rush, I subconsciously knew to not do too much. So after this, I went back into my room and grabbed my phone. I then set off to the couch and big screen to take some medicine and relax. The first person I told was Aunt Sheila. I did that because I knew what her reaction was going to be, and it was what I got when I called. I told her that I walked, and she responded with something similar to, "Nephew! You know you shouldn't be walking! Don't further injure yourself or set yourself back on your care!"

I told her it felt fine, and I was doing what I was told I would never be able to do again. The whole time that I laid there in a hospital bed or sat in a wheelchair listening to these "experts" continuously giving me information for me to give in and quit . . . I defeated those odds. It felt really amazing, and I honestly couldn't keep it in. I spent the whole rest of the day telling people how I defied all odds and walked again. I had so many people giving positive feedback, and it usually was accompanied by concern. That's all right with me, though, because deep down, I knew it felt amazing, and I was on a clear path for still achieving my goals that I set out to do when I was initially injured.

I didn't walk too much after that, though. I only did it to keep the confidence and motivation. I honestly knew that I could cause so much damage if I did too much too soon. On top of it all, I hadn't really sat down and spoken with the orthopedic surgeons since my arrival into Balboa. So I couldn't even have a mental image of what the x-rays were showing. Oh, and I was a good few hours' drive away from Balboa. So if I did cause any further damage, it wouldn't be a pleasant car ride through LA traffic down to Balboa.

One day, can't remember the day or time of the month, Uncle Tim had a day off and wanted to know if I would go to the Navy exchange with him. I had to go with him for his access to base and for him to shop on base. Uncle Tim was a Navy Corpsman as well, one of my inspirations, and I knew he would like to get some Navy apparel. Before I go on about our adventure to the nearest naval base, I would like to tell you of a cool design he made for me to assist me in loading in/out of a vehicle. He designed a special long and smooth board with smaller wooden pieces attached to latch onto the arm of the wheelchair. I would attach it on the arm, hop up on the board, and use the handgrip in the truck to pull myself up. It was tricky getting out, though, because the board was smooth and I would always wear basketball shorts. So if I didn't plan out my exit just right, I would slide down and topple over in my chair. This was an excellent device that he created.

Well, we loaded up fairly early and headed over toward Ventura to go hit up the naval base. It was a good thirty- to forty-minute drive depending on traffic. We arrived on base and went around the whole shopping center just looking at everything. Uncle Tim liked to update his Navy attire as often as he could, and when he did, he loaded up on as much as he could. I actually needed some PT gear so when I went back to base and went to physical therapy, I could actually be in some sort of uniform and be somewhat comfortable. After grabbing some food from the food court, we drove around the base for a little bit, just checking out where the clinic was and some useful places that I might need to know about for later visits. Soon after, we began heading back, just taking our time and moseying along. It was actually really good to finally hang out with Uncle Tim and share corpsman stories with him.

I will give you a backstory on how I became a corpsman in a little bit, but it was because of Uncle Tim.

We arrived back at the house in early evening, and Uncle Tim wheeled me in the house backward due to the little lip in the doorway; he had to lift me up from behind and then wheel me in. So we finally got inside, and it was quiet, but when I turned to the left, I saw people jump out of nowhere, yelling, "Surprise!"

I was honestly surprised . . . and startled. It got quiet, and I saw my papa walking up to me. He leaned down and gave me a big hug and said, "Welcome home, son. I am proud of you." Seeing everyone excited as they silently watched Papa make his way over to me and to hear him speak those words made it feel like everything was going to be more than okay. It was amazing to have his blessing as well. Something I had spent my whole life seeking was his pride in me. Soon after, everyone rushed in to hug me and welcome me home. It was such a great feeling to have all of my family and friends in one location. Plus, it was a great thing to have my family in one place without an argument or a fight. One of the first hugs I got and will never forget was from my goddaughter, or as I call her, my baby girl. She hugged me and just wouldn't let go. I was fine with that, though.

5.

LET THE GAMES BEGIN

Soon after my welcome home party, I was welcomed home, officially, by my parent command. I say that I was "officially" welcomed home by my parent command because I was welcomed by someone from there when I was in Bethesda. My Sea Daddy (Navy Mentor), Mario, flew to Bethesda to visit me long before this "official welcoming." They seemed to discredit Mario's trip to Bethesda as anything to with the command, and they took credit for it. That's fine because I know his agenda was to ensure that I was doing good and not what he could put in his eval or by just following protocol.

I got a phone call from the command Chief asking if I was going to be home on a certain day, and I said I would be there. I made it for a day when Aunt Sheila was going to be home with me so I wouldn't be alone in case I was set to be cornered by the command. Prior to the command coming up, Mario gave me a call and said he wished he could come up to see me with the group, but he didn't want to be in the circus. I told him I understood and appreciated his honesty and integrity. Then we both laughed about how he was the official one to greet me from the command and how they originally took credit for his initiative but now this visit was the initial/original visit.

A few months prior, they told Mario that he couldn't go TAD, or Temporary Assigned Duty, or no-cost TAD, which doesn't cost the command or the government anything, since the service member or an organization pays for the costs. So he had to take his own personal time and spend his own money to make sure his junior doc, or boot, was doing okay.

When the members of the command showed up, I was excited to see the junior members that I worked with before. One of the corpsmen was one who went to 3/7 and Iraq with me. He was in Weapons Company, and I was in India Company. He was the last one to walk in. I could tell that the sight of me in a wheelchair destroyed him. To combat his brokenness, I got up out of the wheelchair to hug him. He told me to sit down, rest, and that he would come to me. I told him that I wanted to stand and hug my friend. He could barely look at me and be in the same room. I later found out why.

The rest of the group was interested in how I was doing overall and how it felt to be home. We discussed the deployed life, and I shared with them my whole deployment and my whole Bethesda experience. I will give you a quick back brief on why I was in Ventura recovering. I was approved by the Navy to recover at home as long as I could make my appointments. Thus, the cause for in-home occupational, speech, and physical therapy and the approval of the in-home assistant devices, as well. Okay, so back to the command visit. Toward the end of the visit I was in fact cornered by the Lieutenant and was told, "You are to be on your doorstep at 0800 in your chair with what gear you have. There will be a van to pick you up, and you will be escorted to the barracks at Balboa. You will check into the Medical Holding Company on the same day. Failure to do so will result in being charged as UA (Unauthorized Absence) and Article 92, failure to obey a direct order."

I thought to myself, *Well, this is the beginning of the end!*

Shortly after being cornered, it was naturally time for them to "get back," and I was beyond excited for them to be leaving. Well, my buddy who I deployed with came in for a few moments to talk to me. I asked him why he was being so distant and told him that everything was okay now. We had gone through training and everything together, then we got stationed at this clinic and worked closely for a short time before we were deployed together into Ramadi in 2005-2006. We never saw each other overseas, but we knew how the other was through our medical comrades. Just a few days before I was injured, we ran into each other on Camp Blue Diamond at the Internet Center. When we saw each other, we hugged and expressed our gratitude to see one another, especially under the circumstances. We soon went back to groups and prayed to reunite again soon.

He told me, as we sat on the couch together, that his unit was hit at nearly the same time we were on that day in late February. He said he heard my last four called over the net as a casualty, and he was just torn from there. By the time I arrived at Charlie Med, the helicopter was near, so I was examined to ensure I would make the flight to Balad Surgical. He brought his casualty in soon after I had been gone, but he had no knowledge of my medical evacuation. He made sure his casualty was going to be okay then asked around if anyone had any knowledge on where I was and my status. He asked a female Army medical personnel, and her only response was, "I don't know, he could be the dead body somewhere in the back." He frantically ran back there looking for me and was relieved when he realized it wasn't me, but the way it was handled was completely unprofessional.

I then knew and understood why he was distant with me. Soon after sharing his experience with me, he was starting to be rushed by the group. I told him to give me a hug. When he did, he started to cry and said, "I thought you were dead. I didn't know how to begin to feel about it and the thought of losing you . . . "

I told him, "I am here now, brother, and that is all that matters. We are here now, and everything will be okay." He agreed and then left.

I shortly began bitching to Aunt Sheila about how messed up it was and that now I had to be all by myself at Balboa battling the unknown. She agreed to an extent but then kept reminding me that they were my superiors and their orders were meant to be followed. I knew that's the way it was and would always be, but it just didn't seem to be a legitimate reason. I would have understood it better if there had been a reason other than, "I order you to do this, and if you don't obey my orders, you will be punished!" Trust me, I did ask for reasoning, and they had none, so to this day, I still have no idea why this deal was broken.

I took my time gathering what I had that I thought I needed in Balboa and packing everything I could. I figured, *Why should I care what I have to take down there when I don't have to carry it?* Well, on that given Monday, I had my bags prepacked and staged at the front door. I sat inside enjoying my morning while I waited for my escort van to show up. When it finally did, I loaded in and headed to the unknown battles that awaited me in Balboa.

My arrival at the barracks in Balboa was actually a great one. The Marine Medical Holding Company staff greeted me, and they seemed glad to have me there. I was soon told that I would be in an accessible room with a roommate. I gathered my stuff and headed down the long hallways to my room. When I read the name on the door to check who my roommate was, I was quite shocked. It was a fellow Corpsman who I went through Field Med School, CTM, and Iraq with.

My roommate was in at the time of my arrival, and we caught up for a little bit. The last time we had chatted was when I was laying in the surgical ward in Bethesda. He called a few times to check in on me from his hospital location, where he was rehabilitating, in Texas. It was a shock to have linked up with him in Balboa again, and to have been roommates in the hospital barracks was a great blessing. He helped me along the way on a few accounts throughout our time at Balboa together.

6.

SCREWED

Soon after I was settled into my barracks room at Balboa, I was contacted by the command that had recently screwed me over, requesting my assistance in a situation. There was a fellow Corpsman from the command that was wounded in combat and was in Bethesda ICU. They needed to use my connections and/or me to be the middleman for them. I found it funny that they were quick to screw me over but when they needed something, they just expected me to forget about it all and jump to assist them.

Well, I did jump to assist them because this was the time to set all emotions aside and just be there for the Corpsman and his family. I made a few calls and told the command to sleep easy because he was in good hands. I then tried to work it out for the command to allow me to go TAD (Temporary Assigned Duty) to go visit him and offer some relief for his family while I was to be at his bedside. They denied the TAD request, not a real shocker to me. I then submitted a no-cost TAD request, no cost to the command or military, and that was denied as well.

For a command that was in serious need of my assistance . . . they didn't want to offer any assistance in return. I didn't let that stand in the way of helping out my fellow Corpsman and his family in their time of need. So I submitted to use my own personal leave and fly out there on my own.

I flew out to Washington, DC, to see this mission through. I flew on the night flight and landed the next morning. I checked into the hotel and went to the ICU right away. When I arrived, I saw an understandably tired and stressed wife standing outside his ICU room. I checked into the ICU and stated my intent for the visit to the staff. Some of them knew me from months before and were surprised to see me again but were happy to know that I had the heart to come back and give back.

I introduced myself to his wife and explained to her that I was there to give her a week's worth of rest and relaxation. I didn't tell her that I was there for the command, because that was complete bullshit. I wasn't there to represent their terrible ways so they could claim my personal trip as their own. I did tell her that I wanted her to go home, pay the bills, and relax, and when the week was over, she could come back. I told her it wasn't an option and I would constantly give her updates and liaison between the medical staff. She then stated how she was worried about money and her travels back home. I went down to the ATM and took some cash out and told her I didn't want the money back and I wanted her to be okay and stress free. She expressed her thanks for me being there for her husband and soon left. I spent a whole week by his side. I sat there in the ICU in my wheelchair holding his hand and watching sports.

Shortly after I was settled in, I was down at the orthopedics clinic discussing my next surgery. After the surgery, I was set to begin a thirty-day convalescing leave period where I could focus on recovering with assistance from family and friends. I hadn't had a surgery since early May 2006, so I figured there must have been a reason for the surgery. I was honestly a little fearful going into it under the hands of a new orthopedic surgeon, but because I knew he was a Naval orthopedic surgeon and had deployed into a combat zone, I figured I could trust him.

Prior to the surgery date, the surgeon told me not to do anything stupid. Well, I didn't think, at the time, that going to get a tattoo was a stupid thing. I didn't think of it as risk for anything. So my little dumb and young self made my way over to a tattoo shop in Pacific Beach with my roommate to get my first tattoo. I decided on an evil joker holding a royal flush. It was something I thought of that would be an image of how I remembered two of our Marines. I got it on the left side of my chest, directly over the heart, to show that my Marines would always consume the entirety of my heart.

I showed up to surgery on Monday morning with a fresh tattoo under my hospital attire. The surgeon came in to discuss last-minute things with me and go over any questions I might have. I had none, and soon I was taken back to the operating room. Once I was back in the OR, I was assisted with the transfer to the operating table. Soon, the staff was connecting the leads to my chest for the heart monitor and in doing so pulled my hospital attire off my chest. The orthopedic surgeon came up to me, noticing my fresh tattoo, and asked a rhetorical question: "What is that?"

To which I responded with a sly, smart-ass remark, "A stupid thing."

He then began to drill into me, verbally, about how I was in violation of failure to follow a direct order. He then asked me how I planned on keeping the fresh tattoo from drying out. I told him that I planned on keeping it from getting dry by being home on con leave. He then laughed at me and told me that due to my not being able to follow his orders, he was going to ensure that I stayed a few extra days to make sure I didn't acquire an infection from my "stupid mistake," and during that time, I wouldn't be allowed to keep the tattoo moistened.

After a few days of a hospital stay, I was on my way back to my room to put in for the command's approval of con leave. I waited to put in my request due to the unforeseen quantity of days that I had recently spent in the hospital. No, not due to my tattoo but for my unknown knowledge on the process/recovery time from an outpatient surgery. Plus, this was my first surgery as an outpatient.

Back to the con leave. So I put in my request, and I thought it went through the proper channels. To my surprise, I was called into the office later that day and was told that it was denied and I'd have to spend my time recovering in the barracks or in the local area. I was given no explanation why, and I had an uncle already in San Diego ready to take me to the family in Ventura.

The procedure that I had done was causing some severe pain, and it hurt to even wheel myself in the wheelchair. I honestly couldn't imagine recovering without assistance from family. I made a bold move, and it might not have been the right move, now that I look back. I called on some big guns in Washington, DC, to assist with this roadblock. I called and left a message stating, "Sir, I hate calling and complaining, but I have an issue. I have no idea why a Petty Officer First Class is denying me con leave after I have just had a major and painful surgery to continue the salvage of my right leg." To make a long story short, 0900 the next day, I was called into the staff office and was "approved" for con leave and heading home to recover.

During the times I was in the barracks and not being on con leave and the leave I took for my fellow Corpsman in Bethesda, I was really hunkered down in there. I took my downtime pretty seriously and kind of enjoyed just sitting back and listening to music and doing research on the various types of amputations. Soon, I was about to embark on a serious battle with military staff that had no understanding of teamwork or how to be sympathetic.

Every Thursday, there is a thing in the military called "Field Day." This section of time is set in place for you to clean everything from your room to your workspace. The consequences of failing a field day inspection vary in severity. The main thing is to get it done right the first time so there is no need to worry about failing and having to redo your work. Granted, different approving authorities have different expectations, but you still don't want to fail.

So there was little me in my barracks room in a wheelchair, non-weightbearing on either leg, doing my best to field day. Believe it or not, I could actually clean a lot from my wheelchair. Well, I did make it easier on myself, though, by using disposable plates, bowls, and plasticware. I did improvise the issue on taking the trash out, which usually resulted in a shower afterwards due to me having to set the trash on my lap and wheel the trash out to the dumpster. It didn't seem to help with the issue of high dusting, though. I figured the command would overlook it due to my injuries and lack of abilities to get to that part.

I had my first room inspection and failed due to lack of high dusting. I put up as much of a protest as I could, but it was all just an excuse; I should have figured out a way to make it happen. I then had to "fix the solution" and go through another inspection later that Friday; otherwise, my liberty would be secured. I thought to myself, *I'm stuck here all weekend, anyway, so I am not even going to bother.* Sixteen hundred rolled around, and they came knocking on my door, and I just opened and said not to even bother coming in because I didn't clean the areas I couldn't reach and I wouldn't risk injuring myself for their craziness.

On Monday morning, I was called in and asked why I was about to be charged with failure to obey a direct order. I stated what I had told the Petty Officer Second Class that inspected my room. I had a doctor's note that stated I wasn't allowed to put any weight on my legs. I then asked them how they proposed to assist me in this situation. This stumped them, and while they were trying to think of a way to help me, I said, "I would like to see that Captain's Mast. Me, not being physically capable of doing a simple task of field daying and the command so quick to burn me at the stake. All the while, they sit and twiddle their thumbs and don't lift a finger to offer advice or simply assist me in one simple task. Hmm, that would truly be an interesting one."

Out of all the ideas they came up with, none of them involved entering my room and grabbing some cleaner and cloth to assist me.

Their only option to help was to assist with the trash when they took theirs out at the end of the day. I had already had that covered with just throwing it on my lap and wheeling downstairs to the dumpster. Even their plan to "assist me" didn't last long before the trash sat out in the hallways, leaving me to clean up the mess again.

I called some friends to bitch about how horrible these folks were, and they told me it was a simple solution. They would just show up on either Wednesday or Thursday to help me completely field day. That is true teamwork and compassion right there, and it was a simple fix. So every week, they would come down and bring some pizza, and we would jam out, clean, and bullshit about all the bullshit. Way better than having some grumpy-ass POG in my room, anyway.

The con leave seemed to go by fairly faster this time around than the previous trip home to recover, and I was back in Balboa deciding what was next in my recovery. I had gone over to the orthopedics clinic to have an afterhours discussion with my surgeon about my options for my left leg. I did this for many reasons, and the main one was simple. When we had previously discussed my surgical options of limb salvage on my left leg, he didn't really seem to have a lot to say about it. I didn't take it the wrong way, but it sure did weigh on my mind for a few months. So this brought me to a discussion with him.

That discussion was fairly short due to the surgeon not wanting to push his straightforward views on my situation. I then began to think, *I should probably do my research on what I need to do next.* I figured the best option would be to discuss amputation and which one would be best for me. I would soon begin this mission by talking with a staff member from the Marine Medical Holding Company, a Marine Sergeant.

I will tell you a quick backstory about my decision on amputation. When I was in the back of the Humvee being taken to Charlie Med at Camp Ramadi, I looked up at the Marine who was over me and told him, "Don't be surprised if the next time you see me I am missing one or both of my legs." Then when I was in Bethesda, my brother was by my hospital bed, and I told him that I was considering amputation. When I looked at him, he was overwhelmed with tears. I then went into damage control mode and told him that I was only considering it and would be sure to give it plenty of thought and do my homework before I came to such a conclusion.

I honestly knew in Bethesda that my left leg was on the chopping block. They didn't seem to have many options for the chronic neuro pain that I was suffering. Remember back to my dad having to create a mallet so I wouldn't break my hand on my cast. The nursing staff from the ward still remembers me for beating my cast into the early hours of the morning. It seemed to become second nature to hit the cast when I experienced the pain. I was taking the maximum dose to treat the symptoms, and it was causing so many stomach issues as well.

So here I was a few months later sitting down with my Sergeant discussing amputations. I was curious what type of procedure he had done and how he went about it. I knew he was doing very well with his amputation and prosthetic because he was injured years before and continued to improve and become an amazing success. That was what I wanted but knew that what worked for one person might not work for the other. He told me this, and he also gave me sound advice on how to gather knowledge, who to talk to, and the appropriate channels necessary for my mission. It was amazing how much knowledge I gained for both paths, and he never guided me onto a certain path.

I took the knowledge I had gathered and discussed with my roommate, who was an above-the-knee amputee (also known as an AKA or AK). He told me that it would be a choice that I would have to make, and I would know when to make that decision. I then told him about some of the family's views and feelings on it, and he just laughed really hard at me and said, "That sucks, bro!" I knew based on the conversation and reading between the lines that I should do what was best for me and not worry about what others thought or said.

7.

DECISION TIME

Before I was to fly out to my brother's graduation in Chicago for his training course, I decided to go have another afterhours conference with my orthopedic surgeon. I went down there knowing what I wanted out of the conversation but needed his non-sugarcoated and honest opinion. When I arrived down into his office, he was running behind on patients, so I agreed to hang out and wait. I waited a few hours for yet another quick meeting.

I rolled into the conference room and looked at him and said, "Sir, I am here to seek your brutal and honest opinion." I could tell this garnered his attention, and I sort of repeated myself and said, "Sir, I am not seeking a sugarcoated piece of medical advice. In my circumstance, what would you honestly say that I should do?"

And he replied, "Amputate. Hold on and wait here while I gather the rest of the ortho docs around here so we can discuss this in full with second, third, fourth, and seventh opinions."

When the other orthopedic surgeons came in, they pulled up my radiology images and reports and then examined my foot. Each and every one of them concluded that a below the knee, trans-tibial amputation was the best option. I then asked if he had done any Ertle procedures before, and he asked how I knew what an Ertle procedure was. I told him that I had been doing my research for a while. He seemed to be impressed with my thoroughness and said I would be his third procedure if I were to decide on amputation. I told him that I knew I had no shot at staying in if I didn't amputate and I wouldn't even have a shot at a decent quality of life. He told me that I had no shot of staying in and I would probably be wheelchair bound for the remainder of my life or, at most, on crutches. I told him that I wanted to get it scheduled and begin improving my quality of life.

The surgery was scheduled, and I was on my way to Chicago to see my brother graduate. When I arrived in Chicago, I told him about my decision, and he did what I thought he would: he got teary eyed. I told him I thought things through, did my research, and had decided that this was what was best for me. He asked if I'd told our parents, and I told him I hadn't just yet. Our mother was flying in a few hours after I arrived, and I said I intended on telling her then. When I told her, she was fine with it and asked, "Is this what you want to do? Is this something that will help you and help you achieve your goals?" I said yes to both, and she said, "Well, if it's what you want, I will support you."

That wasn't even a minor bump in the road. The biggest hurdle was yet to come. Remember how my dad and G-Ma were against the whole amputation thing, one hundred percent against it? Yeah, that's the next major hurdle I will have to describe to you. This was a fairly tricky plan that I had to come up with, coordinate, and accomplish. The big problem with having my amputation in Balboa and Pops and G-Ma back in Ohio was telling them about the surgery and still getting them to come out. I had to devise a whole master plan to have them there for it without their knowledge.

It was actually simple. I just told them I was going to have surgery on October 20th and figured they would show up. Well, it was simple, but I didn't expect the questions, such as: *What are they doing? What leg will they be working on? How will this help you?* I improvised the shit out the answers when my pops asked me, "Well, what are they doing?" I told him it was a surgery that would better my left foot.

Did I feel bad about doing this? One hundred percent! I didn't want to keep information, leave out details, or even lie, especially to my own dad. I felt terrible about it all but knew I had to do whatever it took to have Dad and G-Ma there. The worst part was that wasn't even a speed bump compared to what lay ahead. I thought that was it with that, well, for the most part.

I was informed that there was a new study that showed if I were numb in my leg at least three days prior to amputation, it would severely decrease the risk or chance of phantom limb pain. I told the ortho surgeon that I didn't want to do that because I wanted to feel the full effect of being an amputee and didn't want to take the easy way out. He looked at me as though I was crazy. I told him that I didn't want any nerve blocks of any sort because I wanted to feel the pain so I could look at other amputees and say I knew their pain. He chuckled at me and asked if that's what I wanted to do for sure. I then told him of my other reasoning: Dad and G-Ma. I told him that I only gave vague details to them due to their strong views against amputation. He then said I would eventually have to tell them, but he did understand my need for them to be there.

Dad and G-Ma flew out a few days before so we could get some quality time in and ensure that any pre-surgery things were lined up so the recovery was as smooth as could be. I was blessed and cursed to have my pre-operative appointment done the day before my surgery. Dad, G-Ma, and I were in the orthopedic cast room waiting to begin the pre-operative stuff. Dad was reading the paper, and G-Ma was sitting down and just looking around at all the medical tools/supplies. The surgeon came in and began going over the basic pre-surgery stuff about past medical history, allergies, labs, x-rays . . . etc. Then he came to the question, "Are you sure you don't want a nerve block?" followed by, "You might experience a ton of potentially avoidable phantom limb pain if not."

I noticed my dad moved the newspaper down to the table fairly quick and was whiter than a ghost when he asked, "Phantom limb pain? What type of procedure is he having done here, doctor?"

The surgeon just looked up at me and said, "You haven't told them yet?"

My dad was still pale white and looked at me while asking, "Told me what?"

I looked at Dad then down with guilt and shame and said, "Tomorrow morning, I am having my left leg amputated."

He then responded, "Who authorized this? You can't make that decision with all of the medications you're taking. Doc, is there some place where we can go hash this out?"

They disappeared fairly quickly and were gone for a while. When they came back, the doctor said he would have to postpone the surgery because my dad and grandmother were right about the legality of my decision-making abilities while taking the medications.

He did suggest that a team of mental health professionals could deem me mentally competent if I would like to try that route. I told him that I felt great with my decision and it was well-thought out and planned out. He agreed with me, but he also had to agree with my dad as well. I didn't want it to be called off because I was ready and prepared. I didn't want to prolong the surgery and recovery.

The night before my leg was due to get axed, I was surrounded by a team of mental health professionals to find me fit to make decisions. I figured it was useless, but I had to try, because if I didn't have the surgery, when would I be able to come off the medications and be mentally fit to make this decision? If I weren't on the medications, I would be in so much pain that I wouldn't be found fit, either. I answered all of their questions and did what I could to be as "normal" as possible for having eight or so mental health professionals surrounding me.

They didn't give me an answer, just left the room and entered another one. I was very unclear as to what would happen next and what I would do if I wasn't fit to make the decision to do what was best for my body. After some time, the orthopedic surgeon called all of us into a room and gave Dad and G-Ma credit for raising an issue that he had never encountered before and that he should probably build a guideline of what to do if this were to ever happen again. He then told us that the team found me well beyond fit to make this decision. The team had told him that I was the most mentally sound patient they had ever encountered while on those medications and dosages. He then laid it out to me that it was now one hundred percent my choice to proceed, postpone, or cancel. I told him everything was still going on as planned. I felt bad, but I had to think about quality of life and many other variables that played a factor on the need to continue on as planned.

Pops and G-Ma left the hospital as soon as the appointment was over. I took my time heading back over to the barracks. When I got into my room, I had some friends there waiting for me, and they could just see that it was a rough appointment. They tried to discuss it with me, but I was honestly doing fine. Soon after, they figured I just needed some time to myself. Which was fine with me, seeing it was an early check-in time at the main OR.

The morning of October 20, 2006, I checked into the main OR like scheduled. There was a well-mixed group of family and friends that were there and waiting. After some of the basic paperwork, we took pictures and made light of the situation. Soon after, I was called into the holding area to continue the process before surgery. In the holding area, only one to two family members and/or friends were allowed back in with me. All of my friends wished me the best and then sent the family in. One by one, the family came in and told me they loved me and everything would be okay.

Dad and G-Ma were the last ones in to see me off, and let me tell you, G-Ma wasn't too pleased about it all. Pops told me that everything would be all right and he would be there regardless. I looked to G-Ma for some sort of wisdom or guidance, and to my surprise, I was given a cold shoulder, well, a teary-eyed grandma shaking her head at me. Dad gave me a hug and told me he loved me then began to head out into the waiting area. I thought G-Ma would come over and at least give me a hug and tell me she loved me, but when my dad got up and began to walk out, she got up and began to leave with him. I shouted out to her as she was walking out that I loved her and I would be all right.

I woke up in the PACU (Post-Anesthesia Care Unit) to an individual standing over me and slightly shaking me. When I opened my eyes, I was asked, "HM3 Jacobs, how are you feeling?"

I responded immediately, without seeing who was asking, "It fucking hurts! How do you think I am feeling?!?"

There was a quick voice that tried to correct my terms and who I was addressing by stating, "HM3, that is an Admiral you are addressing!"

I thought for a split second of how to play this one out and decided, *"It fucking hurts, SIR!"*

The Admiral said, "It's okay, HM3, and will be all right. I wanted to be the first one you spoke to when you woke up. I want you to know that you are a hero and you're not in this alone. HM3, get your rest now and know that not only am I proud of you, but Navy medicine across the board is as well."

I said, "Honestly, sir, I really appreciate it, and I am truly sorry for the way I responded out of surgery." He told me not to worry about it and he'd probably have the same reaction if he were to be in my situation. I dozed back off for an unknown amount of time and then was awakened with the promise to be able to go into my hospital room if I stayed awake for a certain amount of time. I must have done so, because I remember it wasn't too long before I was being wheeled out to my room.

I spent five days in the hospital, and those days were full of pain, discomfort, and weird new feelings and pains. I must say that those five days were some of the worst days of my life. I hardly slept at all, mainly because it was difficult for me to sleep without someone I knew around. I just felt too on guard, and throwing in amputating my leg was a bad combo. I did utilize my computer to keep me company during the late-night hours when nothing was on TV. There were a few nights, after the nurses were tired of my late-night music and movies, I asked a friend to stay. He would bring over some teriyaki chicken from a place we frequented in San Diego.

A few months before my amputation, I had decided that it would be best if I had physically proven the orthopedic surgeon in Bethesda. I called while I was still on con leave in Ventura County. I spoke with the Corpsman at the clinic, and he booked for an appointment. I notified my dad and G-Ma of my soon-to-be adventures to Bethesda to prove to that ortho doc that I could walk again. They said they would meet me there, so I then began to make the travel arrangements with my own personal leave time.

Dad and G-Ma greeted me when I arrived into the Washington, DC, region. They had already been checked into the hotel on base. Due to it being a short trip and everyone being tired from traveling, we just ordered in and spent some time catching up on things. Dad and I later linked up with Curt at the on-base bowling alley for a few drinks and caught up with him as well.

The next day, I was woken up by G-Ma telling me I needed to wake up and start getting ready for my appointment. I looked at the time with my sleepy eyes and said, "G-Ma, I don't have to get up for at least two more hours."

She sighed and said, "Okay, honey, suit yourself."

Little did I know how G-Ma would wake me up again. She let me fall back asleep, and as soon as I did . . . BLAM! She picked up my end of the mattress and rolled me out of bed and flipped the whole mattress on me. The whole time, she was yelling, "Don't you talk back to your grandmother! Nor any woman, for that matter. When I tell you to get out of bed, you get your ass out of the bed. Now go get ready for your appointment. This is a big appointment, and you can't be late for it."

I just responded with, "Yes, G-Ma," and I began to hustle around like I was a recruit again. We were off to the appointment shortly after the family Sergeant Major put me in my place. I still didn't understand why we were heading to the appointment three to four hours early, but I sure as hell wasn't about to question G-Ma. Although we did go to the ground floor of the hospital to hit up their food court. I must say that portion of the hospital was pretty impressive.

It was kind of fate that put us in the food court at that time because I was strolling along in my chair with a tray of food, and I saw the ortho doc coming into the food court. I grabbed us a table as I watched to see where he was going to be sitting at. I waved for Dad and G-Ma to come over to our table then continued to watch the ortho doc. I noticed he was getting his food to go, as well as his group of fellow doctors, which wasn't too much of a surprise.

I then stood out of my chair and walked over to him. Walking on my right leg wasn't too bad, but on my left was extremely painful. I wasn't about to let him see the pain, though, and put on a smile and smiled through the pain, knowing I was about to claim first defeat in my path back to duty. He paused, and I noticed he had that look of "I know you from somewhere," so I introduced myself. He then asked what had brought me to the area, and I told him that I had an appointment with him in a few short hours. I then told him, "Sir, I am here to prove to you that I in fact have walked again when you told me I would never be able to walk again without amputating my legs."

His only response was, "Can you do it without the walking boots?"

I was shocked by this question, and it really upset me that he wouldn't be proud or even happy for me, but for him to just jump on the defense and defend his reasoning was rude, arrogant, and disrespectful of my accomplishment. He could have at least showed some sort of care, concern, or pride (even if it was pride in his work). I still attended my appointment a few hours later, and we didn't really speak much in the appointment. What I had flown out there to do I had already done during chow time.

I did head up to the surgery ward after my appointment, though, to go visit the remaining staff. I went up the elevator and then left my wheelchair around the corner from the nursing station and walked around the corner. Some of the staff noticed right away and ran around to hug and congratulate me. They were so proud and so happy for me. They said it was rare for patients to return and they were so glad that I did. They asked how long I was going to be around, and I told them I was set to fly out the next day. They asked me to surprise the oncoming crew before I left so they would have the chance to see me as well.

I returned the next day and was greeted with the same enthusiasm and pride. It is so therapeutic for everyone in such a situation. Both sides see the worst of the patient, and if he or she doesn't return once they have left the medical facility, then those are the last images that the medical staff is left with. So when someone returns and they are doing better, it brings a lot of closure for all that are involved. I know it was from my side because it is good to know that they actually cared so much and were filled with joy and pride when I returned. I will never forget their smiles filled with tears of joy.

The next weeks were long and filled with many long nights. This began a small period of time that laid some of the foundation of why I am who I am today. I hope I can help capture these weeks for you so you can relive them with me.

The phantom pain/phantom limb sensations began almost immediately after amputation. This was something I expected and wanted no sympathy from anyone, not that I had ever wanted sympathy, because I did it all going against medical advice. All in all, the pain and sensation I was feeling was new to me, and I figured this shit would take a while for my body and mind to get used to, but I had no idea the effect it would have on me.

When I was released out of the hospital, I had to start my physical therapy right away. This seemed odd to me because I would be down there to rehab the leg that I just had amputated, but to my surprise, I would be doing the complete opposite. My initial physical therapy was all core workouts and upper body cardio machines. Did this frustrate me? Hell yes, it did. I was kind of pissed off that I rolled into physical therapy and was told to begin working on my cardio on this arm bike. Then when I was done with that, I started working on my core exercises. Those took up my whole hour appointment, leaving me wondering, *When will I get to work on my legs?* I mean, at least let me work on my right leg. Well, I figured they knew what they were doing, and I should just sit back and let them run the show.

A few weeks after my amputation, my old unit, 3/7, was set to have their Marine Corps Ball down in the San Diego area. This was really sweet because it was just a few minutes away from Balboa. It was good to see everyone again and to actually sit down and bullshit with everyone and, to top it off, meet their loved ones. I still put on my dress blues and rolled into the ceremony in my wheelchair. This played to my benefit because I could have someone push me while I carried two drinks.

I did put on a set of corfams, glossy dress shoes. I could do so because of the prosthetic foot that was attached to the cast that they put in place as a neurological trick to combat phantom limb pain. It also felt really great to be able to stand and give my Marines a hug, shake the hands of the great officers that I served under, do toasts, and take pictures with all of them. It seemed like everything was perfectly timed out, and I was blessed to have it so.

Since my release from the hospital, I had these feelings that my orthopedic surgeon had warned about, and I know that the majority of it was my fault for not going with his advice prior to surgery, so I figured it was something I would have to learn to combat and deal with on my own. Luckily for me, I had something that was second nature to me already: beating my cast to hit the nerve in hopes to temporarily calm it. This was a similar but new battle because I had to find the nerve that was causing the phantom pain/sensation.

The orthopedic surgeon told me that I wouldn't have to do that for long because once the cast came off, I could put a shrinker sock on my residual limb (stump or nub) and it would ease the nerve. He told me to continue taking my nerve pain medication as well, and I did. Once the cast came off and the sutures came out, which hurt *so bad*, I was allowed to put the shrinker sock on. The sutures coming out of the incision site for the amputation was so sensitive and was some extreme pain, a new type of pain and something I grew accustomed to after a few surgeries throughout the following years.

Throughout the weeks of hitting the cast again, nerve medications, and a shrinker sock, I had received no sleep whatsoever. It seemed like every time I laid down, my leg would tingle so bad that I would stay up for hours hitting the nerves that I could hit to try and reach some sort of reasoning with them, but no luck.

Right before Veterans' Day weekend of 2006, nearly three weeks later, a friend of mine from Camp Pendleton asked if I wanted to accompany him out toward Palm Springs while he did some stuff to help a friend. I agreed, and the next day, I asked one of my good buddies if he wanted me to visit him and his family. He gladly agreed and met us right outside Palm Springs. He said he had duty the next day, but I didn't care. I just wanted to hang out with him. I felt uncomfortable staying with his wife while he was on duty, and to honor the bro code, I decided to hang out with him on duty. We stayed up all night in the duty hut catching up and shooting the shit. He told me I should probably rest and to crash on the couch. I told him I hadn't slept in a few weeks. He didn't believe me, but he went to the exchange and grabbed some extra strength sleeping pills.

I took a few of those bad boys, and sure, I felt drowsy, but once I laid down . . . the tingling began to hit me. So I just sat up and put in a movie we rented from the video store. The next day, he was post duty, and we all went to grab a nice dinner and then caught an early showing of a movie. The following day, I began my journey back to San Diego, and on the way back, I met with Mario. It worked out really great that I linked up with him as well because I stayed the night with him and his family as well. He too was baffled by my lack of sleep and couldn't offer a good fix for my situation. The next day he took me into our command, and I had the pleasure of seeing some old friends again. I was his excuse to get out of work early because he had to return me to my room at Balboa.

A few more weeks of physical therapy and not being able to sleep went by, and before I knew it, I was heading to the San Diego International Airport on my way to see family in Colorado for the Thanksgiving holiday. This would be my second trip out there, my first being on leave and staying awake and keeping the drivers company (mainly with two sets of two-way radios). This trip, I didn't have a prosthetic leg yet, so I had to crutch my way through the airports. Well, I could have used the carts that are offered for persons with disabilities. I made a huge mistake at the Phoenix Sky Harbor International Airport while making a connecting flight to Denver. I had my big green, former medical, bag and was crutching along through the long terminal connectors. I decided it would be a great idea to attempt to crutch onto a moving walkway.

I know, I know, it was a lame idea . . . I did look at the signs prior to doing it, and they suggested that no wheelchairs or strollers be allowed onto the moving walkways. So I braved it, anyway. I fell immediately, and to top it off, without thinking that my leg was no longer there, I put my left "leg" out and landed right on my stump! I didn't have time to bitch, moan, or even acknowledge what had just happened. The next thing I realized was I had very limited time left on this walkway before it came to an end. I had to improvise a plan quick. Otherwise, I was doomed for round two.

I picked up my crutches and held them both in my left hand and held onto the rail with my right. When the walkway came to an end, I bent down on my right leg and hopped off. I didn't want to sit at the end of the walkway assessing the damage, so I just crutched on to the gate. Soon after I got there, I sat down near the gate and took some medicine right away and then assessed. To my surprise, there wasn't any damage to my leg, just a fair amount of pain. I *highly* suggest to those out there on crutches to not attempt a moving walkway. I was too proud to ride in the cart for persons with disabilities, but if you need that shit, I would say utilize it. That's what it's there for.

My time in Colorado with the family was some good times, and my family had some pretty good initial amputee jokes. During some of the post-Halloween candy sales, Aunt Sheila decided she was funny and was going to buy some chocolate fingers and tell me she found my replacement fingers. Later in the trip, we drove up to Wyoming. For Thanksgiving dinner, we had some fast food chicken. Aunt Sheila was in the kitchen and volunteered to grab me a plate, and without thinking of what she was about to ask, she just went for it: "Danny, would you like a leg?"

I swore the whole place went silent, and I casually responded with, "Yes, Aunt Sheila, I would *love* to have a *leg*!" Everyone stopped and stared in pure horror.

Aunt Sheila just laughed and said, "I know you would like a leg, Danny, but would you like a chicken leg?" Everyone didn't know that I am fine with people, especially my close family, making jokes. I think it's good to make light of the situation and have fun with what we have.

I ended up back in my room after a good week of being with family, and no, I did not sleep during the week I was gone. At the end of that week, I was sitting at six weeks without sleep. I wore my shrinker sock like it was a religious medallion, hoping it would help the ongoing phantom limb pain/sensations. That didn't seem to work as well as I thought.

After about six weeks of not being able to sleep and trying everything conceivable to get some sort of rest and for any amount of time, I was beginning to get really frustrated and was thinking very irrational thoughts on how to fall asleep. I had tossed around some horrible ideas for a few days as I rolled around my room and refused to turn my phone on and speak to anyone. I mean, I didn't answer for anyone. For once in my life, I was having a rough time figuring out a situation. Well, I determined one solution that would work for sure, and I knew it wasn't the best of solutions, but I had to try it.

One night, I looked in the refrigerator and noticed that I had two six-packs of beer, so I grabbed a big glass out of my cabinet and poured as much as I could in there. I grabbed the rest of the beer and rolled back in by my beanbag. I didn't have cable at the time, so I put a long movie on and proceeded with my plan. Please take note that what I am about to tell you about what happened next is extremely harmful and could cause death. I don't support this behavior, and I regret the fact that I did this, especially being a corpsman and knowing the risks. I grabbed the box of sleeping pills and took some out of the individual plastic/foil wrappings. I had enough to cover the palm of my left hand. With my right hand, I grabbed the big mug of beer and took a drink but didn't swallow and threw the pills in my mouth. I then chugged the remaining beer in the mug.

I don't remember the time at night when I took the sleeping pills or the time I woke up the next day. I know it was a good while, though, because it was already in the middle of the next evening. When I woke up, I was covered in my own vomit, urine, and all that mixed into a bunch of sweat. Honestly, I was lucky to be alive, and I knew it, too. To top it all off, I counted the beer bottles that were scattered and broken along the floor. Twelve beer bottles! The last thing I remembered was that I finished the beer in the mug. I don't remember drinking the whole six pack.

So that meant not only did I black out almost right away, but I finished the rest of the six pack and then got the other one. So I must have been irritated that my one and only idea at the time wasn't even working for me. Although after a bunch of sleeping pills and a twelve-pack of beer, it did work for me, and I was lucky to still be around and breathing. I can't not stress enough, folks, that because I made this mistake and it is published in here that I don't support this action or any actions similar to it. It is not worth risking life to do this. I should have sought help from a medical professional instead of self-medicating. It was a mistake (one I learned a huge lesson from), I regret doing it, and I am ashamed to say that I could have ended my life that night because I couldn't sleep. I almost got a hell of a lot more sleep than I bargained for.

After almost ending it that night, I vowed to never do that again and to change many aspects of where I was heading. My first was to take all of my medications and dispose of them right away. I didn't care about pain, phantom sensations, or sleep. I then cleaned up my mess and vowed to not have a drink for a good while. My next vow was to make myself tired in a healthy and natural way, by working out. My final step was to post pictures around my room of those who inspired me to keep on fighting, and I used this as my daily motivation to keep the fight and to do it for them.

I did have a setback soon after I got my path straightened out and I was on a healthy track. I had just about my whole paycheck for all of December taken away by the Navy. I looked into why and found out some serious bullshit. For those who don't know, when the government owes you money, they take their sweet-ass time getting it to you, but when you owe the government money, they take that shit faster than you can imagine. So back to why they took my whole paycheck at Christmas time, thanks a lot, by the way, Uncle Sam. They said I was overpaid by a few months on my "combat pay."

I went down to the Navy Medical Holding Company staff to seek their assistance, and they had no idea what I was talking about and sent me to PSD (Personnel Support Detachment). They told me that I was only entitled to my combat pay when I was initially in the hospital after my injuries, and once I was released, it was to be stopped. This was all new to me, so I just said thank you for the knowledge and their time. It was far from being over, though. I am a very thorough man and wasn't letting it end there. I went back to my laptop and began to research continued combat pay for combat-wounded service members. It was tough to find stuff online, so I called some buddies who may have experienced the same issue, if not one similar. They provided a shit ton of information, and it helped my case out in proving PSD wrong. I couldn't go by word of mouth, so I had to find the exact form, which I did, and I took it in to PSD the next business day.

I had to fill out other official forms and turn in a copy of the proof that I had supporting my case. Combat pay for combat-wounded service members was supposed to continue for one to two years (whether or not they were inpatient or outpatient), and every time they were to have a combat-related surgery that required an overnight stay in the hospital, they were entitled to that month tax-free with combat pay, even after the one to two years after injury. Say the pay were to have stopped after I became an outpatient; they still neglected to abide by the other set of rules, about the month of tax-free with combat pay, anyway. Which was an additional two months and would have been an extra $600-$800 and not making my Christmas of 2006 a horrible and lonely Christmas in the barracks by myself.

8.

BIG CHANGES

The beginning of 2007 was the beginning of some big changes in my life. One day during an evening formation, I noticed a group of ladies that were hanging out in the lounge. After the formalities of the formation, they had the floor to speak to the group. They led off by asking, "Who here has done track before?" I raised my hand, and a few others did as well. Then they said, "How would you guys like to make a big step and complete a marathon?" I thought they were batshit crazy by suggesting that we could go and complete a marathon. I was intrigued by their suggestions and stayed after formation to gather more details. After gathering that I could complete a marathon on a handcycle, I signed up and figured I had nothing to lose and some confidence to gain.

I had signed up to do the Miami Marathon on January 28, 2007, through the Achilles Freedom Team International. There was a group of us, including my roommate, that went to Marine Corps Air Station Miramar and flew on a KC-130 aircraft to southern Florida. Flying on a KC-130 is so comforting. I grabbed my pillow, blanket, and iPod, then I curled up in between the cargo and slept the whole flight. This was my first marathon, so I was fascinated with the whole process, and it was honestly really interesting. I really enjoyed the whole process. It was like discovering uncharted territory.

The morning of the race, it began to rain while we were all at the starting line. For those who haven't done a marathon before, you have to be at the starting line far in advance. So we just sat in the cold rain while we waited for daylight and the start of the race. It was cold, but once we started and the rain stopped, I seemed to dry off fairly quickly.

I finished the race in seventeenth place with a time of two hours, twenty-two minutes, and fifty seconds on a handcycle. It was one of the best feelings I had since my injury. I had finally achieved something I had set out to do . . . and it was physically exerting. About five miles into the race, I thought to myself, *Maybe I should have trained for this shit.* I figured two hours and twenty-two minutes wasn't bad for being new at it. Now that I look back at it, it was pretty relaxing to have one headphone in and listening to some music and the sound of the tires on the pavement. This was the first of many marathons that I have done.

I have since completed eleven full marathons and two 5ks (I walked/ran the two 5ks). Those marathons were in San Diego (June 3, 2007), Los Angeles (March 4, 2007, and March 2, 2008), Chicago (October 10, 2010, and a time of one hour fifty-seven minutes and twenty-one seconds), Miami (January 28, 2007), Washington DC (October 28, 2007, October 2008, and October 2009), Boston (April 21, 2008), West Palm Beach, (December 2, 2007), and Berlin (September 28, 2008). The two 5ks were in Atlanta (June 15-18, 2007) and New York City (June 22-25, 2007). I will go more in depth on those trips as I go through the timeline, and I will explain the major influence and impact each of those trips had on my life and continue to do so to this day.

Following the trip to Miami, we began the long flight back across the county on the KC-130 aircraft. I was grateful that I was worn out from handcycling 26.2 miles the day before. So again, I curled up in the middle of the cargo and passed the eff out. As soon as we landed and were back down in the barracks, my roommate and I just loaded our stuff into his truck and drove up to Mammoth for another trip. He was tired and worn out from the previous day as well but didn't sleep much on the plane, so I drove throughout the night to just outside Mammoth, where he took over.

I was only in a test socket/leg for my prosthetic and probably shouldn't have been heading to Mammoth for a ski trip, but what the hell. I figured it was going to be some good therapy. The ski trip was an amazing trip that showed me that I had built confidence in my physical abilities, especially in my legs. Not only was I able to walk in those impossible ski boots but also maneuver on skis. I will admit that I did have to use the assistant devices during that trip. Trust me, I wasn't all that and a bag of chips with skis, not even to this day. I found out that I had one flaw that I could not get rid of for the life of me: I couldn't turn left on a set of skis. After a recent trip back up to Mammoth, I realized that I still couldn't turn left on skis. So I literally gave up all hopes of ever figuring it out, period. Not for lack of trying, though. I tried to do it on multiple trips but just couldn't. I am better off doing something better and more efficient with my time.

Shortly after the Miami Marathon and the Mammoth ski trip, I continued on my therapeutic healing path by heading to Los Angeles to participate in my second marathon. I had so much fun in Miami that I wouldn't have dreamed of turning down a marathon. It was so peaceful as well to have the road closed and just cruise right on through all the different neighborhoods. It was like a personal tour, and I could take as much time as I needed or go as fast as I wanted and still not miss a thing.

I was in for a major surprise, though, with the initial few miles of the LA Marathon. The start line use to be on a major hill, and it was one-and-a-half miles of climbing uphill to start the marathon. The law of physics—what goes up must come down—was applied in the LA Marathon as well. Once you hit the top of the hill, it was about two miles of downhill awesomeness. We were briefed beforehand on the usage of our brakes, especially turning the corner at the bottom of the hill, which I listened to, but I didn't apply it to my marathon experience. I had a better time in this marathon and picked up a ninth-place finish. I am not sure if I could give credit to myself for my better finish, the massive downhill time-killing acceleration I had, or just the general knowledge of what to expect. I can't be too sure, but that shit was fun, and I think that one confirmed that I was addicted.

After doing the Miami Marathon, the Mammoth ski trip, and the Los Angeles Marathon, I had realized that I was blessed to have been shown the right path of healing and dropping the medications and sitting around the barracks having a self-pity party. When you're sitting there throwing a pity party, nobody wants to join in on that shit, and pretty soon you'll find yourself pretty freaking lonely. I was pretty lonely, and it sucked some serious ball stains, dude. The only people that would hang out with me were people who felt bad about themselves and bitched about how horrible their lives were. After hearing how their lives were and realizing they did it all to themselves, I decided I shouldn't be hanging out with self-destructive douches. So I dropped them as friends and will be forever grateful for Achilles Freedom Team.

There is one other thing that brought me out of my depression, and I owe many grateful thanks to one of the biggest inspirations in my life, Rick Allen and Def Leppard. I have always been a huge fan of classic rock, mainly due to my mother breaking out her old record player when I was growing up and playing her old records. Honestly, I listened to everything Journey and Steve Perry's solo albums during my deployment, and that helped me get through my days. I honestly think Steve Perry has one of the best voices in history. We shall return back to the main reason why I am telling you about this. I was listening to some Def Leppard while cleaning the common areas in our barracks room, and my roommate looked at me and said, "You know the drummer from Def Leppard is an amputee, right?"

I looked at him and said, "No, I didn't know that. Thanks for the info."

When we were done cleaning, I logged onto the computer and read everything I could about Rick Allen and his recovery. I was so fascinated by his strength and will to be back with the band to keep pursuing his dreams, although he was already a famous drummer. I was really impressed by the band's loyalty to him as well, and I know that helped inspire him to come back. After watching and reading everything I could about Mr. Allen and his recovery, I just knew deep inside that I could bounce back and be successful, too. I had my Marines that supported me like his band for him. I knew it was two different situations, but I felt like I somehow knew what he felt and went through.

I pulled some strings one day knowing that Def Leppard was going to be in Irvine. I sent out an email to the management team for someone I knew that is a professional singer and explained why I would like to go see Def Leppard, and they happened to be the management for Def Leppard. So it was easier to get things lined up. I went to see them in Irvine, and I enjoyed the whole show before I utilized my passes to go backstage. When I went backstage, there were all of the family, friends, fans, and groupies. I waited for just about everyone to leave, and as he was walking away, I said, "Mr. Allen, can I have a moment of your time? I am not here for an autograph, a picture with you, or to have you call and chat with my family. I am here to say thank you for helping me break out of my depression." I then lifted my pant leg and said, "Mr. Allen, I was wounded in late February 2006, and hearing and reading your story helped me overcome my depression, and for that, I thank you."

He looked up at me with tears in his eyes and said, "Wow, I don't know what to say." We sat up on some speaker equipment backstage and chatted for a little while. Just chatting with Mr. Allen and getting some personal advice from one of my biggest inspirations still sticks with me to this day. I still think of his wisdom that he passed on to me, and I use it to help inspire my fellow wounded warriors and to continue to better myself daily. If you ever read this, Mr. Allen, thank you again for all that you have done for me and those that I have inspired.

In March 2007, I had to go under the knife for a major foot and ankle surgery. I had to wait until then to get it done because the orthopedic foot/ankle surgeon was on his deployment. In the meantime, I had some injections done until he returned; if I didn't wait for his return, I would have had to have my ankle fused. I waited for his expert opinion, and he decided that he could do a different procedure to help my foot/ankle. We both agreed that it was a better option that an ankle fusion.

He performed a calcaneal osteotomy, Achilles tendon z-plasty, and a correction for hammertoe (claw toe deformity). This procedure was a success for the most part and required another hospital stay. The part that wasn't a success was the correction of the hammertoe. The pin that was drilled into my toe had to be taken out during the procedure because the toe appeared to not have sufficient blood flow after the tourniquet was removed in the operating room. He said if he left the pin in, I would have lost the second toe shortly after surgery. I was already down to my last four toes at the time as it was and sure as hell didn't need to lose one that didn't need to be gone.

The night before discharge, the nurse came in and told me she had to take the Foley out and I had to prove that I had full bladder function before I was allowed to leave. I convinced her to let me deflate the balloon and pull the tubing out myself, due to me being a corpsman and having experience with them before. She laughed and told me I was crazy. I told her to let me do it and I would prove my craziness some more. So she let me do it.

When I returned to orthopedics for my post-surgical follow-up, I was asked if I would like to try having the pin drilled in again, but in the minor procedure room. I agreed, and we began to numb up my toe. He recommended I lay down so I wouldn't watch the procedure. I told him I would be fine to watch. Again, I was declared crazy, which was all right with me. When he drilled it into place, we encountered the same thing, lack of blood supply to the toe, so he backed it out and said we would have to approach the situation later.

One month later, I was back in surgery, but this time with the plastic surgery department at Balboa for a flap revision on my right foot. This was a very simple procedure but a necessary one. The flap was put on my right foot from my right thigh in Bethesda one year and one month before, but then my foot was eight inches wide due to some severe swelling from the IED attack a month prior to that. My foot in April 2007 was down to a normal size, as normal as could be for the time/situation, but the flap was causing some issues. The issues weren't painful, due to numbness on and in the flap, but more cosmetic and interfering with the wear of socks, shoes, and my combat boots. They shrunk it down to a more feasible and tolerable size, and it has been perfect since.

The San Diego Marathon, my third marathon, was on June 3, 2007. The days leading up to the marathon were really fun because I got to meet a ton of the new guys and got to know them and hear their heroic stories. We all hung out and went to the Expo to get our bib numbers, and it was really cool to see all of the new runners clothing, shoes, drinks, energy foods . . . etc. It was awesome to meet other people from their various locations, whether they were local, from Utah or New Zealand. I really liked the San Diego Marathon because it seemed like I was doing a race in my backyard. I knew the area, the terrain, the distance between the terrain changes, and the locations of all the bad spots on the roads. I picked up third place for the Achilles Freedom Team, third place overall, and first in the handcycle division. It was a great feeling to bring the Achilles Freedom a third-place finish because just six months before the San Diego Marathon, they offered me the chance of a lifetime, to come out of my self-pity party/depression. Third place was the least I could do in return, but all that I could offer.

Please follow me in an adventure as we backtrack a bit because I was caught up in telling some other portions of my life/career events.

In March 2006, I was awarded my Purple Heart and took my FMF Board and passed it. After passing, I had my FMF pinned on me by another great Admiral, who later became a great mentor for me and was one of the major reasons why I kept on my fight to stay in the Navy. During that pinning ceremony, I was also pinned to the rank of third class, or HM3, meritoriously. Once someone picks up third class in the Navy, they have one year before being eligible for advancement to the rank of Petty Officer Second Class.

In March 2007, I had a foot and ankle surgery, and I was back on the pain medication. My one and only encounter with a Naval Advancement Exam was in September 2005, while I was in Iraq, and prior to that, I had no knowledge of the whole Navy advancement system. So what I am about to tell you about is a failure within the chain of command. The command knew that I was fairly new to the Navy and was eligible for the HM2 Advancement Exam but failed to inform me of this. This led to *zero* preparation for the advancement exam on my part, which I would have taken the appropriate actions to study for the exam and ensure I was ready.

One morning while I was getting up to prepare for the day, I received a knock on my door. I opened it, and there stood a Petty Officer. I felt the puzzled look on my face and said, "Can I help you?"

He responded, "HM3 Jacobs, the HM2 advancement exam is right now down at PSD, and you have to be there."

I asked, "Well, do I have time to change into uniform or can I go like this?" He said I could go down there in my civilian clothes because I was already running late. I asked, "Why didn't I know about this before?" His only response was for me to ask my command. So I took the HM2 advancement exam with no knowledge of what I was doing or what to even expect.

After the exam, I was asked to look over my award points, and of course those were all messed up. When I went to PSD afterward to straighten the awards for my exam out, I was scolded on why I should do this beforehand and they might not be able to fix it in time for the test. I was really pissed off and told them that I had no prior knowledge of the test and my situation. Then he seemed to ease up and was more willing to work with me. It just amazed me that the Navy would fail to inform me of an advancement opportunity in my near future so I could better prepare for it and, to top it all off, let me take the exam while taking high doses of painkillers. Even if I did have prior knowledge of the advancement exam and studied for it, I wouldn't have done that well because of the medications I was taking. If you are taking any sort of pain medication, you shouldn't be driving, operating heavy machinery, and probably not making career choices. I am not the smartest man in the world, but I would figure that they should have informed me of the exam and let me take it a little bit later when I wouldn't be taking pain medication.

Later on in March 2007, I went into the Navy Medical Holding Company office in my wheelchair. I was still on con leave from my foot/ankle surgery, but I always liked to show face and let the command know that I was doing well. I was tossed a package and told, "Jacobs you have some mail." I opened it up right there, and I could see it was an award of some type. I opened up the award display, and it was a Navy/Marine Corps Achievement Medal for my actions at an attack in Ramadi on January 5, 2006. I will go into more details about that award later and my current continuous battles with the military about it. I know I'm not the first to ever receive a medal in the mail, especially over a year later, but I do think the previous command could have let my current command know about it so they could present it to me in Navy/Marine Corps traditions. Especially because it was a medal earned in combat.

The summer of 2007, June 15-18, 2007, I was in Atlanta for an event for Achilles, the Hope and Possibilities 5k, and attending an amputee conference. This was my fourth Achilles event and my first amputee conference. We were briefed on not to brag about our prosthetic care and the amount of prosthetics that we may have due to the majority of the population being civilians and some of them having never had a prosthetic. Hearing this really made me feel horrible about the quality of life that some have. It really hits you as to how horrible insurance companies can be when it comes to stuff like this and their complete lack of empathy for their fellow man.

I met some good folks on that trip, civilians and former military, and to this day we are still friends. The night before the 5k, a group of us that were with Achilles were hanging outside the hotel and in the smoking area, and one of the former military guys asked if I had done any tricks with my leg. I took about three beers and poured it in my socket and said, "Check this shit out!" I chugged the whole thing, and then he asked if he could give it a go, and I said, "Oh hell, yeah! Go for it!" So he poured in three beers and chugged out of it, too. We ended up passing the leg around chugging out of it for a few hours that night.

The next day was the 5k, or 3.1 miles, and I opted to do the run/walk. I felt that 5k was *way* too easy to do on a bike, but very challenging for a guy that lost his leg eight months prior. I did a fair mixture of running, jogging, and walking. It was a challenge all right, but a good one. Completing a 5k on foot was a great feeling. It was almost as great of a feeling as completing my first marathon since my injury, but there seemed to be a different feel about it. I guess it was because it was done with my legs and not just my upper body. I was excited because I was going to do the New York City Hope and Possibilities 5k a few weeks after.

June 22nd through June 25th of 2007 was the New York City Hope and Possibilities 5k in Central Park. I don't recall the travel date, but I do remember that we took another KC-130 out of Miramar into a military installation outside New York City. Once again, I took my pillow and blanket and curled up between the cargo for another long cross-country trip. It was another nine-hour non-stop flight, but a really comfortable one. We landed sometime in the early evening but were greeted by New York state troopers and New York City police officers and personally escorted to the dinner for the evening. We were running late for dinner, but we still chowed down on whatever was left when we got there. This weekend was a good one to see some old 3/7 buddies that lived in New York City and one who lived south of Boston and had come down as well.

I had the pleasure of sitting down with the two 3/7 friends of mine, BamBam and Timmy, that live in NYC late one night while I was in town. It was the first time we had seen each other since the morning of February 25th. They felt relieved when they finally had the chance to see me up and walking. I am sure a lot of our guys have always worried about my health and wellbeing and are always overwhelmed with relief when they see how well I am doing. I am sure this is the same story for many units across the military. I want to say something to those who are afraid to call and check on your wounded friends: pick up the phone and call them. See how they are doing. Don't wait long periods of time to see how they are doing. This only hurts you in the long haul. It will help you heal, and it will help bring acceptance and peace to you as well. Trust me, it is best to check in on them and bullshit about the fun times.

Doing the NYC Hope and Possibilities Marathon with my fellow doc from our platoon in 3/7 was an amazing experience. I am sure it was a great experience for him as well. I just hope it may have helped bring some closure from our deployment. I know it helped bring a level of comfort and acceptance to me. Don't get me wrong, it was fun to get piss drunk and laugh about the crazy shit we did in the past. Oh man, a buddy that was on med hold with me was there, and we somehow ended up with big random bottles of champagne. We began to walk around the streets of NYC piss drunk looking for a hot dog stand around three-thirty a.m. all because I had never had a hotdog from a hotdog stand in NYC. To my surprise, we actually found one open that early. I am not sure if it was because I was crazy drunk or the hotdog was really good, but that shit was amazing!

I knew after the NYC trip I was due for another surgery, but this one was on my amputated side. The orthopedic team was preparing to cut out a few chunks of heterotopic ossification, or HO. I had some pretty good-sized pieces pushing against the front of my prosthetic, which made it uncomfortable and fairly painful to wear my leg for more than forty-five minutes at a time. I was unsure how long the recovery time was going to be, so I decided to take some leave that I'd saved up for a while. I purchased a one-way ticket from New York to Akron and began a four-week vacation. I will be honest with you guys, four weeks is much too long to spend with family. Sure, it is nice to spend a week or so, but after so much time off, they have to go back to work, and you find yourself hanging around with nothing to do. It probably would have been better to spend two weeks there and then two weeks in the barracks hanging out and sleeping in.

I soon returned back to San Diego, just a few days prior to my thirty-seventh surgery. I went to the Chevy dealership in Mission Valley and began my search for my first vehicle. I knew I wanted a truck, and I knew I wanted to buy an American-made truck as well to help keep jobs here in America. I had received some of my TSGLI (Traumatic Service Group Life Insurance), plus I had my enlistment bonus, deployment money, and an $11,000 grant from the VA for vehicle modifications. So I knew I could walk in with some bargaining power. I didn't reveal my cards right when I walked in. I played dumb for a bit and let the guy showing me around the lot ramble on about what vehicle I should buy and the financing options.

I finally saw the truck that I wanted, and I told him and pointed to a used, slightly lifted 2006 Chevy Colorado. It wasn't 4x4 or a big powerful truck. It was something to drive around the city of San Diego and around the Southern California region. The guy told me that I didn't want that and that I should buy an SUV. I told him I didn't want his SUV and that I was a country boy and didn't belong in an SUV. Then he told me that I would look good and ride in style in an SUV. I replied that real men drove trucks, here was my down payment, and now get me my damn truck. He looked at the amount and then ran inside, grabbed the keys, and pulled it around with a "sold" sign on it.

I then called my pops to get his approval, which was a bad idea. He told me that I didn't need to be spending my money on a truck or any vehicle for that matter. I should stay in the barracks and not waste my money on that garbage. Then he put G-Ma on the phone, and I heard it from her, too. When I got off the phone, I looked at the salesperson and told him, "We have a deal! I want to drive my truck off the lot today as well."

Soon after purchasing my truck, I had to be back at the hospital to go through all of the exams, tests, and radiation treatments for the surgery. The operation itself went well, and I had the usual post-operative care pain. I did run into a problem a few days later, and of course, my family and friends had already headed back to work by then, and this was when I could have used their help the most, but hey, that's how it always works out. So I was experiencing a great deal of pain, and the pain relievers were not touching it at all. I still had the post-surgical cast on, and I figured I should go see the orthopedic surgeon to have him look at it. The cast room crew removed the cast, and the doctor knew it was an infection right away. He told me I would be fine, and he was glad I came in when I did. I went to the pharmacy to pick up my antibiotics and be on my way.

When I was heading to go get some KFC, I grabbed an ice pack out of the freezer and put it on my modified cast when I got to my truck. Almost immediately, I felt relief, and it was a weird type of relief. I must admit I was nervous, but that wasn't going to stop me from my KFC. I got back to my room with my delicious chicken in hand and decided to open the cast to see why my leg felt instant relief. Being in the medical field and especially seeing combat trauma, nothing really impresses or surprises me these days, but when I opened that cast up, I knew I was heading back into surgery. What was red and super glossy just four six hours prior was split open and oozing out copious amounts of a beige color. There was enough to fill an eight-ounce glass, easily.

What did my fat kid self do? I ate the shit out of that KFC and took my time doing it, too. I knew the whole wash-and-clean-out procedure and the length of the hospital stay. Plus only being able to eat the glorious hospital food for those five days. I bet all of you would enjoy that KFC as much as I did in that moment. I did know that I wasn't allowed to eat or drink anything eight hours before a surgery, but I would gladly wait that time.

I got in my wheelchair and headed on down to the Orthopedic Department. I didn't go straight to the emergency room first because I knew there was an ortho doctor on call, and I wanted them to know that I was there previously to see the ortho surgeon who did the surgery. He told me to go the Orthopedic Department if I needed to, anyway. I found the on-call doctor and told him my situation, and he just told me to go check into the ER and he would see what happened from there. I knew what was going to happen, hours of waiting around and being told the same thing that I had found out earlier in the day.

I followed the ortho doctor's orders and went to the ER. The lady at the check-in desk didn't seem to understand my urgency on the matter and decided she was going to treat me like I was the dumb one in this situation. She told me I should go over to ortho and let them know if I deemed the infection to be so bad. I told her I already did that and they sent me to the ER to begin getting checked in and preparing for surgery, like blood work, scans . . . etc. She told me it would be a while to be seen by the ER doctor, so I just unwrapped my leg and told her she needed to update her priority list after seeing what I was about to show her.

After I had the cast open again, I showed her, and she said, "Oh wow! Your whole suture line is busted open."

I said, "Yeah, it is. Now do you see what I was talking about? Look, lady, I am a Corpsman who was in *combat* dealing with injuries you couldn't even have nightmares about! So please trust my judgment and move me up on the priority list."

I then called my connection at ortho and told her how I was

treated by the orthopedic on-call doctor and how he neglected my situation by not even listening to me or looking my leg over. I left a voicemail, and I kid you not, within ten minutes of that phone call, he was by my bedside in the ER doing exams and preparing me for a five-day stay in the hospital. Within a short amount of time, I was being transferred up to the surgery ward to wait for my surgery time. I was in surgery early the next morning, which marked one of three surgeries over a five-day stay to clean my leg out.

After my leg had finally healed, I had to go back to physical therapy, but I was very reluctant to do so. Every time I went in there, I was told to get on the upper arm bike for thirty to forty-five minutes. Then, after that, I had to do core exercises and stretching. So basically, I was going there for middle to upper body workouts . . . but I was there for my legs. Whenever I brought this up with the staff, I was told, "We are the ones with the degrees and we do this every day, so let us do our jobs." After going back and forth with the staff for a while, I just stopped going. Soon after, I began getting harassing phone calls stating if I didn't make my appointments (that I didn't schedule because I had no intention of going back), they were going to call my commanding officer and I would get in trouble with my command. So I went back for a while but notified my command of what was going on, and they told me to just go and bide my time and see if they would work with me on my legs. After trying to settle an understanding with the physical therapy staff, they finally let me work on my legs. Shortly after, though, they fell into their old habits and routines.

After they fell back into their routines and bad habits, I stopped going again and notified my command. So then they called me saying, "If you miss your appointments, we will call your commanding officer (CO) and tell them that you are UA (Unauthorized Absence) for your appointments."

I said, "Go ahead and call my CO. She is awaiting your phone call. I told her about what is going on, and she told me I don't have to go back."

I told my command that I was a corpsman, and I knew how to work out my legs in the gym on my own time and had more time. I knew what I was doing, and I promised them that if I got worse, I'd give in and go back to physical therapy. Since then, I have only had to go back for short amounts of time after a surgery.

9.

GOAL BOUND

After I had recovered from my HO removal and infection, I had to get to work achieving my goal of staying in, and I was running short on time. By September 2007, it was nineteen months after my injury and time for me to stop pissing around and get serious. I had started a series of trips to the gym, and in one trip, I ran into my Marine amputee mentor, and he suggested that I work out with him. I did one workout and realized why nobody worked out with him: he wore me out and made me sore for about a week. I declined his further offers to work out and suggested I stay at my workout level for now.

I continued on a fairly regular path for a while and thought I was ready to try and run the Navy PRT, or Physical Readiness Test. It consisted of a sit and reach, a timed one-and-a-half-mile run, sit-ups, and pushups. I met with one of my recent mentors and awesome Master Chief for a trial at the beginning of the NMCSD PRT cycle. I knew I had a knee issue at the time, but I had no idea how serious it was. So I did the sit and reach, made a joke to Master Chief while doing it, sit-ups, and pushups without any issues. When I started to run, which I thought the running leg was a good idea, the pain in my knee was just too much to deal with, so I had to stop and go see my ortho surgeon. Oh, but the joke, I popped my leg off and put it next to me and touched the toe and asked Master Chief if that counted for a sit and reach. He laughed but told me to be serious.

The ortho surgeon did a series of knee tests, exams, and scans. He heard and felt popping in my knee and told me that I likely had the onset of osteoarthritis. The x-rays confirmed that my joint space was narrowing, and then the MRI showed a torn meniscus and torn cartilage. I told him that I had to pass the PRT before he could do any work on me because I fought this hard and needed to complete my task. He agreed that when I was done with the PRT, he would scope my knee. He then suggested that I do this PRT in the elliptical. I took his advice, for once in the year and some odd months that I'd been his patient.

I reported back to Master Chief on the orthopedic surgeon's findings and his recommendation for my passing the PRT. He set up my time to retake the test. The shitty deal about it, though, was I had to do the whole test over. Oh well, I passed the elliptical portion of the test easily as well as the other portions. This was a major success for me and my chances of staying in because *all* amputees have to go through the Physical Evaluation Board, or PEB.

This is a policy that has been in place for some time. The PEB itself is a long process that includes the command's NMA, non-medical assessment, of the service member and his impact on the command with his injury/illness, along with information from the medical specialists. The doctor in the specialty will present the conditions, facts, and his/her opinions on the situation. The board will then be submitted for the service member's review prior to sending it to Washington, DC, along with the NMA and the medical record.

I knew that passing the PRT would help support my case for requesting to stay in and go back to full active duty. I knew if I could pass the PRT in time, I could add my PRT results in with the command's portion of the board. I did so with plenty of time because

I had to wait four months to send my PEB, anyway. If someone on a medical evaluation board or on a PEB has surgery, their board is suspended because the surgery outcome may affect the board's results. So I had my surgery, anyway, even knowing all of this. The ortho surgeon went in and cleaned up my knee with the scope and fixed my torn meniscus as well. He told me that I had the onset of osteoarthritis and should take it easy on my knee. By doing so, I would have had to stick with low-impact to no-impact working environments. He also told me that the wear and tear from the prosthetic might bring on more cartilage breakdown faster than someone without a prosthetic.

During the four months of waiting, I knew I had to work out and better prepare myself for a possible return to the fleet. Shortly before I knew I was going to have my knee surgery and run the PRT, I had moved out of the barracks and freed up my room for a recently injured Marine. It took one drunken incident for me to do so, though. I went out drinking one night with my girlfriend, and when we returned for her to drop me off, the duty said she couldn't take me back to my room. I told him she was there to ensure that I made it to bed safely and laid down properly so I wouldn't vomit and aspirate and drown in my vomit. The duty said no, she was not to go back there with me. I told him that during the fires a few weeks before, the BEQ manager let her stay in my room with me because her house was in the evacuation area so it really shouldn't be a problem. He told us she had three minutes to make sure I was set up and then back at the quarterdeck so she could leave.

We slowly walked down the hallway, and I punched the walls the whole time and kept yelling, "This is fucking bullshit! A fucking combat-wounded vet can't have his girlfriend escort his drunken ass to bed because some fucking POG doesn't understand jack shit, and that's probably why his bitch ass is stuck on BEQ duty at two-thirty in the morning! I'm so fucking done with this lame-ass bullshit! I am putting in for my housing allowance as soon as the office opens!"

I kid you not, by the time we got to the door, he was walking up behind us saying, "I thought I told you three minutes?"

I said, "I thought you had to understand how to tell time to get in the Navy?" He told her she had to leave now, and I said, "Good, I hope I throw up while laying on my back and I drown in my own vomit and you get charged for my death, you fucking POG!" I know most of this was a little crazy and shouldn't have been said, but I was drunk and pissed off. The next day, I turned in my request to move out, which was approved months before but I hadn't wanted to leave the barracks unless I had to.

I moved into an apartment complex up by Camp Pendleton in hopes that I would soon be stationed up there, well, that and my girlfriend was attending Cal State University San Marcos and she worked at a gym up in Carlsbad. So I would help her out with transportation to and from school and would meet her at her gym and workout so I could be ready for my return to the fleet. It really felt good to be out of the barracks, to own my own truck, and to be set on a path of completing the goal that I set out to do the day I was hit by the IED.

I had a few months before my board was due back from Washington, DC, and I knew with the stuff afterwards I had some good quality time to enjoy some good working out. So I was exercising and hanging out with my girl, and it came time for her twenty-first birthday party, and she wanted to go celebrate with all of her female friends. Well, her party was in downtown San Diego the night before I had to drive to LA to get my marathon stuff so I could compete in the LA Marathon. I decided to go and have a few drinks, anyway. I had more than a few drinks and ended up being the only one who got sick the next day. Now that I look back, I think I had more of a good time because I didn't have a twenty-first birthday party. I had a good friend come to the barracks, and we hung out at Hooters so we could have a beer. Which is one thing that I am really grateful for and always will be. It was just the medications and my medical condition that prevented further celebration, but not the night of her party.

The next day, I woke up and thought I felt fine until I got in the elevator, and the quick descent made it a horrible experience. I went into the bathroom lobby and let it all out. I have only hurled four or five times because of alcohol, and most of those times are because my dumbass will drink anything and mix drinks all night. I know the trick is to stay with one kind of drink. Not this dumbass. I will do shots of Jack and chug Guinness then throw in some SoHo. I give in to peer pressure when I drink, which is probably why I don't do it so much these days.

Okay and we're back from my rambling. It was a long trip from San Diego to LA with beef jerky, water, and Gatorade, since I needed to start hydrating for the marathon. It was a long drive for having a hangover but very refreshing when I got to LA. I got there a little late, so my buddy went to the expo and picked up my stuff for me. Later that evening, I drove us both to the team dinner that a local firehouse put on for us. This was my second team dinner in a row at that firehouse, and the firefighters are always just so amazing and helpful.

The next day was race day, and while we were waiting outside the hotel for the shuttles to take us to the firehouse where our bikes were stored, and near the start line, my buddy popped around the corner with a whole dozen of donuts. He wanted the two of us to carb load on these twelve donuts during the few short hours before the marathon was to begin. I figured I would give it a go—couldn't turn down food or let it go to waste. I think I ate three or four of those massive cream-filled donuts, but when the start time rolled around, I was so full and didn't want to do the marathon anymore, and to top it off, we had an immediate one-and-a-half to two-mile uphill start. I think I finished in ninth place with a time of an hour and fifty-four minutes, so it might have helped with energy during the ride.

I can't remember if it was before or after the LA Marathon, March 2, 2008, when my PEB findings came back. I did get the call saying they were back, and I had to come sign saying I accepted the findings or if I refused and would submit a rebuttal. Once I got down to the NMCSD PEB Liaison's Office, I knew I wasn't going to submit a rebuttal. My findings said, "Fit to Continue on Active Duty," and I was as happy as could be with that! This was one of the biggest moments in my career, and I will never forget the victorious accomplishment that I held in my hands. I signed the papers stating I accepted the findings and did not wish to submit a rebuttal.

I asked what my next steps were in order to get going on my mission to get back out to the fleet. The next steps were to have my ortho surgeon sign off on my Worldwide Assignability Screening so my orders options wouldn't be limited to non-deployable shore commands. This was the onset of the major uphill political battle that I would spend the next few weeks and possibly even months typing out and sharing with you. I like to play by the rules and operate by the rulebook, so I visited my ortho surgeon and had him do his Worldwide Assignability Screening for me. Then I went to PSD and turned the paperwork in to them and stated my intentions were to reenlist and take new orders.

I went to Command Master Chief's office for NMCSD and showed him my findings and my worldwide assign ability papers. He called the command career counselor and had her come over and work on picking me the orders that I would like. As anyone who has been in the military knows, this is a process. This was good, though, because I had to wait on the folks in Washington, DC, to receive my acceptance and for them to accept it and clear me in the system. During this time, I decided to go back to Ohio for a few days and visit with family because I didn't want to get to a new command and have to worry about when the last time I saw family was. I wanted to get to my next command and hit the ground running and prove myself. I didn't want any distractions.

While I was back in Ohio, I received a phone call from Command Master Chief, and he said he had the orders that fit me perfectly, a corpsman at the Wounded Warrior Battalion at Camp Pendleton. I told Master Chief that I would reenlist and take those orders and make him proud. Of course, the next day I received another call from Master Chief saying the orders were taken by the time he submitted them. I came this far and was not about to give up, so I asked him what he had available now. He told me that the School of Infantry was open for a HM3 spot. I told him that I would take those orders and would reenlist when I returned back to San Diego.

When I returned to San Diego, I had a little reenlistment ceremony set up, and I was having one of my inspirations, my ortho foot/ankle surgeon, be my reenlisting officer. He brought his dress blues in that day, and I was in my uniform ready to reenlist for more time and set out on my next adventure. I had to postpone my reenlistment because PSD didn't tell me that it would take a few days to make sure I was cleared in all the systems and to draft up my reenlistment paperwork. I asked my ortho surgeon if he was going to be around a few days later, and he said he was going to be TAD (Temporary Assigned Duty) somewhere and I would have to unfortunately find a new reenlisting officer.

This was pretty depressing for me, but I went over to the C-5 (Combat and Complex Casualty Care) Clinic, where I would go for my prosthetics and physical therapy, and asked a Navy Captain if she would be my re-enlisting officer. She was really happy and honored to. It was a quick little ceremony in her office with one witness, and then we signed the forms and I was set for another term, four years. I will have to get the exact dates of reenlistment and how long I had been in at that time, but you can only reenlist if you're less than one year away from your EAOS (End of Active Obligated Service). I was well past my regular enlistment and only had a short amount of time to reenlist.

I flew out to DC one time and had a little meeting with one of my mentors and inspirations in his office. At that time, he was the Chief of Naval Personnel, and he had pinned my FMF pin on me and at the same time pinned me to the rank of Petty Officer 3rd Class, when I was in Bethesda. We had a good discussion about what I wanted to do with my naval career. I told him I would like to stay in and do what I could to keep on giving what I could to the Navy/Marine Corps. He asked me, "What's stopping you?" I told him that I was National Call to Service, and once my ratings came back, I had to go check into a reserve unit if they let me stay in. Plus, my fifteen months were up when I was overseas, and I had to extend to stay over there.

He said, "Well, Petty Officer Jacobs, what do *you* want to do?" I told him I wanted to stay in and return to the Marine Corps side of the house, and I asked how it would be possible to do so. He said, "Watch this," and he opened his door and yelled out to his assistants, "Jacobs is going to stay in. Make it happen. Anything else I can do for you, Petty Officer Jacobs?"

I was so impressed that I had nothing to say, but I told him, "Sir, I won't let you down, and I will make you proud."

He said, "I know you will, Petty Officer Jacobs. Otherwise you wouldn't be sitting here in my office and I wouldn't have done that for you."

We finished up that meeting, and I told him a few times how grateful I was for his help and reassured him I wouldn't let him down. I am sure he was tired of my excitement and gratitude, but I honestly think I made him proud during my four-year enlistment.

I had a certain amount of time to finish getting ready to go check in to the School of Infantry, Camp Pendleton, California. Prior to my arrival and check-in date, I had some other promises to keep, such as participating in the 2008 Boston Marathon with the Achilles Freedom Team. The Boston Marathon was on April 21st, but the days leading up to it were full of the traditional fun that Achilles always had in store for us. Some had the opportunity to go see TAPS or the firing of the ships saluting battery for evening colors—I can't remember which—performed on the USS *Constitution* in the Boston Harbor. There were amazing dinners the nights leading up the marathon day and a very special day before the marathon. Throwing out the first pitch of the game honored a combat-wounded warrior, a native of

Massachusetts and *huge* Red Sox fan. He threw a perfect strike from the mound to home plate . . . from his wheelchair! He got a standing ovation from the whole stadium. I was so proud of him. This was yet another great moment that Achilles put together to change another wounded warrior's life.

The marathon was a great and amazingly scenic route. There were hundreds of supporters on the side of the road cheering us on as we rode through the streets. During the race, I noticed some pain in my right forearm, and it had been bugging me for a while, so throughout the whole 26.2 miles, I debated whether I should get the plate taken out of my arm or not. Doing all of that debating helped me keep my mind off the actual course, and I managed fifth place for the marathon. I did decide to have it taken out before I got to my new command because I wouldn't have to do the PRT since I would be transferring right around the PRT cycle. After the race, I did my usual and threw on my leg, ran to the nearest fast food joint, and grabbed the biggest burger I could with the largest fries as well and, of course, a massive Dr. Pepper.

I had my plate taken out, which was put in before I even arrived at Bethesda, and it was a simple procedure except they left two screws in my ulna that they said were buried too deep under bone. I didn't mind, though, because the big issue was out of my forearm, and it hasn't been an issue since. I've had only two surgeries on my right arm, which isn't bad for a shattered ulna with some shrapnel still left in my hand.

10.

RETURN TO THE FLEET

had my arrive-no-later-than date, but I wanted to go to the command a few days before and meet the command staff and the junior corpsmen, as well as know where the command was located and time my drive. When I arrived, I was really surprised to see someone I went to Corps School with. It was a shock and also a pleasure to have seen him again. We bullshitted for a while, and he introduced me to the command officials. It was great to sit down and meet with the LPO (Leading Petty Officer), the SEL (Senior Enlisted Leader), and the division officers ahead of time. I figured it would be best to knock out all of the proper stuff first, so when I checked on board, I could get straight to work. I wanted to give them a courtesy heads-up of my situation and let them know that I wanted to be treated like everybody else and not be treated or viewed differently, and it seemed to have gone over really well with the command staff.

The School of Infantry Clinic was a Branch Medical Clinic (direct representation of Naval Hospital Camp Pendleton) and was called 52 Area Branch Medical Clinic, or 52 ABMC. Before I was deployed to Ramadi, I was at 31 ABMC out at Edison Range. 31 ABMC was where the Marines did their field weeks for their boot camp. So we did medical coverage on their hikes, rifle and pistol ranges, martial arts, and various other field evolutions. Well, 52 ABMC was the outlying clinic that covered all of the medical stuff for the Marine Corps School of Infantry. We didn't just cover the Marines going through their initial Marine Corps Infantry Training, be it Marine Combat Training (MCT) or Infantry Training Battalion (ITB). We covered all of the advanced Infantry Training Schools as well, some of which I won't mention.

Since 52 ABMC was an outlying clinic for the Naval Hospital, I had to initially check in there and deal with the typical runaround there. I made sure to turn in all of my paperwork to show my duty status and that I was cleared for worldwide assign ability. I did this because I obviously knew from my previous time at the command that I had a chance of being deployed. I knew that the runaround games with the possibility of me being deployed were going to begin soon, but I was ready to do battle. So I made sure I turned in every paper supporting my desire to deploy again. Due to my "High Visibility" Status, I had to check in with the Master Chief, the Executive Officer, and the Commanding Officer. Everyone was excited to have me on board, and they were happy to assist me throughout my time there and seemed honestly genuine about it.

I finished all of my official checking in and began to get settled in amongst my new peers. It wasn't that difficult to get introduced to most people because of my friend I went to Corps School with. I was in a small holding pattern, though, while I finished some of my command training and waited for an official job title. I had to wait because the command was focused on a series of inspections on the clinic, which was totally understandable. I did as much as I could to help out while I did my stuff. I would run supplies and food to the corpsmen in the field, do advancement training courses for the junior corpsmen during chow time, stand duty, and run administrative stuff to the hospital. During the time that I had free, I was bugging everyone I could in the chain of command for information on how to get my name on a deployment roster or a volunteer roster of some type. I knew the Navy wanted to see how I would do at SOI before just sending me back overseas. Personally, I understand that one hundred percent, but the issue I had, well, I guess I still have to this day, was somebody could have told me that and I would have been fine with that. I think I caused some irritation with the chain of command by consistently bothering them about it, so I backed off for a while.

I knew I had to prove myself and do my part for the command as well. So when I had the chance, I would hit the ground running. Soon enough, I would have my shot, but of course not without stirring the pot one last time. Chief came to me one day and gave me a piece of paper with very little on it, and some of the page was cut off because it wasn't printed correctly. I had no idea what it was, and there seemed to be no explanation from the command leadership or a way to fix the problem that was listed on the document. All the document said was, "Not Medically Ready," and when Chief handed it to me, all he said was, "This is why you can't deploy."

It took me almost two years to figure out what the document meant and how to fix it; I will go more in depth later on about that craziness. My counter to the command "leadership's" lack of helping in my quest was to go above them. I admit how I went about it was wrong, and I did admit to it when confronted later on, which was less than twenty-four hours later. I sent an email to my mentor in DC. Yep, the Chief of Naval Personnel . . . an Admiral. I know I wasn't thinking clearly when I wrote him, because I was used to an open-door program just weeks before. I neglected to consider the fact that I was back out in the fleet and had to abide by the proper protocols and rules and regulations. I told him of my situation and said (paraphrasing), "My chain of command is assisting with my quest, but I am not sure if they (or anyone) can help me with this matter because it is a fairly unique one." We shall just say that when you are an E-4 and in the fleet, you shouldn't just write admirals—or anyone more than a rank above you—without consulting with your chain of command first.

I didn't have my ass ripped by anyone through the chain of command. They left me alone and waited. I was at parade rest outside Chief's office for just a few brief moments before being called in by Command Master Chief. She was *furious*! I am not exactly sure how shit rolled downhill onto her, but she was taking it all out on me. I could just feel the heat from Chief as she stood at attention and stared me down. I could just feel the hate and anger coming from her, and I knew once Master Chief left, I was a goner; I knew I was done for in Chief's eyes. At the end, she said she understood it was a unique situation and I was seeking answers and not malicious toward anyone in the command, which it wasn't. She reassured me that the command, as a whole, was there to assist with anything, but I needed to utilize the chain of command appropriately.

I assured her and Chief that it was a one-time mistake and I should have thought things through before I just sent out an email to an admiral. I had to sign my Page 13, which is a step below from Non-Judicial Punishment (or Captain's Mast), and then I was dismissed. I felt like such a tool by doing something stupid like that, and I knew it would be even harder to prove myself to Chief and the rest of the command, but there was no time for sulking and having a pity party. I looked at it as another challenge and was ready to start working on it.

I was given the position as Senior Line Corpsman for Marine Combat Training Battalion. This was a pretty good job, and it was one where I could prove myself to the command. I did notify my seniors that I picked up HM3 in the hospital, and the whole time I was at that rank, up until then, I had no direct contact with any sort of leadership position and might need some assistance on pointing my junior docs down the right path. They assured me they would be there if I needed them, but they were pretty sure I would do fine on my own.

Being a senior line at SOI, at that time, consisted of being the middle management and a buffer between the junior corpsmen and the command and vice versa. We also were the direct connection and buffer between the Marine Corps side of the house and the Navy side. That part was fairly simple because I was in 3/7 with some of the SOI instructors, and the other senior lines knew most of the instructors from their crossed paths as well. Having some connections, even though they were on the Marine Corps side, was a good thing and may have made some things smoother.

After my training and being appointed as the MCT Senior Line Corpsman, I began to show the command and my peers that I was no different from them. I decided to try something that I thought would impress the shit out of some of the others at the command: not to tell them that I was an amputee. When I checked in to the command, I wasn't in my dress whites because of my cast on my arm. So this prevented the majority of the staff from asking about my Purple Heart or about my leg. Obviously, there were some in the command that I couldn't hide it from, but I kept it from the junior guys and the ones I wouldn't be working with daily. I figured it would be a good way for just about everyone to not see me for my injuries but to see my work ethic instead.

It took a little while to make it around to all of the companies and get to know the corpsmen in my section, as well as the others in the other two sections. In field section, we were blessed to have the administration Corpsman doing the schedule for a while. He had a system that was amazing, but he was afraid to let us do it because he didn't want us to screw it up and have the higher-ups in our office micro-managing our work. When he finally transferred it over to us, we worked in the same office, so it wasn't too bad if we messed up.

After officially sitting down with the Division Officer and giving her the rundown of who I was and my whole naval career path, she told me that out of my nearly four years of service, I hadn't taken any leave for me to just have me time. So I put in for some personal leave that began on August 1, 2008, and it was only for a short time. I took the usual night flight back home, and when I landed, I got a phone call from the command. I thought to myself, *This should be good!*

I answered and was greeted with a friendly, "Where the fuck is HM3 Shmuckatilly?!" (Not his real name, to protect the identity of the individual.)

I said, "Um, what are you talking about? How the fuck should I know where he is? I am on leave and just landed in Cleveland!"

Admin Corpsman: "Is he with you? Did he put in for leave through you that you didn't run? Chief is pretty fucking pissed, dude!"

Me: "I am sure Chief is pissed for an HM3 not being where he is supposed to be, but I honestly have no clue where he might be. He didn't ask me for some time off as a favor, and he didn't put in for special liberty or leave. I have no idea, bro."

Admin Corpsman: "Okay, well, can you make some calls to help me out?"

Me: "Yeah, I got you, bro, but remember I am on leave . . . for me to relax and rest my mind."

Admin Corpsman: "I know, but he is in your section, and you're the only one that talks to him."

Me: "Okay, I will try to get a hold of him and call around to see if anyone else knows anything. Call me if you find out anything and I will call you if I hear anything back."

Admin Corpsman: "Cool, thanks, dude."

Please note that we were the same rank at the time, so it was okay if we talked like that at certain times. I called around and couldn't find anything out, so I called the Admin Corpsman and told him that I didn't hear anything about where this HM3 was at or could be at, but he told me that he had news. He said that this HM3 called Chief and told him he was in Germany and wasn't coming back. This was crazy to me; this Corpsman just became a deserter the same day I left. To this day, I have no idea what caused him to just leave or even why he did it. So much for taking leave and having some rest and relaxation for me.

When I went back home, I was paraded around and had to be on other people's schedules. I did sneak in a few fishing outings, though, but still I was interrupted by work stuff and paraded around by family, so it wasn't just a smooth and relaxing time. In all honesty, though, the whole trip I was afraid of the possible impact that incident may have on my career with having a Page 13 less than two months prior.

I came back, and the command knew that I had nothing to do with HM3's deserter status and, if anything, I was his last hope for a saving grace. Soon after I returned from leave, I read the "corkboard" (NHCP's main page) and realized that I had to begin to get myself and my MCT guys ready for the upcoming PRT. I started to work the schedule around to allow for proper time off and for me and command to prepare. There was a good that came from a bad with the timing of the preparing of the PRT schedule. Some guys, mainly my section because I was handed the newest corpsmen to the command, kept showing up late for field ops. To fix this problem, we said, "For those who have field ops before 0800, you have to be at our 0400 formation to ensure that you will be awake and fed prior to your field op so there should be no excuse for being late. If there is enough time between the 0400 formation and your op, you can utilize that time to work out, do your weekly, monthly, or annual training, or study for advancement. For those who don't have field ops before 0800, you can go to the regular formation at 0700 and then go to your field op or be in the clinic, whatever your schedule says, but you can also utilize the 0400-0700 time for getting your Semper Swole on and getting chow as well."

So this fell into place, and it seemed to work fairly well. Initially, we had all of the senior line corpsmen showing up at 0400 to set the example, but then we had it become optional, and we divided up the days, but even then for about ninety-five percent of the time, we would all show up at 0400 and make sure things were running smoothly and we could handle any issue right away before it became a big issue. This wasn't a bad gig by any means, and I actually enjoyed it because we all got know our guys better and it was a more relaxed environment.

I'm not sure if it exists anymore, but there was a bullshit thing going on called DHMRSI. It was like an online version of a timecard.

It is a good concept, but we had to lie every two weeks about the hours we worked. The field guys would be working from Monday at 0330 until Friday around 1400, straight through, for 106.5 hours straight, then they would have to come in on Saturday to do sick call before they covered a remedial hike for a few hours and then after. So overall, a corpsman, just that scenario, was working about 110 hours in a week, and we were being told the most we could put was forty hours in a week. We were even told where to put the amount of hours and what sections to put them in. If we did it wrong, it would get rejected and then we would have to redo it or they would just correct it to their standards and submit it for us. I never understood why they controlled that; I just told my guys to do what they were told, and I would deal with the command for them. Sometimes, the command would harass us because somebody didn't do his or her timecard "on time." The stupid thing about it was the schedule was updated daily and it was accessible by anyone with a computer. So they could have looked where the schedule was in the command folders and done the member's timecard for them instead of pissing in everyone else's Cheerios. Oh, but if I or someone else in my pay grade didn't utilize all other resources prior, then our ass was smeared up one wall and thrown to another.

One of my first encounters with not understanding the command's thought process was as soon as I was appointed the position of MCT Senior Line. I had a junior Corpsman tell me that he just found out that he was pulled to go on deployment, and he told his family because it was short notice. His family was due to be in town a few days later, but he was scheduled for a bunch of overnights out on this range and wouldn't be able to see his family while they were in. So I asked if I could switch him out with someone else who wouldn't be out in the field, and I was told, "No! That's not going to happen. The schedule is already made, and we can't just modify it whenever."

I responded back with, "Well, I think we can make an exception because it's a pretty unique situation, and how would you feel if he went overseas and something happened to him and you didn't allow his family to see him?" I was still told no. So what did I do? I went out there and stayed on the range for a few days and let him take my place at the clinic so he would work normal working days and go home to his family every day when he was off work. This didn't make the command really happy, though they did respect my loyalty to my juniors and admired my selfless leadership.

It was a good way to begin to show the junior guys that I was there for them and not to screw them over and for us to just focus on the command's mission. For a few months, there wasn't a whole lot of craziness going on. I was just going to meetings and doing field ops alongside my junior guys. I would do the field ops for three major reasons: to get to know my guys better (and how they worked/operated out in the field, as well as to find out their strong areas and their not-so-strong areas so we could build on them and make them well rounded), to see how my junior guys interacted with the instructors and students (and vice versa), and to show them that I wasn't above going out into the field and doing their job with them. I had heard how they would talk about the higher-ups not knowing or understanding what they did out in the field, and I wanted my guys to know that I didn't fall into the category of sitting around and managing from the clinic, which was a tough job, but I wanted to add the managing-from-the-field aspect as well.

Sometimes when we were short on corpsmen, I would have the chance to go out in the field and work their schedules. These times fell around the PRT cycles, Navy Advancement Cycles, holidays, and when some would go on leave. This was a good opportunity for me to go show myself for the command and my physical abilities. I would get out there and do 20k hikes with Flak (with Sappies), Kevlar, and my huge-ass med bag that was typically loaded with supplies. I would load my med bag up with as many sick call supplies as I could so at the end of the hike I could give my sick call supplies to the corpsmen who would be staying in the field.

I'm not going to lie; the first few hikes were rough as hell on me. I thought I would be ready, but nothing can prepare you for hiking with nearly a full combat load except hiking with all of that shit on, and where I was previously located . . . there wasn't any proper way to prepare. I began to get used to the hiking and was in fairly good shape by doing it. What really sparked the command's interest was when the Gunnery Sergeant from one of my companies went and told Chief about how well I was hiking and outperforming most of the Marines out there with my one leg. This was good for my case to have the Marine Corps side of the house noticing what I was doing out in the field and letting my chain of command know about it. Well, I thought it was good for my case, but nothing was going to stop some higher-ranking officials from having their perspective on me and my abilities.

There were a few flaws to not being able to prepare for the field. After a few weeks of hiking and proving myself, I began to acquire sores on my amputation. This was from an improperly fitting prosthetic and from all of my time in the hot weather hiking. I couldn't just get up and go see the C-5 prosthetic clinic. Instead, I had to put in a special request to go to an appointment. The prosthetist wasn't an official medical provider, so he didn't have the access in the computer system to have an appointment schedule. I had to have him email someone in the chain of command and then clear it through them before I could even request time to go get my leg fixed. That process alone could take up to a few days.

My appointments and time off were always scrutinized by the chain of command, and to this day, I still don't understand why. I had to schedule my appointments either in the morning or afternoon and had to go into work and always return to work after the appointment. Let me tell you that I was driving an hour and fifteen minutes or so to get to work every day. I can't bitch about that because it was where I decided to live, but it was a good two-hour drive from SOI to NMCSD. To go from home, work, NMCSD, and then home would be around four hours of driving just to go to an appointment, but no, I had to go from home, work, NMCSD, work, and then home, which made it about six hours or so to just go to an appointment.

I was later counseled on June 20, 2008, on not being able to attend "open-ended/walk-in" appointments because I "missed" an appointment the day prior. On June 19th, I was running late for my appointment because I got caught up dealing with some work stuff and wanted to make it to my appointment in a safe fashion, by being late and not driving recklessly. I called and gave a proper notification. Little did I know that the prosthetics had a Master Chief, who happened to know me, doing a walk through. He could have said to me, "Hey, Doc, I understand you're running late for your appointment. Is it okay if we reschedule? Or you can just make your appointment and be a little late. Thanks, I understand." Remember, there were no official appointment times in the medical system. He didn't even decide to call my chief, which he had his contact info. Instead, he decided to inform this Master Chief that I was late for my appointment and I missed appointments all the time. He told me this, and the first thing I did was inform my chain of command (so I wasn't withholding any information from them). The command took immediate action and didn't hear me out on how the whole process worked, and they took his word over mine.

About a year and a half later, I found out that he had the ability to write notes in the medical system AHLTA, and he was actually documenting all of my appointments. I found my note written by him on June 19, 2008, that clearly showed he contradicted himself in his note and what he told Master Chief. He said under the reason for appointment, "Called and missed appt. Wants socket tighten by five-ply and pad poured," and, under disposition, "Released w/o Limitations. Thirty minutes face-to-face/floor time." So apparently, I called and missed the appointment, but I spent thirty minutes there . . . It made no sense to me, yet I got in trouble and later had to physically suffer.

The next day, I went to Balboa to see him again to better explain my command's issue with me and going to appointments and the hassle that it already was without all of the open-ended/walk-in appointments, and he better understood. I also told him that he couldn't be going directly to a master chief or any top official just to "tattle" on someone. I explained the proper procedures. I told him that, if I am ever in the wrong, call my chief or someone in the same building as me because they wouldn't like another phone call from DC about me ever again unless it was good news. The note on June 20th said (under objective), "Will work with So-So on appt system for prosthetics." I will admit that prior going to SOI, I did completely miss one appointment at prosthetics without even calling, but I believe I was on leave in Ohio and forgot about it, which was no excuse. But I am just being honest and saying I did miss one before; however, I never "miss appointments all the time" like he told Master Chief.

From June 20, 2008, until September 5, 2008, I had no way of making it in for prosthetic appointments due to there being no official appointment system, and I wasn't allowed to go to any open-ended/walk-in appointments. This was the worst time of the year for this to happen because the heat and friction from being out in the field and hiking with all of that weight was causing some serious bursitis issues on the medial aspect of my knee, pressure sores, and the continuation of ongoing issues with the arthritis in my knee. I couldn't just make an appointment to get my socket/leg adjusted because I wasn't allowed to attend those kinds of appointments. I had to modify my prosthetic on my own, to the best of my knowledge, and tough through the pain and severe discomfort with Mobic, a non-steroidal anti-inflammatory that I took daily. Some days, I would have to sit in my truck to eat my lunch so I could take my ice pack out of my lunch and not have my peers or the chain of command see how bad my knee was feeling. I didn't want to show any signs of weakness.

There were a few times while I was stationed at SOI that I had pressure sores, and the only person at the command that seemed to care was the Medical Officer. I would go through the proper scheduling of the appointments and being seen, then I would just request antibiotics from him. One time, before I transferred to the Preventive Medicine Department, I had a pressure sore that was so bad when I would take my prosthetic off, the smell of the infection mixed with the heat and friction cleared rooms. It was awful, but I did my three-day field op, didn't bitch out or even complain, and when I came back from that field op, the command was down my throat for some bullshit reason (I will explain later), but I couldn't go home and rest until I was counseled. Waiting around and not resting appropriately was a partial cause for me falling asleep behind the wheel while driving home.

I was always afraid to go to any doctor because I knew they kept track of my appointments and how much time I spent away from work by going to them. So I kept them as limited as possible, but I found out something from the Admin Corpsman about how crazy the command was with tracking my every move. We had these folders, which were like service records, called "Divo Folders," which was short for Division Officer Folders. The Admin Corpsman told me after a few months at the clinic that my record was the thickest record, and I was the only one that the command made fill out special request chits or not be allowed to attend open-ended/walk-in appointments. There was an HM2, who I later worked for, who had the command's authority to go to her kid's soccer practice and games in the afternoon on certain days without having to go through the paperwork or constant harassment that I went through. I wasn't even sure if she even filled out one special request chit for this open-ended approval. I later found out that her Divo Folder wasn't even one-one-hundredth the size of my Divo Folder, and I was just there for a period of three to four months, as opposed to her time at the clinic.

There was another crazy incident that only happened to me during my time at SOI. I was heading northbound on I-15 from Rancho Bernardo to connect over to Highway 78 westbound and then onto I-5 northbound to Northern Camp Pendleton. This was my usual route, and I had it down to a science. Well, it was easy to drive when it was two-thirty a.m. on a weekday because nobody was really on the freeways at that hour. I was cruising northbound doing a tad over the speed limit, part of my having it down to a science, and I noticed this car coming up behind me fairly quickly. I knew what this meant, so I began to slow down and merge over to the right in anticipation for the red and blue lights to come on. Sure enough, they did.

The California Highway patrolman got out of his vehicle and slowly walked up to my window as cautious as could be and started talking to me from my blind spot; well, I was blinded because of their spotlights in my mirrors, anyway. He asked why I was speeding and if I had been drinking or in any immediate danger or having a medical situation that required my speed down the interstate. I chuckled and said, "I will be in a real medical situation and danger from my chief if I am late for formation." He chuckled and came up to the window and asked how I received my Purple Heart. I told him, and he said he was a doc as well. He told me to slow it down and leave a bit earlier from then on out so I wouldn't have to be doing anything above the speed limit. I told him thank you and went on my way to work.

I turned on my Bluetooth and tried to call the other senior line guys to let them know that I had been pulled over and I might be late. None of them answered their phones, so I decided to send a text to inform them of why I might be late. One responded with, "Dude, I hope you're not going to be late because the one day that Chief is here at 0400 is today."

I responded with, "I don't plan on being late, but being pulled over kind of took some time away from regular drive. I didn't factor in being pulled over this morning on my drive in."

I arrived onto base and made it to the clinic *at* 0400. Well, in the military, if you're not fifteen minutes early, you're late. Of course, Chief was furious, and he let me know about it. He started ripping into me in front of my junior guys, saying, "Way to show up on time and be the perfect example for your junior guys! There is no excuse for being late! You should add an extra thirty minutes to your commute to counter any of this bullshit! Did you get the officer's badge number so I can call and verify this? How do I know your lazy ass didn't just come from a bar and this is your excuse? Next time you get pulled over, you better ask for a fucking ticket or I'm charging you for being UA!"

When this occurred, I was the only Senior Line Corpsman with a collateral duty and working on that after all of the other senior lines went home for the day. Some days, I would get to work at 0330 because my guys had the 20k hikes, and then they were out in the field until Friday around 1400. So I would get out there at 0330 to make sure they had what they needed and if they needed additional supplies, because they couldn't get into the clinic over the weekend prior to their Monday 0330 push time. I would give them my supplies out of my bag and hook them up with chow before they pushed. Depending on what needed to be done in education and training, I would have to stay until ten or eleven at night and then make the hour or so drive home just to shower take a nap and do it all again. So there were nights where I would be falling asleep driving home just to sleep for two hours. Honestly, some days I wished I fell asleep behind the wheel and crashed so there would be an investigation launched to find out why I was working so hard and why the command was lying about the hours we were working. I know I wasn't alone in how many hours I was working because a lot of the junior corpsmen were doing that in the field, but I just thought it was bullshit how they kept it a little secret. I am actually surprised that not one person fell asleep behind the wheel.

I did keep the one speeding ticket I got from the command, though. It was nowhere near base; it was outside Bakersfield, actually. I was pulled over for doing seventy miles per hour in a fifty-five-mile-per-hour zone and was issued a ticket. I signed for it, paid it, and did the traffic school all before I went back to work off of leave. I just didn't want to give Chief any more ammo in his hunt for my head. He somehow seemed to have enough ammo, though, without me giving any away.

I'm going to backtrack for a tad here and tell you of another Corpsman who checked into SOI about a month after I did. He was a fellow combat-wounded Corpsman, although his injuries weren't as severe as most; he was still one of the Purple Heart members amongst the HM ranks. He had dealt with the same political battle that I did with wanting to go on deployment but was also blacklisted. This Corpsman was just as motivated as I was, if not more, to have the possibility to go back on another deployment. We talked every single day about how great it would be for the command to let us go back instead of forcing the turds who didn't want to go, or were too afraid, on a deployment.

The command's argument was very vague and didn't seem to make sense. They claimed that we needed to let everyone have a chance to go. Which was bullshit because I have known people to have gone on multiple deployments out of the clinic before their time was up, and it was like they were handing out tickets to the World Series or something. *"It is a random selection made at a higher level."* This was another lame excuse because I was told on multiple accounts, in passing, "You will never go on a deployment out of this command, and I will make sure of that," or, "With your injuries, you are such a liability to yourself and others." Oh, and, "The mountains that you hike here are like hills compared to the mountains in Afghanistan, and I know if I can't hack it over there, you wouldn't be able to handle the days over there."

Over the years, I have heard all of the excuses and will share them as I go. I admit that the first month or so, it was rough for me to hike the hills and mountains at and around SOI, but as the time went by, the more I hiked, I was out-hiking some of the instructors and almost all of the students. I would hike the whole time going from the tail end of the students and hike faster than them so I could watch their gait and to see if they were perspiring. I would hike all the way to the front of the company and then turn around to walk backward and watch them some more as they passed me. I would continue to do this until they stopped for a safety break or at the end of the hike. During those times, I would remain around and do sick call for those times as well. During those hikes and every other field evolution, I had never felt that my injuries caused harm to me or anyone.

The funny thing about the whole excuse about me not being able to hack the mountains in Afghanistan, when anyone higher than the clinic chain of command would come through or call and see how I was doing, they would brag about how many 20k hikes I had done and how all of the Marine instructors were impressed and bragged about my abilities. They also wanted the bragging rights to another accomplishment of mine, and they did for sure.

In late September 2008, I took some personal leave to go to Berlin and do the Berlin Marathon with the Achilles Freedom Team. I was supposed to do it the year prior, but for some reason, it was canceled with Achilles. When 2008 rolled around, and Achilles said it was still going to take place that year. I did what was required in order to take leave and travel over to Germany. The command made a big fuss about me taking leave and going to Germany to handcycle a marathon, but they wouldn't give a shit if I sat on my couch and drank my sorrows away on leave. But, seeing this would possibly bring any attention to me and the command, they got worked up over it, just like anything else. In all reality, as long as I had the leave days, I was responsible, and I wasn't causing chaos and was bringing a good light to the command and myself, they shouldn't have gotten all worked up.

There is one circumstance that I agreed with the SOI command on. I was asked to do some training with the US Paralympics' Sitting Volleyball Team. I told them I would be there and do whatever training I needed to do in order to make myself better. I was a little greedy and forgot that I was placed on a medical board just a short time prior due to my ongoing knee issues. I completely forgot about the fact that I was on a medical board, and I probably shouldn't have been out and about doing physical training for any organization. I was kind of bummed out at the time but also knew from the military aspect of it all that it wouldn't be wise to cause further injury to myself and affect my medical status.

I was placed on a medical board, and as soon as I turned in the paperwork, I was pulled from field section and placed at the front desk to fall under the ancillary services department. This was a really depressing phase, not just for me, because I was leaving the place where all of the other combat corpsmen were and going to the section filled with all of the deployment dodgers and POGs (Personnel other than Grunt). I was also leaving my junior corpsmen in the hands of some folks I didn't think I trusted to lead my juniors. It wasn't for the lack of their abilities, but I just had a certain way of leading, inspiring, and protecting my guys.

When I was transferred over to Ancillary Services, I was mandated to sit at the front desk and do nothing but customer service. I was told that it was due to my limitations on my medical board. However, as I am currently typing this, I am awaiting my medical board for my medical retirement and am allowed to stand duty, go TAD to different commands, and do my regular medical work or just about whatever. I am not sure if it was due to lack of knowledge or training on how to handle a case of this nature or if I was just being screwed around with. It wasn't pleasant because I was constantly cut down in front of junior corpsmen and the Marines that were in the lobby as patients or patient escorts.

In one incident, I had a junior Corpsman ask me to help him with a procedure, just watch over him and make sure he was doing things properly, and to possibly help with some understanding of the procedure, why it was done. I agreed and began to get up and head toward the treatment room. Well, little did I know, Chief was standing behind me, and as soon as I stood up, he grabbed my shoulders and slammed me back down in the chair at the front desk and told me that while I was on this medical board, I was to sit at the front desk like a good little broken sailor and not do anything else. If he caught me doing anything but working the front desk, I would be charged for disobeying a direct order and dereliction of duty. This reverted back to when I checked in and he told me that he would burn anyone in that command because he was chasing the "Star" (the Silver Star that goes above the anchors to represent the rank of Senior Chief). I knew that I would have to be on guard, more so than I already was with not willing to trust anyone.

This was kind of a shitty deal because the actual clinical staff always bounced to chow right before their actual time for chow, and they took the full time getting back from chow as well. The two-hour chow times were to allow those who drive to and from work and from off-base the opportunity to work out and help keep the PRT failure rates down. This was a complete waste of time. Having two hours for chow just allowed people to travel out farther and get more crap to eat. I admit, there were the few that would get their PT on, and I respect them for it. In the field section, we used chow time wisely. We would go get our food and then come back to continue our work or study for advancement.

There was one other thing that was severely messed up about that place; it might be in a lot of other places, as well. It was the use of the smoke deck. Only those who used tobacco products were authorized a break, and those who didn't . . . well, you would be shit out of luck. Sometimes, in the field section, all of us senior lines would go and conduct business out on the smoke deck. It was a place where we didn't have to worry about thin walls or sharing an office with another department. So when I was stuck at the front desk for hours on end and needed a sanity break, I was denied because I didn't utilize tobacco products. I should have said, "No, I don't, but I need to ease the pain by doing a shot out of my handle of Jack."

Let me explain why I needed a break. There were mainly two reasons. I couldn't stand working inside a building doing customer service bullshit and being treated like a criminal, and wearing the new working uniforms didn't make my knee feel too good, especially sitting with my legs bent, which caused my knee more pain. The term for osteoarthritis is "theater knee." Whatever I said, though, was deemed as an excuse and I was just trying to weasel my way out of things. To counter all of the political bullshit, I decided the best way to deal with my sanity was to give in and get a can of dip so I could get up and move my knee. In some political battles, it is best to temporarily join them. I only had to do this for a few months before my board came back.

For being someone who was always trying to weasel his way out of doing things, I sure was in charge of the clinical services a lot because the HM2 that I worked under seemed to be gone to more appointments and family functions than anyone I had ever known. Oh, and by the way, she never had to fill out a special request chit for each thing she did nor was she constantly harassed by the chain of command for the amount of time she spent away from work.

Right before September 2008's HM2/E-5 exam, Chief put on my midterm evaluation that I needed a special eval for the exam due to my short amount of time at the command and I didn't have the best of evals coming out of the medical holding status. So I would have gotten an eval based on my time at SOI and the work I had put in for the command. I was really excited because I thought everything was finally about to come together for me and I would pick up HM2 so it wouldn't be so bad. Chief handed that form to the LPO, or Leading Petty Officer, and told her to get it ready for me. Quick background on her at the time: pregnant and never left her office. A few weeks before the exam, I asked the ALPO, Assistant Leading Petty Officer, to check on it. He followed up on it and told me she was working on it. I gave it about another week, and when I hadn't heard anything, I asked again. Of course, the answer was, "She is still working on it."

I lost all hope right then and figured I would have to do amazing to advance on this cycle.

When I went to Chief and asked him why I hadn't received my special eval yet, he told me that it was never a guarantee and I should only count on three evals to be for-sure evals: Periodic (regular eval), Frocking (when promoted), and Transfer, none of which I qualified for, so I was left standing there with my dick in my hand. I figured if I did well enough, I could at least have the PNA points, pass but not advance, which I had already racked up a few of those bad boys. So a lazy LPO not following Chief's instructions may have screwed a junior sailor/corpsman out of advancement, and she just went about her day like nothing happened. I one million percent guarantee you that if I pulled any of that shit on a junior sailor/corpsman, I would have been in front of the man for multiple UCMJ (Uniform Code of Military Justice) counts and booted out with loss of benefits. Speaking of which, that shit was held over my head for my whole time back out in the fleet. I would have never even had a second chance like some people.

There was a guy at SOI that got out after I had been there for about a month or so. This Corpsman had been through some serious shit overseas, and I've heard his experiences and have talked to some of our mutual friends about it as well. He was busted for a few DUIs, and one was a shady bullshit charge that the highway patrolman hooked him on. He plead guilty and admitted that he wasn't dealing with things the right way. When asked, "What can the command do to help out?" we suggested that they have more to do in the SOI region so we weren't so isolated and leaving the only option to drink. What was actually done about it? Nothing. Yeah, they built some new barracks, but that just made it comfortable drinking. If I had any pull, I would have transferred him to a command that offered more, had more going on in the local area, and offered him the option to hang out with friends or hang out on base where there were things to do. The SOI command didn't have anything nearby, but if he could have transferred to the 13 Area Clinic, he would have been close to the base theater, the football fields, and the Wounded Warrior Battalion so he could volunteer and do something and feel useful again.

I took the advancement exam with only my transfer eval from my two-year recovery . . . and SOI and the whole NHCP command was okay with that idea. I couldn't complain to anyone outside the chain of command because of the stupid Page 13 I had for jumping the chain, which I rightfully deserved, but I was in a seriously f-d up situation with no one to turn to for help. I figured, oh well, at least I might get some PNA points off of it.

Soon after the Navy Advancement Exams, the PRT cycle began. I was recently put on the medical board and couldn't do anything physically exerting because of my medical conditions, so I was waived for medical reasons. I will go into more depth on this portion later on, but for this period in time, I was just waived from the cycle. Remember the PRT cycle of 2008 for when I tell you more about this at a later time, of how this cycle almost f-d up my career even more.

About a month after the holidays, my medical board came back with the results: "Fit to Continue Active Duty." I had figured this would happen because of my ongoing terrible luck with things. The whole time my board was in DC and I was waiting results, I was hitting the gym non-stop. I wasn't allowed to do anything physical for the military during that time because of the limitations that were placed on me, but I wasn't going to have the board come back in February and then not be allotted the time to train for the PRT shortly after the February time. I can't remember if it was that PRT cycle or a different one, but I surprised everyone by actually running the PRT.

Working at SOI and being treated like I was the biggest turd the Navy had ever had really pissed me off. I never showed it, though. I just took it all in and released it in different ways, although it took me about a year before I finally realized that I still had two more years in NHCP's dirty little secret. I went on a three-month rampage of taking it out on anybody and everybody. I wouldn't answer family or friends when they would call; when I looked at my phone and saw that they were calling, I would either press ignore or just not answer and not call them back. Those that I would talk to, I was extremely short with and just didn't care about anything or anybody. I did this because this was how I was feeling about how the command was treating me. I still did my job to the best of my abilities and looked after my junior guys, which I didn't take it out on them (except for one).

It was some crazy bullshit to constantly be lied to, filled with empty promises, given no help when I would ask, watching shit bags getting treated better than I was, and just the complete lack of acknowledgment and respect of my hard work and dedication. My mid-term eval reflected my hard work and dedication, but that was something that wasn't on a permanent record, so of course it didn't mean shit when it was supposed to count. Just some more false hope for this guy.

Being a combat-wounded service member back on full duty, minus the few months I was on a medical board status, I was being treated worse than corpsmen that were undergoing Non-Judicial Punishment, or NJP, for domestic violence, driving under the influence, Basic Allowance for Housing or BAH) fraud, and various other offenses. It honestly surprised me that this would be what I was greeted with when I returned to duty. I remember when I checked in, I told Chief that I didn't want to be treated like I was some hero and wanted to be treated like everyone else. I didn't expect to be treated like I was found guilty of domestic violence accompanied with a DUI, for my second offense.

Oh yeah, some of the shit that went on at SOI wasn't even swept under the rug. It was more of a cover up than that. There was serious favoritism going on in that place, but when I hosted a bowling night for my *whole* section, I was accused of favoritism and fraternization. No, that was called "sailorization." I held that bowling night so the families could see and know me as their loved ones' direct bossman and so they could put a face to me and feel comfortable approaching me about any issues their loved one may have. It was also a team-building event so the section could get to know each other better. But no, because I was doing this with the whole section, it was viewed as favoritism instead of something useful.

Another thing that I did for my guys that was viewed as wrong was going out into the field to make sure my guys were doing good and doing what they were supposed to be doing. I also liked going out into the field to make sure the Marines felt safe with their Corpsman. I was told that my job was to be the middle management, which meant I was to run the show from inside the office or clinic. That really didn't sit well with me, because I hated that type of leadership! I hated people that micromanaged from an office and had no idea what was actually going on in the field with their juniors. It just didn't make sense. I still did my own thing anyway to make sure my guys were doing well and were doing their job. I was constantly scrutinized for it, though. In the long run, those that fell under my sections were better corpsmen because of it.

In February 2009, my medical board came back "Fit to Continue on Active Duty." I figured it would, and as I stated earlier, I prepared physically in my off time so I would be ready for the PRT that was going to happen in the upcoming months. Soon after I was cleared in all of the systems, I asked to be transferred back to field section so I didn't have to sit in the clinic again. This was a short-lived trip, four months, over to field section before I got effed in the A again.

During my short four months back in field section, we got a new Chief, and he was a Godsend. I remember feeling a massive sigh of relief when the outgoing Chief introduced him. He was by far one of the best chiefs I'd ever worked for and I would work for again, any day. I honestly felt like I didn't have to walk on eggshells around him like I did the previous Chief. Granted, I still gave him the respect that I did for any chief, okay, maybe more respect. As with any new boss takeover, there were some changes. These were all for the better, though. He allowed more leeway with some stuff, abolished some other stuff, and implemented some stuff, too.

Life around the command was better soon after the chiefs were done doing their official transfer of commands. Things changed for the better, and it was a quick turnaround. With the new Chief, there wasn't a whole lot of explaining what you needed and/or wanted to do; he was all about trusting in our abilities and trusting in us to make the end result the best for valorization and the command's mission. With Chief allowing for such a work ethic, it took so much off of the stress levels. I know everyone has their different leadership techniques, but Chief's were more beneficial on the mind.

Although we had a new chief and things were turning for the better, we still had the same higher leadership within the command. The higher leadership was more of a dictating-from-the-back-office type of leadership. I think the command would have been a better place if the leadership was like it was before, making time to mingle with the juniors in order to get to know them on a personal level as opposed to treating each sailor as though he/she was just a body filling a billet. I understand that things get busy as one is directing a whole command, but still take thirty minutes out of each day and make it better for the juniors by getting to know them so when you make an appearance out of your office you don't seem like a feared dictator that is solely fueled by rumors.

Here's a perfect example of "dictator." One of my junior Corpsmen had an error of judgment by leaving his gear after doing a hike (followed by sick call). The Marine staff called Chief and explained to Chief how he had a corpsman's gear. The crazy thing about it was I was signing for my eval when Chief got the call. So I asked Chief if I had his permission to handle the situation appropriately without violating any rules or regulations. Chief told me to do what I deemed necessary to make sure that neither he nor any of the other juniors left their gear. I ran ideas past my fellow senior lines, and we came up with the best idea. Everyone in field section got the glorious opportunity to wear all of their gear around (unless it was in the direct way of patient care) while mustering every hour on the hour for some knowledge/Q&A on why gear accountability was important as a corpsman. All of us senior lines wore our gear while carrying out our work/missions for the day as well.

During one of our formations toward the end of the day, one of the higher-ups came out of the clinic and was heading out for the day. I noticed him, told the detail to stand by, and when the officer was due to pass, I called everyone to attention. I stood in front of the detail at the position of attention and greeted him appropriately, and he greeted us back. He carried on about his way, and I told the group to stand at ease. The Q&A continued, and soon after, I was called into Chief's office. Chief asked why I did not salute a naval officer, and I told him that I was wearing flak and Kevlar and saluting was not custom. He told me that I had to prove whether or not it was customary to salute or not to salute, and why, while wearing flak and Kevlar. So this "leader" couldn't pull me to the side and address the situation at the time; instead, he greeted us accordingly and then went to his car to call Chief and have Chief do his dirty work. It was taught through the enlisted ranks to approach a situation, no matter the rank, and resolve it at the source first and then utilize resources if need be.

So we spent many hours looking into the customs and courtesies while wearing flak and Kevlar. After many hours of research, we landed at the conclusion: It was at the discretion of the command/officer because on the Navy/Marine Corps side of the house, there is no "do or don't salute" answer. This just proves the type of leadership that was there at that time.

11.

FINALLY A BREAK

O ne of the gunnys that I worked with requested me and some of my junior guys that needed some good training for an upcoming deployment. I had some juniors who were slated to head out with 3/4 on a pump to Afghanistan, so I rearranged the schedule in order to have them go on this field op and to have their other field ops covered. This was going to be a three-day non-stop training evolution, and the guys were pumped. When the time rolled around to take off for the training evolution, I had a different junior Corpsman approach me telling me that he changed his phone number. I told him that I was heading out on this training evolution and was going to be gone for three days, so he needed to update his phone number on the recall roster by informing the admin department so they could update it and reprint the recall roster. I also told him to notify the other senior lines so they had an updated contact number and they could call him if his schedule changed or just whatever they would need him for.

I left soon after, and he went about his day as well. I had some time to call and make sure that he did what he was supposed to do, but there was no cell service in the mountains and valleys, so I would keep trying to send a text to one of the seniors or admin. Of course, it was late in the day by the time it sent and even later when I got a response back. I thought nothing of it and carried on with the missions. I went from supervisor to field bubba in no time, though. I didn't mind at all. I loved being out in the field, anyway.

We hiked down some sides of a mountain that didn't even have animal tracks or trails. We had to go down that side of the mountain regardless. As we were preparing to head down the side of this mountain, I took out an 800mg Motrin and downed it because my knee was beginning to hurt just a bit and I figured it was time for one, anyway. I did have a serious issue going on my leg at the time. I had a decubitus ulcer, or pressure sore, on my amputated leg. It didn't help that I was in the field for three days hiking around in the ninety-five-degree heat, but one of my juniors had a medical situation that required him to leave the mission. This allowed for me to get out and prove myself some more.

So we took off down the side of this mountain to try and be down at the mouth of the valley by nightfall. Once we got down to the riverbed, I turned and looked back up and said, "Wow, not too bad for a one-legged man."

One of the sergeants didn't even look at me as he said, "Doc, now is not the time for jokes. We are all tired, hungry, and need to make it to our extraction point."

I responded, "I will shut my pie hole, Sergeant, but that wasn't too bad of a hike down that mountain."

At that point, the Sergeant came back to me and said, "Doc, who is this 'one-legged man' that you keep referring to?"

As we continued walking toward the mouth of the valley, I said, "Sergeant, I'm the one-legged man."

He then proceeded to tell me to shut the fuck up and that there was nothing visibly wrong with me. I told him that nothing was wrong with me physically, but I was missing my left leg below the knee.

He told me again to shut the eff up and there was no way that I could be missing my leg below the knee or at any spot for that matter.

So I lifted up my pant leg and showed him. He couldn't believe it even when he was feeling it out. I told him that I was being truthful and kind of proud of myself for making it down that mountain without any issues. We didn't have much time to stand around and flap our gums, so the Marines just glanced at my leg and verbalized how bad-ass they thought it was of me to still be full active duty and continuing on with my career. Then we were back to patrolling toward our staged camp for the night.

At daybreak, we packed up and needed to get back up to the top of the mountain for helo extract, and then we were done. We soon began our trek back up the mountain, in a more fashionable manner this time around. Once we reached a certain spot on the mountain and I had service, I checked my voicemail. As I listened to my voicemail and hydrated, while in the shade, I heard the madness that was going on back at the clinic. Oh, and of course, all of the madness was being pointed in my direction. When I arrived back from my field operations, I was not authorized to leave until things were sorted out.

Of course, nobody would explain what was going on, so I had to sweat it out for the remainder of my field op, which wasn't healthy to be stressed out while conducting combat training in ninety-five-degree heat (with ninety-percent humidity). As I was listening to all of the hate voicemails and trying to hydrate, First Sergeant walked by and asked, "Doc, what the hell are you doing?"

I said, "First Sergeant, I am doing what it takes to stay hydrated. We had a doc drop from heat-related issues yesterday, and I am the senior one out here and am the only medical guy for this platoon, so I need to stay hydrated for you and your Marines."

He just looked at me and my leg then said, "Doc, I don't know you all that well, but I have a feeling I trust you."

At the top of the mountain, I linked up with the other two docs, and we did our own debrief on the field op. I asked if they had fun, what they thought about the training overall, if the Marines answered any questions they might have had. They were very pleased and excited as well. I was just pleased that Gunny's Marines taught some stuff to my junior docs, who were set to deploy within the next six months. I did have something in store for these guys, though, and it was a pretty sweet payoff. Gunny hooked them up with their first helicopter ride in the service. I gave up my spot in one of the helos so all of my junior guys could ride, and I hiked back down to the clinic. I stopped by and checked on the Marines that were back early and made sure they didn't need any medical assistance. I then headed off to the command to find out what everyone was all up in arms about. I gave them a heads-up that I was en route back and five minutes away. They told me that I should stay outside until my presence was demanded inside. I just figured at this point I was sure they were making something big out of nothing and just using this as an excuse to get rid of me. That worked for me because I was interested in preventive medicine, anyway.

I was covered in the black charred stuff from fires and dirty as ever, so I just laid on the cement in the shade. I must have stayed out there for an hour or so, which really pissed me off even more because they knew when I would be back from my three-day field op. So they had three days to do all the paperwork for my "incident." On top of not having the paperwork done in a timely fashion, they decided it was a good idea to hold me there at the clinic after I just did three days in the field with little to no sleep, and to top it all off, I had an infected pressure sore and hadn't taken my leg off in three days. So that was really nice and considerate of the command.

I was finally called into the office, and of course, it was like I went on trial right away without a lawyer or a chance to advocate for myself. The incident that they were so worked up about was a dereliction of duty/failure to obey orders on *my* part in regard to the junior Corpsman who changed his number and neglected to notify the admin department as per my orders. After I heard them out on why they were disgusted with me, I explained what really happened, and I had witnesses to prove it. They told me it wasn't necessary because they had already informed the higher-ups of what happened and their solution to fix the problem. I had to sign the counseling chit and then only had a few days to do a proper turnover to the new oncoming senior line for MCT.

I was disgusted by the fact that some of those senior lines took a junior's word over mine, that I was fired over a "he said/she said" ordeal, and that my credibility apparently wasn't worth much to them. I was actually glad to be done with their little clique and focused on something more meaningful, and it all worked out in my favor, anyway. One funny thing about it all, I had to go introduce the new senior line Corpsman to the Marine staff at the MCT weekly meetings, and the same Gunny that I just did that three-day field op for was going to go over and talk to Chief and tell him he should move me back and fire all of the other seniors. I told him it wasn't worth it, that I would be happier doing something as far away from that as I could.

I submitted the request chit to transfer over to the PMR (Preventive Medicine Rep) office to begin OJT (on-the-job training) instead of being back to a front desk sick call jockey. It was approved, and before I knew it, I was working in a relaxed environment and for a pretty awesome boss. The job was easier, tedious, and never ending. It was just a better place to work, though, because of the relaxed environment.

After just a few weeks of doing OJT and waiting for my spot in the two-week PMR course, I was on my way down to the Preventive Medicine Unit (PMU) next to NHCP. The course was a lot of classroom time and viewing a ton of PowerPoints. During my chow times and the time after class, I would go next door to the Wounded Warrior Battalion and visit some of my fellow combat-wounded friends. It was good to drop in and make sure they were doing all right. I happened to run into a fellow Corpsman who I had served in 3/7 with. So we caught up and shot the shit about the good ol' days.

During my visits, I was asked by the Wounded Warrior Battalion West (WWBN) Corpsman if I was offered the chance to work at the WWBN would I take that opportunity. I told him, without hesitation, that I would be more than honored to work for him at the WWBN. He told me that it wasn't a for-sure thing, but every time he asked around about a combat-wounded Corpsman working for him at the WWBN, my name always came up and was always at the top of anybody's recommendations. He told me that we would be in touch and he would let me know either way.

After the two-week course, I headed back to SOI, with the knowledge of the possibility of me departing that command and going to do something I reenlisted to do. Just knowing of the possibility of my departure and going to change lives made me happy in a way that SOI could have never offered. I recall being questioned about my happiness and motivation. I just told them that my two weeks of being away rejuvenated my motivation. I wasn't lying because the conversations and the events that took place during those two weeks did rejuvenate me.

I didn't hear anything for a week or so, and then out of the blue on a Wednesday afternoon, Chief came in and said, "HM3, Monday morning you are to report to the Wounded Warrior Battalion per Command Master Chief."

My response was a motivated, "Aye-aye, Chief."

I began to clean out my locker and finish passing on my work to the others in PMR. I felt bad about leaving them, especially after recently being transferred into PMR. They knew how much this transfer to the WWBN meant to me. They knew based on the many hours we had spent talking about my frustrations with the command not understanding or even attempting to understand how much I gave to prove to them that I could do everything they could do and more.

Before I start to write the next chapter, I thought you should know that I prayed *every single day* that I could switch spots with every single person that I worked with, be a younger rank or higher up, so they could walk in my combat boots. I prayed that each and every one of them would spend fifteen minutes being me. I don't want to be a cocky mo-fo, but I am one hundred percent sure that they wouldn't be able to handle being mentally beat down constantly and knowing that I did everything they did and then some . . . but to be told it wasn't good enough and to be consistently stripped down mentally.

I'm not going to lie; I had some amazing times at SOI and inspired many great corpsmen, but the bad outweighed the good, and my memories of SOI are mostly terrible ones. There were many times I thought to myself, *Why do I continue on? What is stopping me from checking into the psych ward and letting someone know how I really feel?* There were many times I actually thought about driving down to the psych ward instead of driving into work. Sometimes I thought about how easy it would be to turn to the bottle or to drugs, but I kept telling myself that I needed to push on and continue to pave the path for my fellow wounded docs to follow. I am a man that has never quit anything, and I didn't plan on doing so during those times. I knew that I had fought that far, and I couldn't quit then; I would have given up three years of hard work and dedication. I couldn't allow that to happen.

12.

A NEW, NEW BEGINNING

On Monday, August 31, 2009, I checked into Wounded Warrior Battalion West. I was told on Wednesday, August 26th, to check in on Monday to the WWBN and that I was to be the Company Corpsman. I showed up around 0800, but the HM2, the LPO, assumed that I would be there prior to 0700. So he yelled at me to "freaking hurry it up and change over! Gosh dangit!"

I rogered up and said, "Aye, HM2!" I didn't have any official orders or any instruction to check in at a certain time. I grabbed my camies and a stall in the common head. The whole time I was putting on my camies, I kept muttering to myself, "I knew I should have showed up at 0600 and changed then. Shit, shit, shit! I am not going to have a great first impression by showing up late and not even in uniform! Now he is going to just send me back to SOI, and that's not what I want by any means! Well, I will make it up to him from here on out . . . I got this shit." Instead of explaining that I didn't have actual orders that told me when I had to check in or explain that I had some serious arthritis in the amputated leg's knee so that's why I didn't want to drive for an hour with a compression sleeve causing me additional and preventable pain, I figured an excuse wasn't something that he wanted to hear from his new HM3.

I really hit the new job well and took off running with the system in place while creating my own methods of madness. In September 2009, it was easy to create a system that worked best for me and those I worked with at the battalion. In a matter of weeks, I had a system set in place that allowed for a smoother flow of assisting the patients that were stationed there and a better system that helped the company staff in their accountability of their Marines, well within the medical side.

It was hectic at first, but once I had my system in place, it allowed for a more peaceful LPO. I had heard that he hadn't really had a break since he worked there and was getting burned out. So I made it my mission to ease his workload and give him some time off. Within a few weeks of showing him that I had things under control, I told him that he should take some time off. He kind of scoffed at the idea of taking leave and being away from work. I know he feared taking leave because the place would fall apart without him. Honestly, I feared that a little bit, too, but I would have never let him see that because then he wouldn't have taken leave.

It shocked the whole battalion when they heard he dropped a leave request, but it was long overdue for him. The first few weeks of working there, I had to handwrite all of the patients' medical appointments in my calendar and then write them on the whiteboard for the company's accountability. Although technology is far beyond what it was in 2004-2005 when I would track Marines' previous appointments, medications, medical notes, immunizations, etc., I still had no system set in place that could easily account for them while protecting their identity and medical information at the same time. So at that period in time, I would look at every Marine's schedule in the system and update my calendar, and as soon as I did that, I would update the whiteboard. Once the board was updated, I would then go out to the formation and announce the names of those who had appointments and what time they were. I also told them to see me off to the side if they needed a reminder of their appointment specifics. I would get some feedback sometimes of a Marine not knowing about some appointments. I looked into it, and sure enough, it was a lack of communication during the time of the appointment being booked or afterward. I am not pointing the blame on anyone, but I did fix the communication error by not only looking up the appointments daily but having the one who booked the appointment call me directly so I could update my calendar and notify the Marine and his/her section leader. I mainly did this because I hated when I would see that they missed an appointment and it was "not their fault."

Doing this part of the new job was easy for a while, then it got progressively worse because the number of patients kept increasing but the number of staff members, being medical staff, remained the same. Manually keeping track of every Marine's medical appointments and military and civilian facilities kept a guy busy. I didn't mind, though, because that gave my boss a break, and I quickly built trust and a good working relationship with the staff and patients.

After about six weeks of manually keeping track, attending medical appointments with the Marines, updating records, and attending all of the medical/staff meetings, I was allowed to be the safety Corpsman on some of the wounded warrior events. One of the first was to go with and participate in a skydiving event. It was actually pretty awesome. My job was to just be the Doc and watch over my Marines. That was an easy trip in comparison to the following one.

My second Corpsman coverage at the Wounded Warrior Battalion was a fun one but also challenging. I went with a group of bike riders to the San Francisco area. We were to ride from the VA in San Francisco to the VA in Los Angeles, down Highway 1. This was a fun journey because I was to ride down the coast of California with a group of wounded Marines. What an awesome opportunity!

We arrived in San Francisco in the WWBN bus a day or two before the trip was to begin to allow for shopping, sightseeing, and a complete gear/bike check. I was happy to have that extra day or two as a buffer so I could be selfish and get some amazing clam chowder. By the way, San Francisco has the third best clam chowder, compared to Boston and Dublin. Okay, back to the trip. So the buffer allowed me to hack my lungs up a bit. I was coughing for days and couldn't shake it for the life of me. It was so bad that Chief was telling me I was going to have to ride in the van if it didn't improve, and he saw me coughing up blood the evening we began our journey.

The morning of our trip, we loaded our gear into the WWBN bus so we could keep our stuff separate from the rest of the groups. Then we headed over to the VA for our opening ceremony and to begin our adventure. I began with my camel pack—it was a big bag with the water pouch in it—loaded with three liters and a ton of medical gear. It's a good thing that I had that bag full of medical gear because within the first fifteen miles someone started to skid out going downhill after being cut off and wrecked big time. I stopped and gave some medical supplies to the civilian doctor who had stopped and was calling for a paramedic. There was nothing further I could do, but it was a good thing I had supplies.

The first day's ride was seventy-five miles or so. Remember the cough I previously spoke of? Yeah, that bitch really started hitting me hard about sixty miles into the ride. I wasn't coughing up blood, though, because the previous night, Chief told me that if I didn't magically make my cough better, I was going to be in the bus riding at the tail end of the group. I didn't like that idea, mainly because those that had done the trip a year before said riding in the bus behind the whole group at five to ten miles per hour for seventy-five miles would not be fun. So I went out and bought some Vick's VapoRub and a shit ton of cough drops. About sixty miles into the ride, I kept my promise to Chief (I promised him that if I felt, in any way, my health was in jeopardy, I would stop riding, get into the bus, and notify him of my current status, my signs and symptoms, and what I was doing to ensure that I was taken care of) and stopped riding my bike; I rode in the bus for the remainder of the day. I notified Chief that I stopped riding my bike and hopped in the safety bus, and I was having a slight issue with breathing once I hit the hilly areas. I could have finished the ride, but I didn't know the course, and I couldn't go against Chief's orders.

It was a beautiful trip cruising down the California coast on Old Highway 1. We only ran into one area of people not really supporting our bike ride, and I believe that was when we were starting our second day in the Santa Cruz area. I am still unsure what the deal was with the few people who had issues with our bike group. I had my headphones on and was chatting at the same time as well. Oh well, not everybody will be happy with a group of cyclists taking up a lane on the road. Although I thought the Northern California area preached road sharing and alternative methods of transportation. Other than one bad experience, it was a peaceful and smooth ride. It was so beautiful and the scenery was peaceful as we cruised down the coast at about fifteen to twenty miles per hour.

I can honestly say that cycling from San Francisco to Los Angeles down a scenic coastal highway was some of the best forms of mental, physical, and spiritual therapies. Even though I was physically exhausted at the end of each day and ride, I felt amazing. Sit back and imagine this in your mind and tell me that what I am about to explain isn't soothing and mentally relaxing.

It's a sunny day with a temperature of about seventy-five degrees, and you're on a bike just letting your legs mindlessly pedal at your comfort speed. You feel the breeze from your ride and as you're cycling along the beach. You can feel that breeze off the cool Pacific Ocean, and you can hear the waves crashing onto the rocky beach. You glance over to your right and see the waves crashing and birds flying about aimlessly. You just think to yourself about how amazing the view is and how great the feeling of the cool ocean breeze is as you're cruising alongside a good friend.

Just imagine hundreds of miles alongside the ocean over a period of five days. When you stop for the day, you stop in a beach town along the way to enjoy a good snooze, but only after a few slices from the local pizza joint. It is such an amazing form of therapy. I have never understood why this isn't a form of therapy offered over being heavily medicated by a mental health specialist. I will later go over the ideal version for my perfect therapy, the place where I go to recharge my batteries. Answer this question, and as honest as can be: Would you rather have your medical insurance pay for or assist with the costs of sending you to your ideal therapy location/activity (if you have a medical condition that requires this and it is a healthy therapy) or for them to pay a pharmaceutical company to make a medication to cover your medical issues, a medication with a massive list of side effects (that may require more medication to cover the symptoms/medical issues if you have a side effect)? I'll tell you right now, if I had the option of a pill or bass fishing for my anxiety or PTSD, I would choose bass fishing *every single time*! I'm just saying that there are better alternatives than medications in most cases.

Back to the daily adventures at battalion. In October 2009, the Wounded Warrior Battalion West's barracks were almost complete, as well as the Hope and Care Center. My time at the Wounded Warrior Battalion was the most pleasant since my return to full duty. Granted, my days were filled with busy advocating work, but I was surrounded by many who had some sort of understanding of my injuries and my desire to remain on active duty and to go back and give more.

There were some that I worked with that still had their doubts about my abilities. They instinctively focused on my physical appearance rather than my proven capabilities, to that point. Let's reflect real quick on my physical accomplishments to that point: passed multiple PRTs (with standards way higher than the minimum for my height/weight/age category), completed multiple 5/10/15/20k hikes (with full gear load and throughout the mountains of Northern Camp Pendleton), ski dived, rode a bike hundreds of miles down the California coast, and participated in pre-Afghanistan training with instructors from SOI (in ninety-degree heat, throughout the mountains, multiple ongoing days in the field, carrying a combat load, and all while having infected pressure sores on my leg).

So when I mentioned all of that to those who doubted me, they would then bring up a bullshit excuse about how I could be seconds slower with medical gear because I have two fingers that are partially amputated. It's all just another physical appearance thing to try and throw back at me. Yet again I can throw things back about how many procedures that I had performed at the SOI clinic.

So during my time at Wounded Warrior Battalion, I would speak of returning back to a deployable unit and be an FMF corpsman again. Some of my fellow corpsmen would laugh at me and bring up my physical injuries. I am unsure if they thought that they would bring me to reality by saying stuff about my injuries or what they meant by it, but I know one thing: it just fueled my fire to return to a deployable unit.

My time at Wounded Warrior Battalion was from late August 2009 until April 2011. During that time, I enjoyed the work that I did, even though it could be just busy work, such as printing out medical records, but I knew that it was to help better a wounded warrior. I could rabble on about great the work I did and my accomplishments, but I would rather write about my whole experience as a wounded warrior as well.

One of the greatest things that I enjoyed about being a combat-wounded corpsman and working at the Wounded Warrior Battalion was the initial moments I would get with the wounded, ill, and injured Marines and sailors. During those moments, I would let them know that I was a combat-wounded Navy corpsman and their brother. I also let them know that if they felt the need to just drop on in and BS with me as a fellow wounded, ill, or injured service member, my door was always open. We could discuss anything, and I wouldn't pull the medical card unless what they were discussing with me caused, or would cause, harm to themselves or others. This allowed for a more peaceful and less resentful battalion.

After running the second PRT cycle for 2009, I was reminded of an issue that had been bothering me since I had my last foot and ankle surgery in 2007. A quick back brief, I lost my fourth toe, and for some reason my fifth toe would try to fill in the gap between the third toe and the fifth toe. So in 2007, the foot and ankle specialist put a plate on the outside of my fifth toe so it would hold the toe in place. It did its job, but for some reason, the stupid toe just wanted to keep on trying in its mission to fill in the gap. So when I would do any physical activity, it caused pain, but I didn't complain about it until after the second PRT cycle of 2009. The only reason I did complain and begin planning to do something about it was mainly due to where I worked and the understanding of the staff.

I never complained about the pain or about anything from the moment I knew it was possible to return to duty. I wouldn't risk the chance of my return for another surgery and months of recovery. When I was at SOI, I asked how the whole process would work if I were to have a surgery. I was told this: "HM3, you can have whatever surgery you need, and we encourage you to take care of yourself. However, as soon as surgery is completed, you are to report back here, and then you will be riding the desk until you are well enough to get back to duty. We are understaffed, and con leave is a recommendation and is approved by the command." I would never have a surgery to be released and check back into SOI just to ride the desk while recovering and in pain. I mean, I was already in pain, but at least I could get away from the clinic by going out in the field for a while. So that is why I never had anything done at SOI, except some minor injections in my knee.

However, I knew I was at a command that was understanding, so I had begun to plan the surgery out. I planned it out so I could ensure my wounded, ill, and injured Marines and sailors would get appropriate care during the holiday season. That in itself was a big mission, but I will get into further details later. I also stayed around and didn't take any personal leave through the holidays so I could cover for the rest of the medical crew and ensure they had adequate time off to be with their families, seeing as I would be on con leave for my surgery soon after their return. During the weeks building up to my surgery, I had everything done and planned out for while I was gone for my surgery. Everything was done and set for HM2 so he could run things smoothly and basically on an autopilot. I also timed it out so I would be recovered and set for the first PRT cycle of 2010.

During the holiday season, it was rough to get medical care for any average Joe. So when the Wounded Warrior Battalion had a battalion doctor that was on borrowed time from his or her specialty, it was even tougher to get a few Marines seen for their complicated cases on a daily basis. We were blessed to have the kind medical folks at Camp Pendleton Naval Hospital, and we made it by squeezing the Marines in during the few slots that were made available. I knew that everyone headed home and desired quality family time, so when I couldn't get my Marines seen, I would sit and wait with them during their ER visits.

The last I heard, the two battalions under the Wounded Warrior Regiment had their own battalion medical officers and staff that support the battalion medical officer (battalion MO or just MO). I never understood why it took so long for the higher-ups to make billet for a battalion MO. Every other Marine Corps unit had a battalion MO. I knew the military budget cuts took part in the delay and the paperwork to create a billet, but the war started in 2001, and almost a decade later, they finally got a few settled into the battalions. It made no sense for a doctor to be doing their job within their specialty to then be burdened by a group of Marines with some complicated cases. I am no politician, but hey, that's probably because I have enough sense to have seen that problem and have spoken about the solution during some meetings, just to then be told, "Doc, that makes sense, so stay in your pay grade."

After the holidays, my surgery drew near. I was hoping that during this surgery they could pull the broken screw out of my tibia.

I snapped the screw that was holding the plate on my right fibula in place. The main screw went from the lateral portion of the fibula to the medial aspect of the tibia. Somehow, I snapped the screw in the *middle* of the tibia! It wasn't like a small snap; it was a clean snap that separated completely. Surgery was set for early January 2010, marking my first surgery since April 2008. I was awed by the length of time between surgeries because of the unresolved medical issues. I don't understand another thing, another political thing: why would the government give the same amount of recovery time for those who are wounded, ill, or injured who desire to get out and stay in? I am sure I could have used another six months to have my foot and ankle worked on again.

The holiday timeframe was a busy one for me. I didn't take leave for the holiday season because I was set to be on con leave, so I just let the other docs use their leave to be with their families. I took the ninety-six-hour holiday weekends to spend with my local family and friends while being on call for any emergencies that the battalion staff or patients might have had during those blocks. The few days that I had to report in and do busy work around the office, I spent preparing the office for HM2 and Chief so while I was gone on con leave, things would be on autopilot again during my absence.

Once the New Year rolled around, I did a proper turnover and headed down to the Naval Medical Center San Diego's main operating room for my forty-seventh surgery. My pops came out for the surgery to help me out because this procedure was built up to be a big one. I was set to have my fifth toe amputated with some hardware removed, two plates with the screws attached. The two plates were the ones along the lateral aspect of my fifth metatarsal and fibula. The plate on my fibula had been bothering me for years, and I had wanted it out but had never had a good timeframe; well that, and I was always afraid that the hardware held my foot and ankle together. I had never guessed that my ideas behind the hardware holding my foot and ankle together throughout the four years was scientific, but I never wanted to risk it.

I thought that, having a toe amputated, I would have been kept overnight for any possible pain control or something, but it was an outpatient procedure, and I went home soon after surgery. My pops drove through the traffic slowly to not upset my stomach because of the anesthetics and not having anything in my stomach from a whole day. I was still in and out throughout the car ride, but I sure was thinking about an Arby's roast beef sandwich in my refrigerator. So when I got home, I crutched right on in the house and started chowing down. Umm, yeah, I didn't last a whole thirty minutes before chomped-up roast beef and bread came right back up through my throat and nose. I must say that I was more impressed with how amazing that shit looked like the same sandwich that I ate a half hour before. I just settled with some crackers and water then propped my leg up to help with the swelling while I dozed off to sleep off the anesthetics.

My thirty days of con leave caused a lot of stir craziness. I wasn't supposed to be up and about, but when I saw that the ceiling fan was causing Romeo's hair and dust to be blown around on the ground, I waited for the ultimate moment to make my move. I waited for my pops to head out the local Goodwill for his leisure shopping to hop up and start sweeping and mopping. It hurt like hell, and I could feel my foot swelling up, especially in the area of my newly amputated toe. I kind of did a rush job the first few times because I was afraid of getting caught, but I couldn't bear the thought of asking my dad to clean the floor or just continuously walk around cleaning. Although that was the main reason for ol' Poppers to be there, I just couldn't ask him to walk around with disinfecting wipes cleaning every little tile or slab of wall. I would rather help out and enjoy more of his company than anything, so that's what I did. I think he caught me on, like, the fourth time I was up and cleaning. He yelled at me and told me to sit down and rest and to let him do what he was there to do.

Toward the end of my con leave, I was begging God for the time to hurry up and go by so I could have some independence back. I was looking forward to going back to the battalion and getting away from the home life again. Granted, I was still in pain and deciding on whether I was going to attempt to walk with a space-filling orthotic in my shoe or shit can that garbage and not rely on another medical device to assist me; the quick answer was to cut that shit out of my shoe. In all honesty, the spacer was there to help assist with any balance issues I may have had after losing my fourth and fifth toe on my right foot. It is a good idea in theory, but it just seemed like an annoying object that was going to be in my way and possibly cause more problems than what it was supposed to help.

My begging was answered when HM2 called and offered me the gig of a lifetime. He asked when my con leave was finished and then offered for me to be the Corpsman to assist some wounded warriors that would be attending Super Bowl XLIV, or forty-four. (I will save you the time of looking it up like I had to . . . and I was there!) I told him, "I would *love* to!"

I then brought up the fact that I would have to come off con leave early to try and go PTAD, Permissive Temporary Assigned Duty, and I was very unclear on how to cancel con leave early and then get the command's approval to leave again. I was unsure that any command would approve of canceling medical-related leave, especially from having a toe amputated, to then fly across the nation to medically monitor wounded, ill, and injured service men and women. So I went completely around that by checking in off of leave and then taking "personal" leave. I was beyond thrilled to use a few days of charged leave to go to the Super Bowl and to be there with my friends and brothers in arms.

So the craziest thing happened to me when I checked in at the hotel in Miami. Before I get into that personal story, I would like to thank the amazing folks in Miami-Dade County, the locals from within and around Miami. The welcome that the wounded warriors (from the Wounded Warrior Regiment, Battalion, and the Semper Fi Fund) received was beyond phenomenal! The greeting at the airport, the USO, and throughout the whole weekend was just so . . . speechless, really. Thank you again to you kind folks in Miami-Dade County and the surrounding areas.

Throughout the years following my IED attack, I had tried to return to Bethesda, Walter Reed, Naval Medical Center San Diego, and various other rehab installations to mentor the wounded, ill, and injured as they came home. Well, one year, I met an extraordinary gentleman and a hero of mine since. I will not go into great detail about this gentleman to protect his identity, but he is one tough dude. He shared his story with me, and I felt an overwhelming feeling to thank God to be in the presence of this hero. Throughout the day, I got to know him and his family better. He and I exchanged contact info, but as life goes on, we all lose touch with people sometimes, especially when we all have to heal while trying to maintain a career.

I checked into the hotel in Miami, and when I did so, the group that was taking care of all of the wounded warriors told me who I was to be rooming with, and I couldn't believe what was happening. I was going to be rooming with the gentleman that I just spoke of for the next few days! I was so excited that I couldn't wait for an elevator and took off up the stairs with my luggage. I soon realized that trying to run up thirteen stories with two suitcases and a backpack was a real bad idea. I exited the stairwell and waited for an elevator to take me the rest of the way. I arrived at the room and was disappointed yet happy to find that he had checked in but was on a tour in the local area. He was back soon enough, and we stayed up the entire night shooting the shit and comparing our ups and downs throughout our careers as wounded warriors.

During our conversation, I found it *very* intriguing where the Navy had decided to send two combat-wounded Navy corpsmen for their first duty station upon returning to duty. Well, as you know, I was promised the initial job at the Wounded Warrior Battalion on the West Coast, and when I lost that battle, the next option was the School of Infantry, the Naval Hospital Camp Pendleton Clinic detachment. Well, the first place that they had sent my fellow combat-wounded Corpsman was to the School of Infantry Clinic on the East Coast. It makes me question their theory behind it. I can't make any assumptions as to why, but it is kind of odd, though.

The whole trip was full of events but nothing really demanding on my foot. Most of my job was to monitor medication intake, monitor alcohol intake for all patients, and monitor everyone's medical conditions throughout the whole trip. It was easy for me to do this because I knew everyone's medical conditions and the medications they were taking. Plus, it was easier for wounded warriors to discuss their medical situations with me because I had the knowledge as a medical provider and as a fellow wounded warrior. It did kind of suck that I had my surgery a few weeks before because I was taking pain medication and I wanted to have a few brews with the guys when we would be out at dinner or at another event. It was an ethics thing; I possibly could have had a drink and have been all right, but then the Marines would have their doc abusing power . . . and right in front of them.

Being a man and being at Super Bowl XLIV is something that is unexplainable. It's so simple and complicated to try and explain. I am more of a diehard baseball fan than anything, but being a man and in the Super Bowl atmosphere was still astonishing. I couldn't even imagine being at the World Series; I would probably be so excited I would stroke out or something. It was difficult to figure out who I would cheer for in that Super Bowl. I wanted the Saints to win because it would be their first title, but then again, it's the Colts, and Peyton Manning was such an amazing quarterback that it's hard to not go for the Colts. I never did figure out who I was cheering for; I guess it's like every other Sunday for us Browns fans.

We soon returned back from the Super Bowl trip, and I began to help with moving the office into the building. I was excited for the bigger office and to have Alpha Company a little way away from the battalion headquarters. The move actually caused more work than it actually helped because the military decided to not drop the proper connection lines for us medical folks to access the Navy and Navy medicine side of the house. So now if somebody needed something simple like their appointments printed off, I would have to walk over to the other building, which was a distance away, and log on to print it off. Doing actual medical stuff didn't bother me when it came to bouncing back and forth between the offices. I did start a list of requests for non-urgent medical information to lessen my runs on my busier (meeting) days.

Around the time of Alpha Company's move, I ended up moving from Temecula to San Marcos. My friend, whose house that I had been watching while he was deployed, was due back early. I just couldn't deal with the price of driving from Temecula to the middle of Camp Pendleton. I was spending hundreds of dollars in gas to get to and from work daily. Being in San Marcos cut my drive in half. Plus, that moved me closer to all of my friends again. Living in Temecula for the short amount of time temporarily killed friendships. I had great friends that would drive and had driven the distance to come see me, but still it was a lot to ask of people.

I am going to skip from mid-March until May 2010 to protect some sad and depressing things that had occurred within my family. To protect the privacy and out of love and respect for my family, I refuse to discuss the tragic events that occurred, and I will leave it at that.

During the first PRT cycle of 2010, I had passed the push-ups, sit-ups, and the sit and reach with no issues. When I had started the cardio portion of the PRT, I began to experience some intense pain at the very end of my residual limb. I would have stopped the PRT, but like many things, I had procrastinated and was doing the PRT on one of the last days. I knew I had to tough through it for the next ten to fifteen minutes and then go have it examined. Before I could even get seen, I had to take out my padding in my prosthetic and cut a small area out to relieve the pressure from walking. I had to do this a number of times before I figured out a possible cause for so much pain. The x-rays that I had done had revealed that I had HO growing in again. So I scheduled another surgery, and again I had intended on this one being another dual-purpose surgery. This next surgery would remove the HO from the distal end of my residual limb then perform my second knee scope.

As you remember, I had my first knee scope in November 2007, and I was told that I had the onset of arthritis. By May 2010, I had felt my knee degenerate from all of the usage. I knew it was uncertain how much damage my knee had taken since November 2007 until I was under the knife already, but based on the shit that I did to it throughout the few short years, I knew it wouldn't be good, although in a sick way I was excited to see how fucked up it really was.

So in May 2010, I had returned into the operating room at Naval Medical Center San Diego for my second knee surgery (and all before I even hit the age of twenty-five). The orthopedic team had removed two chunks of additional bone growth, heterotopic ossification, from the end of my stump and performed a knee scope. I had some damage to my knee, including a posterior horn meniscal tear, frayed/torn cartilage, and some serious cartilage loss.

Prior to the surgery, I gave my word on participating in a softball game at Petco Park, home of the San Diego Padres, which was to be a mix of some San Diego Padre players and a selected group of wounded warriors. Well, I had my surgery and didn't want to back out, so I put on my leg, even though I was supposed to be only crutching around, and headed to the stadium for the Memorial Day softball event. Although I was in so much pain from just wearing my leg and walking from the front gate to the center field entrance to the field, I wasn't about to bitch out and not honor my word to those who had put this together. Once the teams were set, my team took the field, and I ran out to second base like I had done my whole life. After running and diving around, we finally made the three outs, and I felt some sloshing in my gel liner. I trotted over behind the wall of players that awaited their turn to bat to take off my leg and drain the blood and sweat that was seeping through the suture line. I would do this every time we would come in to bat. I was honestly hoping that nobody would notice, but after the game was over, a former pitcher for the San Diego Padres called me over to the makeshift mound and named me the inspirational player of the game because he noticed me draining the blood and sweat from my leg in between the innings. I didn't want to be put on the spot, but he said it personally inspired him, so I guess it was well worth it.

I had tried to do some research to see if there was any correlation between below knee amputees and rapid degeneration of the knee due to prosthetic use. My results came back with nothing. When anybody would give any feedback, it was along the lines of, "Well, if your knee hurts and you have arthritis, maybe you should slow down and not be so active." What kind of BS is that? Why should I be robbed of my youth because of something that could have been examined and fixed? Instead, the system thinks it's easier and less cost efficient if they slap a prosthetic on you and send you on your way to be another system's problem.

As you can tell, I spent my con leave period from the May 2010 surgery doing my research and talking to fellow amputees. My results from chatting with other amputees were, "Yes, the system is fucked up and we all have pain. It's just the way it is, bro." I figured as such, anyway, but I wasn't going to slow down or give into the ways of the system. I grew up with the mentality to never give up or back down, and I sure as hell wasn't going to let it happen after I had already achieved so much.

During my con leave period, I had given into my family bugging me to go to Vegas for a little reunion. I figured it was fairly harmless to be in Vegas on crutches with alcohol. Don't worry, I didn't get hammered and fall all over the place with my crutches. I was not worried about anything. I had family to take care of me, keep me company, and booze while I was at the card tables. It was going good for a while until something out of the freaking blue hit me.

My leg started opening up slowly, and these little strings came poking through my skin along the suture line. I was unsure what the hell was happening, so I just started taking pictures to document the crazy shit my body was doing. I emailed them to the folks over in orthopedics, and they told me I should probably come in to get it checked out. I scheduled a time to head on in but then realized I had to drive back that night to make the appointment in the morning. So I just left the family in Vegas and headed back throughout the middle of the night.

The next morning, I went in to see the ortho surgeon, and he told me that my body was rejecting the Vicryl sutures and if any more came to the surface to just cut them out. He trusted that I could take of this at home because I was a corpsman, but he told me to just make sure I documented where they came to the surface, their appearance (partially absorbed, still tied . . . etc.), local reaction, and how many. I eventually had to extend my con leave for two weeks because I had one bad encounter while doing laundry.

It was a hot day, and we used the apartment complex's facility. I was on my way back from carrying the basket of done laundry when I notice my gel liner was starting to slip in my prosthetic a little. I chalked it up to being a hot day and my leg might have been sweating a little bit, but then I realized by the time I got back to the apartment that my leg didn't sweat anymore. So I set the basket down and slowly took off my liner. Sure enough, there was a small cup's worth of blood inside my leg. The cause was another damn Vicryl suture coming to the surface. I had my best friend (let's call him "Bruce") there with me, and I asked him if he wanted to help cut this bitch out of my leg. I then realized I was asking an Infantry Marine if he would like to cut something out of somebody, and it was a stupid question, because before I realized what I had asked, he already had a knife out. I told Bruce, "We will be using a suture removal kit, not a hunting knife, good sir." He was slightly bummed but then flopped down with the scissors while I pulled the suture high enough for him to cut, which was slightly painful, since I was pulling on an internal suture. Just a few days after we cut that one out and it had closed up, another popped up in a different location, and it was time to cut another. This went on for a few weeks.

Before I knew it, my days of sleeping in and enjoying time off were done, and I was heading back into the battalion. For those that aren't military, you may not understand, but so much can change in not only one unit with forty-five days, but within the whole military. I came back to half of the battalion being new patients and new staff members. So not only did I have to catch up on the initial intakes, but I had to adjust to how these new staff members handled business as well. I adjusted quickly, and everything was back to business as usual.

Little did I know that my days at the Wounded Warrior Battalion were coming to an end, not on my account, though. I will get around to that soon, but let's stick with keeping the timeline of events here. In August 2010, I went into the gastroenterologist for a flex sigmoidoscopy and a colonoscopy because I was having bright red blood in my stool and sometimes uncontrollable bleeding. (Yes, I took pictures of that to document as well. Actually, the pictures turned out to be some of the best pictures I had ever seen.) Back in April, I had lost my daughter, and I had been trying to be the shoulder for everyone else to cry on. Well, I forgot about making sure that I was okay. Apparently, I handle stress and the variety of other emotions that occur when we lose a loved one, and the government doesn't give a shit. I was diagnosed with a one-time severe depression episode, and during that phase, my lower GI tract took the brunt of it all.

After everything appeared to be normal, minus my one-time severe depression episode, I just went back to being me and went about my days. I was told I needed to seek professional help to assist me with the loss of my daughter, but I continued to refuse, and eventually people just gave up trying to tell me to go see the wizard. I was not going to walk down the dark path of seeing a wizard and being prescribed a shit ton of meds that would just mask the inevitable. I handled things in my own way, and it didn't include walking around like a zombie on meds. I handled things by staying strong in my faith, sharing my story, mentoring others, and engaging in physical fitness.

October 10, 2010, was the day of the Chicago Marathon, my first time doing the Chicago Marathon and my first time back on a course in about a year. This was my return to the Achilles Freedom Team since my previous chain of command was harassing me about not wasting my time doing marathons. This, by the way, was fucking bullshit that my command had to know about my personal leave time and how I spent it. This was later brought up in my career by someone from the same chain of command. Anyway, I was back with the Achilles Freedom Team and as happy as could be to be back with family.

I had actually been doing some training for this marathon by doing pure upper body strengthening and endurance with indoor rock climbing and hiking in the desert. This actually paid for about the first twenty miles, and then I realized I didn't train hard enough because I started to lose some gas. I was booking it for the first half and then starting to lose it soon after. I realized that I should train for more than six weeks before the next race. I think I still beat my personal best, but not by much, and finished in the top five for handcyclists.

Just a week after the Chicago Marathon of 2010, I was back in the operating room. This was to have my hand worked on for the first time since Bethesda in 2006. It actually might have been Balad Surgical or Landstuhl, Germany, when I had my fingers worked on prior to October 2010. Anyway, I was having a revision of my partially amputated index and middle fingers plus a joint fusion on the distal joint of my left ring finger, although I should have gone with the advice of my family and friends and not had my ring finger fused. I had been doing indoor rock climbing and had gained some movement and strength back in the finger. I was proud to have gained some flexion and strength, but it was in constant pain, and the x-rays showed that the joint was an "S" shape. I still should have listened to my family and Bruce on that decision and waited.

Shortly after my hand revision, my fingers began to get red, swollen, and glossy. I went in to the Orthopedic Department at the Naval Hospital in Camp Pendleton to have it looked at, and the surgeon told me she didn't think my fingers were infected. I told her that I had been a corpsman for six years now and had encountered more infections in my six years than she could ever dream of. She didn't argue after that and ordered some labs and then some antibiotics. She told me that if it got worse to come back if need be.

Thanksgiving 2010 was fairly interesting because of my recent surgery on my hand and my lack of ability to utilize my hand. You guys should know that I *love* food, and that by default makes Thanksgiving and the Fourth of July my favorite holidays. Normally, I make myself two plates of food so I don't have to make so many trips. Not that year. I had to change my fat kid routine and get up and make many trips.

In early December 2010, I had been checking my Navy Knowledge Online, NKO, account for the HM2 advancement results daily. I had been with the Wounded Warrior Battalion since August 2009, so I had an early promote eval and was hoping that helped me with my advancement exam for the second cycle of 2010. Plus, I took the Navy's EAP course at the hospital's command when it was offered before the second advancement exam cycle.

I decided to log into my NKO account during chow time to see if there was any updates on the advancement exams, and Bruce was sitting right there when I logged in. It showed "Selected for Advancement," and I yelled at the computer, "You've got to be fucking kidding me!" Bruce was pretty startled then caught on to what was going on, and he started laughing. I was so stoked. I printed that page off then went to eat the biggest, greasiest cheeseburger to celebrate. I called my LPO and told him I would be back a few minutes late but would explain why when I returned. He said that was fine. When I returned back, I showed him my print-off, and then we went over to show Chief and the rest of the medical staff. They were all pretty happy as well and told me now that I am a second to start acting like it. I just chuckled and said, "Hey, I don't have the two chevrons yet, so I can still be the same old strong-headed self." They all chuckled as well.

The end of 2010 landed me in the orthodontist's office to have a device put in for my upcoming corrective jaw surgery, Surgically Assisted Rapid Palate Expansion or SARPE. It is actually a pretty cool procedure; you guys should look it up. Anyway, they had to put this device in so when the surgeon was done splitting my upper palate I would have to turn this spacer two times for x amount of days until my upper jaw was as wide as my lower jaw again.

Around the holidays of 2010, I had to start thinking about new orders, extending, and/or reenlisting. My projected rotation date, or PRD, was approaching in May 2011, and my end of active service was in April 2012. I was in an odd situation when it came time to picking orders because I wanted to extend my time at the Wounded Warrior Battalion so I could just ride out my contract. I had only eleven months left on my contract, at the PRD timeframe, so I didn't plan on reenlisting and taking orders elsewhere or being denied a C-School again. I was doing great things at the battalion and making a difference with a lot of the patients and other wounded, ill, and injured Marines and sailors. So I figured if I was good at something (especially something that I could relate to with others and improve their health) and enjoyed it, then why leave and go back? I did have a plan for a possible return to the fleet, but I soon realized how few were there for me when I needed them.

Well, the Navy has a timeframe for picking orders before the Navy picks orders for you. It is a way for sailors to be more proactive in their order selection. But I was almost screwed over because I was assigned to a different command, and my old one wasn't able to keep up with me daily to know what was needed from them to assist with my career decisions. Seeing as the Wounded Warrior Battalion was right next to the Naval Hospital in Camp Pendleton, I would take a later lunch on some days so I could begin to look at what duty stations were available in case I made the decision to stay in for another enlistment. I was thinking about getting out, because if I reenlisted, I would be contracted for over ten years, and I would have to stay for the full twenty-plus years, which wouldn't be bad, but I felt like it was time to move along.

I would have applied for a C-School, but I had been denied a few times during that enlistment, my second enlistment, for various C-School applications, and there was no understanding from the Navy's side of the table. I was denied C-School applications because the Navy wanted corpsmen who were in their first enlistment and E-1 through E-3, with an exception for E-4s. I was a newly pinned E-5 and with a possible third contract, so I would have been stuck as a regular "General Duty" Green Side Corpsman or 8404. I could have waited to go for IDC, Independent Duty Corpsman, for a C-School, but then I would have to wait a few years, and at the command I was working at, it was next to impossible to complete a checklist for some prior training and experience for letters of recommendation or just to be prepared.

I shouldn't have had to wait on that because of the "standard" prerequisites. As you may recall, I was originally enlisted as National Call to Service, or NCS, and that meant eighteen months of active duty then finishing my time as a reservist. I was a little after eighteen months when I was injured, so the Navy allowed me to extend my active duty contract as I continued my rehab. By the time I was recovered and passed the medical board's decision, I had been active duty for three years and eight months. If I had signed a five- or six-year contract originally, I would have fit in the timeline. But I signed an NCS contract and was graciously allowed to reenlist into active duty again (which was unheard of but it was approved). I had a unique circumstance and should have been considered for a C-School. I know that there are rules in place for a reason, and by choosing some of the C-Schools, I would have only been allowed to promote within that field for so long, but I would have adjusted fire later on in my career. I was just going to ride out my contract doing a job that I enjoyed doing and wanted to do for as long as I could because I was helping wounded warriors out.

After the holidays, I was scheduled for my first major jaw surgery. This was a stressful one for me. After my injuries, I had all of my surgeries on my arms and legs, so for a surgeon to cut into my face was a little nerve-wracking. I was just a little worried about having my face worked on, but I knew I needed it. I was told that if I didn't get this done, my teeth would be done for. I had some serious crowding going on and an underbite, and my upper jaw was eight millimeters narrower than my lower, so my back teeth barely came together, which caused eating any meat to take forever to chew. I am not exactly sure how much of this was from before my time in the service, seeing my dental record was lost or misplaced after I was injured. I don't know why the Navy didn't offer to perform these surgeries and put on the braces soon after I became an outpatient. They could have performed all of my dental and orthodontic work while I was just focusing on physical rehabilitation. That makes too much sense, so of course it makes sense as to why they didn't offer it before 2010.

In late February 2011, I went into the operating room to have my SARPE done. I plopped over onto the operating table while they attached all of the leads onto me. After they had prepared me and the anesthesiologist was about to put me under, I asked him to hold off so I could "get my Jesus on" just before being put under. He agreed and then asked if I would like the OR to be quiet, and I said it didn't matter as long as I was able to pray. I closed my eyes and began to pray. I was surprised when someone grabbed my hand and bowed his head with me. It was the oral surgeon. I wasn't only surprised, but I was immediately overwhelmed with comfort. I finished my prayer, thanked the surgeon, and nodded to the anesthesiologist that I was ready to go under.

The surgery wasn't as bad as it looked in the videos I watched prior to my procedure. It wasn't bad because the surgeons have to move the nerve in the area, and doing so numbs up the area for the most part. Although there was some serious pain, swelling, and discomfort, this honestly helped with the healing process. I was kept overnight for observation and pain control. The best part of the surgery was after the initial surgery and hospital portion. It was the part of turning the key device in my upper jaw twice a day. This part was the greatest because my upper palate was separated by one millimeter at that time, so as I turned it, I could hear and feel the bone separating even more! It was so cool and such an unusual sound.

13.

NOW IT GETS INTERESTING

hile on con leave, I received a phone call from the School
of Infantry. I knew that the number was a standard Camp
Pendleton area phone number, so I answered, knowing it
could be from the oral surgery department, the battalion, or someone
from the Naval Hospital/School of Infantry. It just so happened to
be the School of Infantry. It was the Senior Enlisted, the Command
Chief. I knew he was the Command Chief, and he and I had a brief
encounter a few months before. He wasn't too impressed by me
during our first meeting, and I actually had it coming because I was
kind of a smartass to him.

Let us backtrack a few months prior to this phone call. I went up
to the School of Infantry Clinic to pin some junior corpsmen to their
newly advanced rank. When I showed up, I parked in the handicapped
spot, which was the only spot open, and I was the last one there, though
I wasn't late. So we went through the whole ceremony, and just before
I headed back to work at the Wounded Warrior Battalion, Chief came
up to me and said, "Congratulations on picking up HM2 of the United
States Marine Corps." I knew what he was getting at because I wore
the Marine Corps cover in my Marine digital camouflage uniform
instead of the lame Navy cover. I knew I was technically at a shore

command, so I should have been wearing the one without the Marine Corps' Eagle Globe and Anchor. I honestly did it because I wanted to rebel against the Navy because I'd spent a shit ton of money on uniform items when they lied to me about reimbursing me after my deployment. (The quick story on that is prior to me being augmented out to 3/7, I was told to just leave my gear at the command, and when I returned from deployment, they would give me my gear back. By the time I returned to active duty after my deployment and injuries, my stuff had disappeared. The command said they would reimburse me for any new uniforms. When I went back to duty, however, and had to do a whole sea bag inspection, an inspection on all of my standard-issued uniform items, I had to buy every single uniform item again. Of course, the government failed on their end of the bargain. So I refused to buy new items if I really didn't have to.)

My response to the Chief's comment was, "Oh, thanks, Chief. It's been a long time coming."

I am unsure if he knew that I knew, but he proceeded to "instruct" me on what I needed to do to correct myself. "HM2, that means go buy the appropriate rank for the appropriate Navy cover that will accompany that uniform." I figured I had let it go too far and just rogered up so I could be back in time for the afternoon meeting with the case managers for the WWBN.

I hope that is a healthy enough back brief on my short encounter with this Chief, but I don't think it was enough for him to call me and do what he did. I was heading home from a follow-up appointment from my recent jaw surgery, and I hadn't taken anything for the pain because I had to drive myself to and from the appointment, so I was a little on edge and easily irritable, to say the least.

The phone rang, and I hurried to sync my phone and Bluetooth so I could find out who was calling and for what reason. I answered, "This is HM2 Jacobs."

On the other end was a naval "leader," and he says to me, "Hey, Jacobs, this is Chief Don from SOI."

I said, "Good Morning, Chief. What can I help you with?"

He replied, "Whenever you're done with your paternity leave or whatever the fuck you're on, you are to report back to SOI."

I was really thrown off by what was happening, and I tried to repeal my case, but he wasn't having it. I said to him, "Chief, I copy all, but I thought my time was going to be finished off while as a medical liaison for the Wounded Warrior Battalion, as per Command Master Chief?"

"That was true until the command changeover. Now there is a new sheriff in town."

I replied to Chief's orders, "Roger, Chief. I just had a massive jaw surgery, and I will be back off of con leave within ten days, so can I get a few days to do a proper pass down with the corpsmen here and then transfer back up?"

He agreed that would be for the best. I used the rest of my con leave to not rest but to start working on taking orders to a different command. I was not going to extend and stay at that terribly isolated outlying clinic. The funny thing is that if that Chief really wanted to stick it to me, he could have waited until I signed the extension and then pulled me back. I am glad he didn't do that, though.

Soon after that conversation, I called my family and vented out all of my anger about the whole situation and then started to contact the command career counselor at the Naval Hospital Camp Pendleton. I was less than three months out of my projected rotation date, or PRD, so I would have had to take orders based on the needs of the Navy. At that time, the Navy had a new rule stating, and I am paraphrasing, you had your choice of orders within the six- to nine-month window of your PRD, and anything within the six-month window was based on the needs of the Navy. So I decided to call my detailer to explain my situation while acquiring letters of recommendation from fellow corpsmen and Marines. I will explain that whole crazy debacle in a bit.

The detailer was a busy man, and I knew how overworked they could get, so I tried to keep the command career counselors in the loop so they could try to relay messages on. The one major part of my acquiring orders came from the assistance of a former Marine First Sergeant and fellow member of 3rd Battalion/7th Marines. He overheard me talking about how frustrating it was to not have anyone understand where I was coming from and to not have some command support. He asked me what I wanted to do, and I told him I would like to return to the Infantry, and he asked me to make sure that's what I wanted and not what my emotions wanted.

I took some time to ponder it all, and I came back with the same answer. He asked how he could help, and I told him it was in the hands of the detailer. He asked for his number and email so he could personally contact him. I shook his hand and hugged him for just making the initial contact. He told me to not get too excited because there was a good chance that I could not get the orders based on the rank requirements and needs. I told him I understood but was just grateful for his assistance because some military members, and civilians, that I had served or worked with since my return to duty had doubted my abilities if I returned to the Infantry. I must say that they never doubted my abilities stateside or with a non-infantry unit, which made no sense. He told me to not focus on their negative comments regarding my situation. First Sergeant received contact back from the detailer saying that the orders would be up for selection soon and he would do his best to get me the orders I desired. He also said that he had never been contacted by a Marine recommending a corpsman, or sailor, to go back to a Marine unit and to inform First Sergeant and myself that my medical information was not on my record or profile so he wouldn't have known any difference between me and another HM2 fighting for the spot. The main issue I had with this whole order selection was not having anyone Navy, especially within the fellow corpsmen realm, backing me on my career because they refused to have the faith in me based on my abilities, that I had proven time and time again, but based on my physical appearance (which could only be seen out of uniform). That just frustrated me a bit. I, however, knew that the Marine Corps had my back.

After all of the orders stuff had begun, I had to finish up my con leave, which actually gave me a few days toward the end to catch up on my rest before climbing back into the long days at SOI. I wasn't too happy about returning to SOI and leaving the WWBN hanging because they had just lost another HM2 to new orders, and I felt bad about leaving things in the hands of a new crew. I told them to contact me if they needed help with anything, though.

It was amazing to know that I would be returning to SOI knowing that I would be getting orders out of there soon after my return. It was also something that I couldn't tell that command, because then they would try to stop it—and they actually tried. The Chief that came in after I had returned to SOI kept asking me to extend. Finally, I gave in and told her I had already made contact with my detailer, with the assistance and recommendation from my First Sergeant, and had something in the works. She was an amazing Chief and leader, by far one of the best I had the pleasure of working for, and once I explained my situation and what the detailer said, she was on board and told me that if I needed any command assistance to let her know.

Just a few days after my return to the School of Infantry, my orders posted, and I had finally received the orders that I had been waiting for: 1st Marine Division, Camp Pendleton, CA! I *finally* got them! This was a personal and career accomplishment. It wasn't without many sacrifices and severe dark phases . . . and it wasn't over just yet.

I knew once my orders posted, I had some more leg work to do, pun intended. I had to pick my check-out date, pick my PCS leave dates, reenlist, and do a worldwide assignability screening. I scheduled the assignability appointment, as well as any other medical stuff that correlated with the screening. I then contacted one of my inspirations and asked him if he could do my reenlistment ceremony, and he was more than thrilled to do it. I picked my check-out date and my leave block. I was so stoked that everything had finally fallen into place.

I went through all of the prescreening requirements and then went into the appointment. I didn't hold anything back during that appointment and told the doctor about every single medical condition so it couldn't come back to me about withholding any known medical conditions that could possibly hinder my ability to perform a task or job in the future. I just had a feeling that if I held anything back, it would come back to me. I was medically cleared to perform the duties that would be assigned to me at 1st Marine Division. This was amazing news, but I knew that there was still room for error, so I didn't gloat too much and knew that I was still at a duty station and there was work to be done, although I did kind of drop my pack . . .

Prior to setting everything up to lock on the whole orders deal, I wanted to go give Command Master Chief of 1st Marine Division the heads up on the situation. An appointment was set up, and I went down to discuss the whole thing with him. He was pretty cool about the whole thing, at first. We discussed the expectations from a command perspective, and I also expressed my desire to just be one of the guys and not a special case. We agreed that would be a good idea, but we both understood that this could be a big media thing after. He asked what I wanted to do and where I would like to go within division. I told him that I would like to venture over to Combat Trauma Management to be an instructor. He said he would like to work on the numbers and see where an HM2 would be best. I left the meeting feeling pretty good about the whole thing and also relieved knowing that I gave him a heads-up on the situation and we discussed it thoroughly.

Anyway, I headed down to NMCSD the next day for an appointment and to discuss the reenlistment ceremony with my doctor. On my way back from that appointment/meeting, I was contacted by 1st Marine Division, their manpower unit, and was told that I was not returning to 1st Marine Division because I was not medically cleared. I was then asked what other orders I would consider. I was honestly in shock and had quickly fallen into a dark depression. I just told whoever was on the phone that I would consider a different deployable Marine unit. It was honestly one of the most depressing phone calls that I had ever received. I didn't even know what to think about the whole thing and what was going on.

I rushed back to SOI to figure out what was going on or what happened. I found in my medical record that the doctor who had signed off on my worldwide assignability had changed her decision for some reason. Before the papers magically disappeared, I scanned them and emailed them to myself and a few other trusted sources as evidence. I had found out that someone had come up from 1st Marine Division and spoken with the doctor then left. I had no idea who it was or what was said, but whatever was said turned her decision. I went to speak with Chief about the matter, and I was more concerned about my order selection at that moment rather than who was trying to dictate my career based on my appearance and not my abilities. I had realized that I hadn't reenlisted yet, so I told Chief that I was going to request a command transfer and finish out my contract and not reenlist. She told me to not act on emotions and to take the rest of the day to ponder things and that she would look into what was going on and would have answers after formation the next morning.

I called my dad on my drive home to discuss things with him, and he told me not to hang my head, to keep fighting and not back down. Those words were encouraging but still a tough pill to swallow. I went home and thought about everything. If I took orders to a deployable unit, not a grunt unit, I could use it as a stepping stone, but I wasn't going to let the military know that I was considering that as an option. Instead, I stuck to my guns and didn't show them any weaknesses.

Chief kept her word and pulled me into her office for a discussion. She told me that someone did come up to have a discussion with the doctor and that the doctor didn't know how to respond, so she changed it based on the information she was given from division. I don't fault her by any means because it was a complex situation. I was told to stand by while Chief called my detailer to figure out if my orders were dropped and/or changed and, if so, what my options were. Chief really had my back on this, and I really appreciate her for honoring her word.

I am not exactly sure what happened, but soon after everything went down, I received a call from 1st Marine Division and was told that I was still set to check in for duty on June 15, 2011. I was beyond excited because, whatever happened, I knew that would be the end of the politics and drama dealing with me just going to 1st Marine Division. It was a peaceful moment, so I proceeded with my reenlistment ceremony.

The reenlistment was a great ceremony, and my doctor, and an inspiration of mine, did an amazing job by making everything happen so perfectly. He was a little nervous but did an amazing job and said some amazing things. He opened the floor for me to speak about what was going on with my career and where I was headed and how this was such a big deal, not just within the military but mainly within the Navy, because the number of combat wounded was significantly less than the Marines and Army. So a successful story on the Navy side of the house was even bigger and more inspirational within the ranks of the blue side. There was even a special guest, a former commanding officer of mine, who was the Admiral of Navy Medicine West at the time. It was such an honor to have him remember me under his command, and to have him stop in and congratulate me was even more mind blowing than I could have imagined.

After the dust settled from the politics, drama, and "leg" work, I had taken my ninety-six-hour liberty so I could finally relax and begin to plan my block leave for my transfer leave. Around that time, I had a whole eight to ten full working days left anyway, so I spent the remainder of my time doing another turn over and then turning a lot of my free time into sitting down to mentor all of the junior corpsmen who were remaining at the SOI command for a while.

I will never forget the day I left there, one of the best days of my life. I honestly haven't been back to even visit or to see if it's the same miserable place that I had left it, twice. Anyway, there was a multi-farewell ceremony. It was a great ceremony put on by some great folks. I had worked with an HM2 up at the SOI command for just a few weeks, and he knew how much I loved the Marine Corps, and we all knew how much he loved the blue side of the Navy, because he was fresh to the HM rate because of a lateral move later in his career. So while some who were with infantry units would reminisce of the good ol' combat days, he would try to counter our awesome war stories with his shipboard duties. So he had a paddle for me wrapped with the Navy's blue digital cord mixed in with some pink as a joke so I could take that to my next command, 1st Marine Division, and have to explain the blue and pink. It was pretty funny, and I loved it, but I was the type of guy who would have never put it up in my office, anyway. It does still sit by my nightstand, but I am not the type of guy to decorate my workspace with "I love *me*, look at *me*" stuff. We all had some good laughs that day, though. Soon afterward, I headed back down to the Naval Hospital to officially check out and move on to the next portion of my career and life. Although there were way too many bad memories, I am still grateful for them and the people I met during those times.

14.

FINAL FIGHT

On May 31, 2011, I checked out on two weeks of leave. It was an amazing feeling to be on leave and checked out of SOI. I think the better of the two was just the fact that I was to never return to the School of Infantry. I was really stoked for my leave, though. I had been planning a fishing trip to the cabin out in Branson, Missouri, for about a month. This was the first time in my career—at that time, I was six years and nine months into my career—that I had taken leave to do something for me. I would say that I couldn't ask for a better trip, but then I would be lying. It would have been better if the large-mouth bass had been biting better on my fishing days, but it was still an amazing trip with my family and friends.

I was excited to use this leave block to celebrate and to wind down from my first full duty station since I was found fit to continue my active service. It was pretty amazing, but after a while, I was starting to go over every scenario of my soon to be near future, especially on the whole command's issue with me. I tried to not let it get to me, and it was easy for the most part because I was doing what brought me peace. Toward the end of the trip, I noticed it was starting to wear me out. It wore on me so bad that I left my all-time favorite hat in a family member's car and didn't even notice until I got back to San Diego. Then I realized that my dumbass self had let this next assignment get to me so much that I left my hat in Missouri and I might never see it again. I was even more pissed at myself because I searched everywhere online and realized that there were no other hats of the same kind for sale *anywhere*!

I returned to San Diego a few days before I was set to check in at 1st Marine Division. I always enjoyed being home at least a day before I was to check back in off of leave for two reasons, and they kind of tie into each other. One, I have always enjoyed being prepared, be it having uniforms being ready, having my medical gear lined up, having a fresh haircut, ensuring my vehicle had no issues, etc. The second reason was so I could try to not appear to be a turd, and being back at least a day before allowed for me to prepare properly. I just knew from my nearly seven years of service that I would need as much time to prepare for this next duty station, especially with my situation; I could not give the higher-ups anything that could even remotely prove them right.

Sure enough, I spent the whole day before my check-in date picking up my dress whites, inspecting them thoroughly to make sure they were inspection ready, getting my new ribbon stack that I had professionally stacked, picking up new dress shoes, getting a new FMF pin and freshly rolled neckerchief, getting new crisp white undershirts, and getting a fresh haircut. I had spent the same evening preparing my work bag with PT clothes, my work camies, important medical documents, my current medical record, my DIVO file (Division Officer Folder) from SOI, and my other commands and one piece of paper that I wanted my new command to look at and take care of when I sat down to discuss command education and training things.

On June 15, 2011, I checked into 1st Marine Division and in doing so set US Navy history. At the time, I was unaware of this fact. June 15th was a pretty standard day. Show up in your dress uniform with your official documents and just begin the whole check-in process. There were a few checking in with me, and there was a command function going on as well, so it was a fairly slow day, which I didn't mind. After doing a half day of just the paperwork portion of checking in, I was told to just come back at eight the next morning in camies and to have my dress whites just in case I had to put them on to do the circus dance for the higher-ups as part of the check-in process for them. On my way home, I stopped by the dry cleaners and dropped them off so they would be ready for the next day just in case.

The next day was more check-in stuff but not in the typical dress uniform. I skated out of finishing the check-in while in whites. I was really happy for that because honestly the dress shoes caused a lot of pain and discomfort in my foot and knee on my amputated side. My combat boots felt amazing on my foot and knee, so I wasn't complaining; I had bought a custom set of boots from Oakley and had a custom orthotic made for my foot. I was bugging my buddy who worked over in the manpower section about where I was going to go within division. I had requested to go the 7th Marine Regiment because I would have been back with 7th Marines, and they were set to go on deployment within a few months of my arrival back to division.

I was also told that if I wanted to be an instructor with the combat trauma management course team, I was going to have to deploy in order to prove myself worthy and to also "do my time" as a grunt doc. I explained to those who didn't know me about how many lives I had saved when I was with division before, yet that wasn't good enough. Then someone had the balls to tell me that I had to go through Combat Trauma Management (CTM) again. I told one of my best friends, Baskee, who ran CTM, and he said, "No way, bro! That's the dumbest thing I have *ever* heard of! You don't have to redo CTM." I figured that there was no expiration date on CTM certificates. I mean, it was bad enough to have enough courses and open seats as it was, so to send docs through it again made no sense to me. Another thing that I thought was pretty freaking hilarious was my best bud who ran CTM was in the same CTM course with me six years prior, and we were deployed to Iraq in the same timeframe and he personally knew my reputation from my deployment as well. So he put his foot down and signed off saying that I was good on CTM. Well, another thing that was interesting was the fact that many other corpsmen were endorsing me to be an instructor at CTM, and somehow, that was denied, and I was told I would have to go on another deployment to prove myself worthy of a spot as a CTM instructor. It was just a funny concept of me going overseas and doing a full year, maybe slightly shorter or longer, as a battalion aid station doc and not practicing combat trauma; because of my situation, they wouldn't let me go outside the wire into combat, so how could I even practice my combat trauma skills? Makes no sense so I just had to laugh and play their mindless games.

Before I knew it, I was told what battalion I was set to check into. I was heading to Headquarters Battalion (HQBN), Battalion Aid Station. I knew why they assigned me to HQBN, and that was so they could keep a close eye on me and easily manage me from right next door. I can't prove that, but when you have been playing the political game within the system for a few years, you have an understanding of the whole process (especially when I was told, unofficially, that there was a chance that I could be going to the 7th Marine Regiment, 1st Marine Division Detachment 29 Palms).

I just decided to play the game and give up a pawn during this match and thought to myself, *Well, I shouldn't complain too much because I at least made it to 1st Marine Division. Yet they could honor their word and have some faith in me, especially after everything I have been through to return to where I am today. Oh well, time to continue the games for now.*

I had my orders from manpower drafted up and then escorted over to check into the HQBN BAS. I was honestly excited to be with a new command and to prove myself within that command. I, however, had no idea what kind of shitstorm I was walking into when I checked into HQBN. I didn't figure that portion out for a few more days but gathered some information real quick when Senior Chief, the Command SEL (Senior Enlisted Leader), told me that I was to be the HQBN BAS Assistant Leading Petty Officer, or ALPO. This didn't click right away, but there were many others of the same rank in the BAS, and none of them were the ALPO.

It didn't take too much for me to be checked in the command because I already had computer access, both Navy and Marine Corps sides, due to my previous commands and the access I needed to do the medical liaison between the blue and green sides. The only thing that I really needed was to go around to the different Marine shops around HQBN and introduce myself to them and build my contacts. The biggest contact issue I had was within the BAS. While trying to sit down, or just working side by side, with my fellow BAS docs, I had begun to realize that morale and motivation were the biggest issues for these guys, and they were not willing to work with me right away. They viewed me as an overly motivated leader coming in with empty promises. I was a new motivated leader and knew that my words were taken as empty promises because they already had so many promises made to them and that just ended with no leniency and very little liberty. So I made no promises but just listened to the bitching.

Let me explain about how bad this command's morale level was and why they just didn't care to improve it. On my first full day at HQBN BAS, we had to report in early for formation. We were then released for morning chow and had to be back for the pre-sick call formation. When afternoon chow time rolled around, we had another formation just to be released for a thirty-minute chow break and then back to another formation. At the end of the work day, it was . . . another formation. Just a reminder, I am not complaining about being stateside in a HQ BAS with a thirty-minute chow break; I am explaining the lack of motivation. After being on the front lines in Ramadi, Iraq, eating expired MREs and knowing that our guys were still out there sacrificing, I would never complain about a chill job.

Another thing that slammed the motivation was a thing called Command General Inspection, or CGIP. The previous inspection percentage was a whopping thirteen percent, so Senior Chief had ordered a twenty-four-hour duty as punitive punishment, and the Corpsman who stood the twenty-four-hour duty had to verify twenty medical records, no matter how big the record was. Trying to verify twenty records during an overnight duty, which was really twelve hours, was nearly impossible. It wouldn't be possible if you had the record of a malingerer or the record of a First Sergeant with eighteen-plus years of medical care; I will explain how I fared out when I stood duty, but I have some other stuff to explain first.

After doing my check-in, I jumped right on in with the regular medical care to be another helping hand. I showed the command that I was certified to help with preventive medicine, so I hopped in there when I could to assist the HM3 that worked in there and the HM1 that oversaw everything preventive medicine. I was soon assigned to be the Assistant Leading Petty Officer, or ALPO, and I gladly accepted the job because I knew I was a new Petty Officer Second Class and motivated to help bring some sort of actual motivation to the command. I was also assigned as the command's Limited Duty Coordinator and Liaison for the BAS and the battalion.

One of my first missions as the ALPO was to get to know my fellow BAS docs and to hear their complaints. So when the BAS slowed down during the day, I would call in all of the juniors first and then all of the docs of my rank and higher. I used this new position, ALPO, to get to know them a little bit. I would ask the ones with families, "Does your family hate when you have to do overnight duty and miss their special moments? What would you do to make things easier here so you can go home happy every day?" I swear to you that their whole perspective of me and my purpose there changed with those few words.

I took all of their concerns and promises to work and make things flow smoother at the BAS to the Leading Petty Officer, LPO, and to Senior Chief. I told them that I could turn the BAS around in just one week if they worked with me to lift the thirty-minute chow to the normal time as a starter. They agreed, and I told the group to meet with me when they were done with sick call. When sick call was done, I told the duty to assume their post and I would personally relieve them when it came time for them to get chow and for the rest to be back in two hours. If I had a camera, I would have been able to capture their joy. I then told them that I wanted everyone to be responsible; otherwise, I would yank their privilege.

Around late June, the duty schedule for July 2011 came out. When it did, I was standing next to the HM3 that worked in preventive medicine, and he was immediately pissed and bummed out about the duty schedule, and I soon found out why. At first, he wouldn't tell me, but I told him that he could trust me. After chitchatting with him for a while, I found out that he had been on duty for the past two major holiday weekends and even had a request chit, that was approved, saying that he would be exempt from the next duty weekend, so he made plans to be with his family for the Fourth of July weekend. I told him I would take care of it, and he told me it was okay and that he got it it's the military and it happened. I told him, "Not if I can help it."

I went into the LPO's office and had a little chat about what was going on and how stupid it was that they didn't consider this Corpsman and his request chit and family plans. The LPO said, "Well, HM2, once the schedule comes out, it can't be changed, especially with the holiday and how others already have plans and money invested into their Fourth of July, ninety-six-hour liberty."

I responded with, "Well, HM1, what about this sailor's promise from the command to not be on the next holiday duty schedule, his financial investments into the weekend, and his family plans?" I could tell command lacked interest in honoring their word to this doc and in the command's moral. I just told the LPO, "You know what? Fuck it, I will cancel my plans for the weekend, and I will take his duty so he doesn't have to be the bad guy to his family any longer!"

The only response was, "Well, HM2, if that is what you think is best, then it's your call."

I opened the door and slammed it behind me, saying, "It is my call, and that is what is going to happen."

I went over to the preventive medicine office and told that HM3 that I fixed the duty and to not worry about it, to call his family and let them know that they were going home for the holiday. He was so grateful and gave me a big hug thanking me for taking care of him. He then asked who took his duty so he could switch him a duty day. I told him it wasn't necessary. He kept pushing to find out who so he could show his gratitude. I told him that I was the one that took his duty, and I could see he felt bummed about it, but I told him that I wasn't on the July roster so he shouldn't worry about it. I told him that I did it because I wanted to ensure his happiness at home because it reflected at work, and his family would always be there, but the military was temporary.

I spent my Fourth of July in 2011 on HQBN BAS twenty-four-hour duty verifying my share of twenty-five medical records. It wasn't that bad, to be honest. I had a TV with cable and no one around to bug me. I had a cooler full of sandwiches, chips, and a variety of snacks. I did have one patient come in during my twenty-four-hour shift, but that was to prevent this Marine and his command from transporting him to and from the Naval Hospital. I did the dressing change on this Marine and drafted up his SOAP Note, or SF-600, for the next provider. The rest of the time I just enjoyed the terrible shows on Telemundo or the other channels.

Soon after the July holiday, it was time for the BAS to focus on catching up on the medical care for the small units coming home from deployment, preparing the main body for a deployment, and preparing for the upcoming Command General Inspection, or CGIP. This made for some busy times around the BAS, causing many late nights working on the CGIP stuff. A fellow HM2 and I took care of things around the BAS during the day to make sure the medical care for the battalion was taken care of, and then we would stay into the late hours of the night for the CGIP. We busted our asses preparing for the CGIP for a multitude of reasons, but we had some major reasons for doing it. The previous CGIP had a failure rating of thirteen percent, and we were told that if we failed this next inspection, the Battalion Medical Officer (Battalion MO) and the Senior Enlisted were to be shit canned. We happened to like Battalion MO and Chief, and we felt that they hadn't been there for that long, so we busted our asses to ensure their job security and reputations.

This other HM2 took over as the ALPO and education and training, and I moved to a few other departments. I took over the administrative department, limited duty and safety. I also became the assistant to education and training while remaining an assistant to preventive medicine. Needless to say, I did as much as I could in every department around the BAS. During my work around the BAS, I could tell why there was a thick rumor around 1st Marine Division that HQBN BAS was the worst BAS to work at. Let's just say that it wasn't easy rewriting the SOPs (Standard Operating Procedures) for a few different departments, especially the administrative department. I want to say that was the worst SOP to rewrite because I never worked a day in admin before in my life and the admin SOP defined the battalion and how things were run. Oh well, we shall say that the admin department, and a few other departments, received an overall rating of one hundred percent on the inspection.

Preparing for the upcoming deployment was a crucial part of my future with 1st Marine Division. If you recall, I had to go on this deployment in order to make it over to CTM to be an instructor. Well, that and the day I was hit, I vowed to return. I was told that I needed to do one thing to prepare myself for the HQBN deployment. I had to stop my medications for my arthritis prior to deployment. I just had to figure out how to stop taking medications for severe arthritis in my left leg, the amputated side.

On a medication refill appointment at the pain management clinic at NMCSD, I spoke of my intentions to quit my medication with my doctor, and he offered a possible solution. I was intrigued and trusted this doctor, for he and his crew had been by my side through so much to that point, so we discussed the option and decided to go through with a five-day trial study.

This five-day trial was to implant a nerve stimulator into a nerve that branched down to cover the inside portion of my knee, the most painful part. The trial device was soon in place, and it was a huge success. During those five days, I had no need to take any medicine for the pain in my knee, although I still took Motrin as a precaution to prepare for the end of the five-day period. We then began to prepare for the surgery to implant the permanent device.

The planning for that surgery was an extensive and very thorough process. My doctor and his amazing pain management team had thought of everything possible. They wanted to place the device in the right location, as well as a comfortable spot, and ensure the leads weren't in a spot that my leg, liner, or sleeve would interfere with. We even went as far as to have me put on all of my gear and to label, on my skin, where my gear lay when I was standing, kneeling, and sitting. Once the landmarks were made, they then did an ultrasound imaging of the possible locations to determine the best spot for the device and leads as well. Once a location was determined to be the ideal location, more pictures were taken, and then the paperwork was drafted to prepare for the procedure.

I had previously spoken to the command and told them that this would be so beneficial to the Navy, the command, and my health. I had worked for the same Chief before, from SOI, and he knew how much this meant to me and that this could be huge for the Navy for me to redeploy, so needless to say, he was on board. He briefed the whole chain of command, and they were on board with everything. So everything was set in stone and the paperwork was all signed and was ready for the procedure. Prior to my fiftieth surgery in August 2011, I had done a ton of work to prepare my fellow coworkers and to do a proper turn over for my con leave. I did a proper turn over and told Chief I would let him know, so he could brief the higher-ups on my condition, when I was out of surgery, and my progress.

I had my fiftieth surgery, and although it was an eight-hour surgery, it was a success. The pain management team did another phenomenal job. I passed the word to Chief, and the BAS chain of command, that the procedure went well and I should be up and about soon. My con leave was a standard thirty days, although there was no proven recovery time because nerve stimulators are not placed in limbs too often. They are more focused into the spinal region. I knew I wouldn't require the full thirty days, but I figured I would use the time to align everything for a deployment and to start preparing my whole family for my return overseas.

During my con leave, I received a phone call from Chief, and he had to be the one to deliver the bad news. He called to inform me, "HM2, you are being pulled from the deployment list because you still require surgery. I am sorry to have to be the one to inform you of this. Enjoy the rest of your con leave, and we will see you back here. Take care, HM2, and keep me in the loop."

I just responded (although very depressed and heartbroken) with, "Aye, Chief, I understand." I am not sure if that was his call, which I doubt because I don't think he had the power to pull me for medical reasons, but nonetheless, I was crushed. I didn't know, or care, who made the call. All I knew was that it was a cowardly way to prevent a man from his dreams and to negate his years of hard work to finally accomplish them. Whoever made that call didn't realize what my deployment could have done for the Navy, in a positive way, and I had realized that it was probably a reasoning of, "If HM2 were to get injured again or, worse, killed while deployed, how would this look on us?" or, "Well, what if something were to happen to his leg while he is deployed? Then how do we handle that?" There was always a counter to their reasoning, although we may never know what their reasoning was.

First of all, if I were to be injured again or killed, I'd counter that with: I reenlisted after the fact of my injuries sustained in February

2006 and thus fully understood the risks. Secondly, I know for damn sure that nobody in the Navy would let me go back into combat, so I would just be a BAS doc the whole time, anyway. The prosthetic issue, I would take a few legs with me, and I have the basic knowledge to work on and adjust my own leg while doing professional training on it, so don't feed me that bullshit excuse. All it really was was bullshit excuses from someone (or a group of someones) who had a focused mind set on the physical appearance and not my abilities that I had proven time and time again to these closed-minded folks. These were the same folks that placed limitations on a limitless individual. I just wished that they would have created a board and let me have a hearing of some sort so I could have proven myself in front of this board.

I know I can't go back and have a "redo" for that moment in time nor should I live in the past and cloud my future. I will say for the purposes of writing this and having the blessing of a healthy healing process that this has offered I will touch on some things. I should have seen that coming, and I should have known that they would either use the medications, the leg, or the surgery as an excuse to pull me from the deployment. I mean, they tried to change my medical documents to prevent me from even being there, so why would this be different?

With all of the political bullshit the Navy had put me through over the seven months leading up to me being pulled off deployment, again, in September 2011, I had just had enough, and I couldn't physically, mentally, or spiritually deal with it any longer. I had proven myself time and time again, but it didn't seem good enough to most of the people that had a say in supporting me. At the end of this book, I will go over a list of accomplishments that I had had since my injuries, and you can see everything in a list. I will just get back to the story for now.

So I walked over to 1st Marine Division Mental Health and asked for a walk-in appointment. The Corpsman asked if I wanted an appointment for later, and I told him it couldn't wait any longer and I needed to be seen as soon as possible. They asked me to fill out some paperwork in the waiting room while they went to speak with a doctor. I told them I feared that I may relapse into another PTSD episode. I filled out the paperwork and waited while I texted the ALPO and told him I was at division psych and I had no idea how long I would be, and it might not be a promising outcome and not in a terrible destructive way but medically.

I went into this walk-in appointment and held nothing back. For many years, I had let so much build up or I just let go but no longer. I was to turn twenty-six in a matter of days and was just tired of spending my life getting the runaround and not getting really far. I mean, don't get me wrong, I am glad to be who I am and where I am today, but at that moment in time, I had no view of the bigger picture or even a glimpse of some light at the end of the tunnel. I felt that this was my only option before I ended up having another PTSD episode.

I went in and gave the psych doctor a very thorough background of my career, injuries, and struggles with each. He seemed to be very impressed with how well I had dealt with things until that point and my minor relapses into reclusiveness and lack of caring for many people and situations. I told him I was dropped from the care of a previous psych doctor because I stopped going without her officially releasing me, but my appointments were so scattered, and I relied on my religious beliefs to help me through things. I told this doctor that I had the faith that my religion had led me to where I was and had guided me through everything so far as well. I know it's crazy, but I would rather fall onto my religious beliefs than explaining my feelings to strangers and coping with pills that just prolong the return to reality.

I explained to the doctor about my mental struggles in dealing with the Navy and those who discriminated against me and my abilities. I explained how I was physically and mentally tired of being in so much pain for pushing myself beyond the regular standards that were required of corpsmen in the same job. I felt like I was injuring myself further by trying so hard to prove myself over and over. I told him of doing 20k hikes weekly, while at SOI, as well as all the other hikes I would do and all of the last-minute scheduled Afghanistan training that I took part in while it was ninety-five degrees outside while hiking unknown distances on unmarked and unknown terrain. Yet that wasn't good enough for the command when it came to helping me achieve my goals and aspirations. Oh, but they went around bragging about all of the great things that I was doing and how the Marine Corps staff and instructors loved what I was doing and how motivating it was to them and their students.

I then explained about my "PTSD episodes" and how they affected others. I mean, I was never violent during my episodes or ever wanted to bring harm to others, but I just had a switch where I turned off and checked out for x amount of time. It seemed like I became a zombie or a programmed robot. I would look at my phone when someone like my mother would call and ignore the call, listen to the voicemail, delete the voicemail, and then not call until the switch somehow came back on. During my phases, I felt like I placed a mask over my face, and then when I got home, I took it off. I would look loved ones in the eyes and tell them that I didn't love them anymore and I would love to live and die alone . . . etc.

He said I needed to go see my primary doctor because he and I both agreed that I shouldn't physically continue on this path and that it wasn't good for me and my future. I set up follow-up appointments with him and then headed down to orthopedics at NMCSD to work on a Physical Evaluation Board. This also fell at a good time because I just had the nerve stimulator placed in my leg to cover the medial knee pain, the most painful portion of my knee, and it hadn't really been helping, anyway, so I felt that my knee was doomed and that in itself would place a huge damper on my career. At that point, the nerve stimulator wasn't doing too much; I mean, it was helping but not doing too much.

In late September, I had begun my check-out process, and of course that was another time for the Navy to mess with me some more. I had my check-out list, and I went through most of the list pretty quickly except for one part. I had the part of checking out of CIF (Central Issue Facility), and for those of you who know what this place and process is all about, you will understand what I am about to tell you.

So I waited around in the CIF line for a few hours, and when I was finally at the check-out counter, I was told that I had geared checked out and needed to bring it in before I could get the coveted CIF stamp on my check-out sheet to check out of 1st Marine Division and head to 32nd Street's Transient Patient Unit, or TPU. I told them that was absurd because when I checked into 1st Marine Division I never went to CIF to check out any gear and I had no intentions to until I knew I was going on deployment or out into the field, and my job at HQBN was all admin and BAS work. They printed off a list of everything they said I had checked out, and you will not believe what they had listed!

I apparently still had all of my deployment gear checked out from my Ramadi pump in 2005-2006! I honestly couldn't believe it, yet I could because this was just my luck. I explained to the lady that it was impossible for me to ever bring that gear in so I could get the CIF stamp and checkout. I contacted my Platoon Commander from 3/7 India Company and told him what was going on, and he was in just as much amazement as I was. He said he would write a letter for a combat loss of my gear. I thanked him for that, and naturally he had that done within a matter of a day or two. But, yet again, it didn't end there.

I took his combat loss letter into CIF with my Purple Heart and my Theater Medi-Evac documents, and that wasn't good enough for them. So the next step was to submit all of my evidence in a routing form to my current Commanding Officer in hopes of his approval for a combat loss. I went ahead and jumped through these hoops that lasted days on end in hopes that I wouldn't have to pay for this gear. I wouldn't have paid for this gear, by the way; I would have snapped and raised some hell because I had paid enough, and I would not be held accountable for somebody not doing their job.

Anyway, back on track. I finally received the approval from the HQBN Battalion Commanding Officer, and I ran it over to CIF so I could check out and be done with the whole political runaround nonsense. I honestly was so worked up and so stressed out during those few weeks of trying to clear my name of this craziness. I just couldn't believe it. I mean, I could, but it just seemed to be so unrealistic. During my research of what to do if the combat loss wasn't approved, I had read some terrible things that just really pissed me off, and I wanted to do some terrible things to the idiots of which I am about to explain. So I read some forums and some families of fallen Marines, Sailors, Airmen, and Soldiers being billed for the gear of their fallen loved ones! That shit is unacceptable! I mean, who are these idiots that would even approve of sending that bill to the loved ones of a fallen hero?

I spent weeks stressing out and being pissed off even more over how the Navy was trying to stress me to the point of a heart attack and/or a stroke. I honestly almost had an actual stroke when the HQBN Chief told me what he had told the MEF, Marine Expeditionary Force, Master Chief: "HM2 Jacobs understands that the rules are to report to TPU and depart the deployable command, but he would like to stay at division to help around the BAS."

Chief told me he preemptively told the MEF Master Chief that was my intentions, and he was sorry he didn't have the chance to talk to me first, but he assumed that I would have said that. I told Chief that I did not want to do that and wanted to focus on my health and wellbeing during my processing out via medical retirement. He seemed upset, but he said he would call the MEF Master Chief and inform him that we had discussed the options and I was choosing TPU. That actually made me really happy to know that it was finally time to focus on my health.

In December 2011, I had finally transferred out of 1st Marine

Division and headed down to TPU to begin the last phase of my career but not without the Navy getting some more shots in at me. I figured if I left 1st Marine Division, it would have been the end of the blows, but I guess I shouldn't have assumed that the punches were done flying until the day I was officially out.

The TPU staff that I had encountered during my nine-month stay at their command were amazing. I am honestly pleased to have had them as my last chain of command because it was a breath of fresh air compared to my recent commands. They were very helpful with what I had going on and my crazy medical schedule.

Around the end of the holidays, I had begun to get into the Orthopedic Department at the Naval Medical Center San Diego in order to have my knee examined . . . again. For some unknown reason, I was still having some serious knee pain, and it was very troubling. It was really difficult to explain to the pain management doctors that I was still having severe knee pain although they had just implanted the nerve stimulator in my leg to help with it.

Due to the implanted device, it was difficult to get an image of my knee without having to go in with a scope to check it out, and that's what was going to have to happen. The orthopedic surgeon who was working with me already knew my situation and knew that I had some serious arthritis from previous knowledge and the MRI done in August 2011. The next step was to plan the scope with a possible procedure that may assist with growing a form of scar tissue that acted as cartilage called fibrocartilage. This procedure would be a painful one called microfracture.

The plan was to go into surgery for the knee scope and to possibly perform the microfracture if the pockets of full thickness cartilage loss were small enough to try and create fibrocartilage. In late February, I went into surgery planning on waking up to severe pain from a microfracture procedure and being told that I would spend the next six months doing physical therapy to gain full function of my knee again.

Doing the whole pre-operative set up was a pretty funny one. I knew that the orthopedic surgeon was a fellow Cleveland Indians fan, so while the operating staff was preparing me for the surgery, I was talking Indians baseball with the orthopedic surgeon. That was by far the best pre-operative time I have had so far. As usual, though, right before I was sedated, I got my Jesus on and then nodded to the anesthesiologist that I was as ready as could be for surgery. Within a few moments, I was out cold.

When I woke up in the PACU, I was told that the procedure went extremely well and that I would have no need for any more knee surgeries for some time to come. He said I still had tri-compartmental osteoarthritis, but it wouldn't be as bad as it had been. This was some of the best news I had had regarding my own health and well-being. I did want to follow through with physical therapy because I had the time to work on my knee and the mindset to focus on myself and not worry about hurrying up to get back to whatever the Navy wanted. During my con leave, I focused on properly strengthening and stretching my lower body. Although I was on con leave, I was on medical hold at Naval Base 32nd Street, so I had all the time in the world to finish my physical therapy and all of medical appointments, which was a first for me in my career.

In early 2012, I had to finish up all of my disability and compensation appointments with the VA. I shall say from experience that this actually helped the claims process along faster than if I were to have just finished out my time and done it after my departure from active service. As mundane as it seemed while I was trotting around the San Diego County region to attend all of these VA appointments and re-attend the ones that needed further attention, it helped out the claims process timeframe.

For the next few months, I won't be discussing more than medical stuff, and it's simply because I was just checking in twice a day into the medical holding unit. I checked in to med hold in the morning and either got my Jesus on then napped it out in my truck or went home and napped. My times were mainly focused on my spiritual, emotional, and mental recovery. Not to sound like too much of a hippie but these portions are just as important for the healing process. I won't preach too much in these regards, but just know everything is all intertwined and tuned into each other.

In May 2012, I was scheduled for the main operating room for surgery number fifty-four. This one was my second and final jaw reconstruction. I knew that this surgery was going to take away my ability to eat again. So I turned my fat kid up a bit and just gorged out so much during the weeks leading up to surgery. The first jaw surgery I didn't know what to expect with the whole "liquid/soft diet" garbage, but the second one I was really building up for, especially seeing as to how they were detaching my whole upper jaw from my skull.

There wasn't a whole lot I could do to prepare for the second jaw surgery. I mean that in a physical and preventive manner. Usually before I have any surgery on anything, I do a complete deep clean of my truck and my place so I can do my part in preventing any bacterial infection. I go as far as scrubbing the walls, counters, tile, and bathroom with bleach, and then I shampoo the carpets and spray them with disinfecting sprays. A little overboard, you may be thinking, but when you are preserving what extremities you have left, the extra care and caution is a must. Especially when you have had multiple staph infections, random bone infections, and strep group B infection. The strep group B infection nearly took my right, and healthy, leg above the knee. I am thankful that Naval Medical Center San Diego narrowed the infection down and treated it accordingly. Phew, that was a close one, man.

Let's journey on back to Camp Pendleton's main operating room, shall we? As I recently stated, I was back to the surgical scene again for my second and hopefully final jaw surgery. Like the first jaw surgery, this piece of work had to be planned out to the fullest detail because the oral maxilla facial surgeon and his team were about to completely detach, reconstruct, and reattach my upper jaw. So, to say the least, this needed to be one hundred percent on point and at the perfect time, and May 2012 was that time.

The morning of the surgery, I reported to the OR check-in location, and since I was running a little bit late, I had to rush my whole preparation process for the surgery. Seeing I was the first case and the case was set for a four-hour slot, I needed to be in and on the operating table at a certain time. Not that it mattered too much because of the whole preparing once I got in the holding area and on the table.

Within a matter of twenty minutes or so, I was back in the holding area with my leg off and contacts out when the anesthesia team for my surgery case came over and began all of their pre-surgery preparations. This was usually a really quick process, although very thorough. While this pre-anesthetic process was going on, the head surgeon from OMFS came in to talk about the surgery and what to expect. He then began to make a special wrap on my head for the procedure. This wrap, which I was sure looked ridiculous, was made to hold the breathing tube a special way for the surgeon. Probably why he made it himself.

As soon as the wrap was on and my contacts were out, I was being wheeled back into the operating room. As per my usual routine, I moved on over to the operating table and asked the anesthesiologist to hold on the meds until I finished getting my Jesus on. To my surprise, the head OMFS surgeon came over and put his hand on me while I prayed. I finished getting my Jesus on and thanked the OR staff for making it quiet in the OR and the doctor for praying with me then nodded to the anesthesiologist that I was prepared. Off to the land of deep darkness I went, and to my surprise, I didn't land in the bright skies above.

When I awoke in the PACU, I was extremely sleepy, and to my dismay, I found out why. It took me a little longer than normal to wake up in the PACU because the anesthesiologist had to push some extra medicine to control my blood pressure about forty-five minutes into the surgery. Apparently, I could feel the pain from the surgeons cutting into my skull and detaching my upper jaw from my dome piece, and my blood pressure jumped fairly high, and I started to bleed so much that they had to stop the cutting and regain my blood pressure and pain control, thus causing the deeper sedation and extra medication. I am honestly unsure of the blood pressure levels and how much blood loss there was, but I do know that it could have turned uglier real quick.

After the surgical team regained my blood pressure and controlled my pain, they continued on as planned. The procedure didn't take much longer than they had scheduled it for, even with the blood pressure and pain control issue. I awoke in the PACU a while after. I say a while because of the extra amount of medication they had to use. I then stayed in the PACU for a while longer, about three hours, because of my sleepiness and lack of desire to move up to the surgery ward.

From my point of view, and this is the scariest part of it all, I just gotten done getting my Jesus on while the OR room staff prepped me for the procedure, and I was then put under general anesthetics. Again, from my perspective, I was woken up in the PACU by a nurse, and she wanted me to be awake and alert for a certain amount of time so I could then be transferred up to the surgery ward for the remainder of my stay. Little did I know why I was so tired after this specific procedure. I just knew that I was super tired and extremely annoyed with this nurse for not letting me sleep the meds off. I finally faked the funk enough to transfer up to the surgery ward just so I could then go back to sleep. During all of this moving and transferring around, I had no idea about the complications that I had encountered during the surgery. Since then, I had vowed to always be awake during any surgical procedures to occur in the future.

I was to stay a few days at the Naval Hospital Camp Pendleton on their surgery ward. I did so, mainly for pain control, but also for the constant monitoring from the nursing and corpsmen staff as well. The staff on the NHCP surgery ward took very good care of me during my stay. I was honestly blessed when a single room finally opened up and they allowed me to transfer in there so I could have some privacy and a TV that was closer to my bed.

I hope by this point you guys have all figured out two things about me: I like to keep a busy schedule, and I hate staying in hospitals. So what I am about to tell you is a funny story about how I tied those two things together. Be prepared to laugh at this and to also be mad about how I may have neglected myself for a whole day or so to just honor my word, although me doing that has led me down a great and blessed path.

The day after I transferred into the single room, I had it in my mind to be checking out (discharging, if you will) of the hospital. I knew that the next day I was to be a guest of honor at an event in Los Angeles, near the Los Angeles International Airport. I promised a good friend, Justin, who was mentor and coach of mine, that I would attend this Memorial Day event with him. Now, I would not tell the hospital staff that I would be heading to Los Angeles the next day, but I did tell them that I needed to be discharged from the hospital by that evening because I still had shit that I needed to do in my personal life. After hours of the nurse pleading with me and trying to convince me that intravenous pain control was more effective than oral medication, she gave in and spoke to the doctor and his staff to discharge me. So around five p.m. that day, I was checked out and heading to my nice cozy bed.

That night, I was fine controlling my pain and discomfort on my own and throughout the next morning. At a certain time during the day, I stopped all medication and prepared myself to head up north. I drove about two hours from San Diego County on into Justin's house in Orange County. During the hours leading up to my two-hour drive and during the long drive, I was hurting pretty badly but knew I couldn't back out and not honor my word. So I just toughed through it knowing that once I arrived at his place, I could take some medication since he wanted to drive from there.

It was a good thing that I arrived at his house early and we left at a decent time. Soon after we left, we would then spend the next few hours in the glorious Los Angeles rush-hour traffic on the 405 northbound. Once we arrived at the location, we realized that we were still a little early, so we went to go shoot the shit and grab some chow. I had to settle for the soup because of my surgery, and he crushed about eighteen to twenty wings. Justin, his lady, and I then headed into the lovely event. We all hung out throughout the event, and they both still couldn't believe that I escaped the hospital to be there. I told them I wouldn't have missed it for the world. It was a pretty cool event that they had honoring the troops from past conflicts, recent and ongoing conflicts, and of course those who were to ship off to boot camp to carry on the torch. It was an honor to be with veterans from WWII, Korea, Vietnam, the Persian Gulf War, and those from OIF/OEF. They then had an enlistment ceremony for a few hundred soon-to-be service members. I tried to go around and shake the hands from the many generations of veterans.

Soon after the event was over, I made sure to not take any more medicine so I would be able to drive home after I returned to my truck. During the drive back to Justin's house, we had a very in-depth conversation about the transition from doing something we loved on into the land of unknown. We both discussed the difficulty of keeping the faith in the plans of the man upstairs because we'd get overanxious with what we wanted to do and what we wanted to happen. This conversation couldn't have come at a better time in my transition out of the service. It was something that had been on my mind since the thought of reenlisting after my injuries. It was a very beneficial chat, and I was hoping to put some of our thoughts and ideas into action later on toward the end of my time in service.

I did my usual travels home to Ohio to visit with family and friends during my con leave. One of my best friends, RyRy, was set to get married to his lovely lady, and I liked to fly back home to catch an Indians game or to Akron for what was then the Akron

Aeros games with my pops and then to do some fishing with my fishing buddy. On this con leave trip back home to Ohio, I started writing my book about my time as a wounded warrior staying on active duty. I remember sitting there one night at my dad's place and thinking of my whole transition plan and what might assist me in that process, and writing about the good and bad of staying in as a combat-wounded veteran was one of my ideas. I thought of it as a therapeutic way to help ease the transition and let some of the grudges and bad memories go.

My thirty days of con leave ended, and I was back to 32nd St Naval Base for my medical holding musters. I had about as much of the sitting and waiting as I could take, so I would escape over to NMCSD to see my PEB (Physical Evaluation Board) liaison's office to bug her about the stage that my PEB was in. Up until July, I heard nothing. So I went from not hearing anything on the status of my board from March/April until July. When I found out the information in July, it was dated for June, so somewhere in the system it wasn't showing the status of my board and just had been updating the same "no update" nonsense. This drove me nuts knowing that I could have heard something on my board and signed things sooner if things would have been communicated better within the systems somehow.

So in July 2012, things were finally being reviewed and approved before sending the board to the PEB offices at NMCSD for my review and disapproval or approval. This reviewing process could take some time depending on the amount of stuff within the claim. I knew my claim was fairly large, so I anticipated a few weeks before I would hear anything back. My assumption was right; the weeks led me into yet another month of just waiting around to hear more word on how much longer it would take before I was to be medically retired.

In early August, I received a phone call from the NMCSD PEB liaison's office requesting my presence for the review of my board. The funny thing about all of this was in July when I found out that things were updated in June and no one told me . . . I found out my ratings then. So I knew my ratings before NMCSD called me in for the review. I went down there knowing I had a pretty sweet deal, and I was going to accept the findings or disability ratings for both the VA and DOD. I even went out and bought a brand new pen on the way down just to commemorate the moment as a small token for myself.

Things changed a little bit over at 32nd St Naval Command once I signed my findings. I was sent to another portion of the medical holding side, and there I went back to work until I was to start my terminal leave. I honestly didn't mind even though I was dealt a shitty job—urinalysis observer—because I had a light at the end of the tunnel. I just knew all I had to do was show up where I needed to be, keep my mouth shut, and keep my nose clean, and I was to be a retired twenty-seven-year-old dude.

In August, I burned about two weeks of my terminal leave to see one of my best buddies in northwestern Ohio for a few days then went over to Fort Wayne, Indiana, to see a good buddy. There, he did an amazing piece of work on my right arm. Then I headed down to Danville, Illinois, for an event. That was an amazing and peaceful two weeks, probably some of the best leave I had taken in my eight-year career. It was peaceful to just hang out with my buddy and his lady in their relaxed hometown. Fishing on the riverbank in the light rain listening to some country music brought a peaceful state of mind to me and helped the thought of transitioning out.

After a few days in Ohio, I headed to see another good friend in Indiana. He was an amazing dude and had done one tattoo on me before and had drawn up another for me. So he spent about six hours working on my right arm, and afterward, we went to get some food. I soon headed over to Danville throughout the night to greet the group for the event that was to take place there over the next few days. Once that was over, I then returned back to the great city of San Diego to pick up the quick-paced life of the city again.

That leave had ended, but I found myself back in pain management having the surgeon examine something I had noticed while on my trip. My leg was having some issues with the nerve stimulator pack in it. I was unsure whether it moved or my body was rejecting the pack and pushing it to the surface, so we were in talks to repack the stimulator pack into my leg. We had decided that doing the procedure in early October before I retired would be best with the combination of my terminal leave so I wouldn't have to wait to get things straight with Tricare before proceeding.

I worked all of September for 32nd St and on all of my separation paperwork for the VA, for the Navy, and for the command. During those last few weeks of working, it was so nice wondering what it was going to be like to be a civilian soon and to never have to worry about the bullshit anymore.

In early October, I took all of my completed separation paperwork, my con leave papers, and my terminal leave paperwork over to the Naval PSD on 32nd St to get everything straightened out before my surgery. I can honestly say that I would have flipped and not have kept my mouth shut if I spent all of this time straightening things out to be prepared and then I had to come in after surgery. You shall see if the Navy failed on not being prepared.

I signed and accepted my DD214 and PSD and all of my paperwork as well. I then returned back to my command to officially check out with them and then headed back to PSD to let them know that I no longer had a command and I was all checked out on con leave/terminal leave. They told me to enjoy life as a civilian and best of luck with my surgery and whatever other future adventures that might be ahead of me. I thanked them and headed out.

The very next day, I was in the operating room for surgery number fifty-five. This was fairly a minor procedure, and I was happy it was just a minor touch up so my recovery would be a speedy one. It was a quick recovery and, sure enough, took about a whole two weeks. Then I was just about to be done with it . . . or so I thought.

The good old Navy had failed after all. It was Friday, October 26, 2012, late in the morning, when the Navy decided to call my phone. I knew it's the Navy, but I rolled over and went back to sleep. I signed my DD214, and so did the Navy. So why the fuck were they calling me two days before I was to be out and done? I had no idea. I think it went back to them having a red flag in the system when my name popped up.

The phone rang again and again and again. So me being pissed off at this point, I answered with an angry, "*Hello*?!"

I was greeted with, "This is 32nd St PSD, and we are looking for Petty Officer Jacobs."

I said, "This is soon to be *civilian* Jacobs. Who is asking?"

The voice responded with, "You've been UA for the past three weeks and you need to come in ASAP."

I then responded in a low-toned, pissed-off voice, "Um, actually, no, I am *not* UA. If you would check your rosters again, they would reflect that I am on terminal leave and have been for three weeks. Plus, I have my DD214, and I will not be wasting any gas to come play your stupid-ass games."

Whoever was on the other line quickly responded with, "I'm looking at our DD214 check-out list, and we didn't sign your DD214, so you at least have to come in and sign for it even if you have been on terminal leave for three weeks."

I quickly spat back, "I am not driving down there, wasting half a tank of gas, just to play your little games. I will email whoever your boss is my *signed* DD214 proving that you're inadequate at your job and calling service members while they are on terminal leave enjoying a nice sleep. How about you fix yourself? Because I swear if I come down there, I will destroy your world. Now call me back in ten minutes because I will get up and scan my DD214 into an email in preparation to send this to your boss."

He then called me back a few minutes later saying I was good to go and to not worry about anything. They didn't update the list in the system, so I was on a hit list. Still, I hate when people jump the gun without doing their full research. Oh well, it was straightened out, and I was on my last weekend in the Navy. It was an amazing weekend just knowing that Sunday night, October 28, 2012, was my last minutes in the Navy.

In the weeks and months leading up to my retirement, I was worried about what to expect when my time was up. I knew sitting around and not doing anything wasn't my gig. I had pondered for a long time about what my days out of the Navy would bring me, but I had no clue what I should do. I knew that going to school and then later getting a job of some sort was an option. One thing I knew that would keep me busy was writing all of this out while I tried to spend as much time as I could with the people I had been neglecting the whole time I was trying to prove something to the Navy.

Well, I ran into an unexpected answer to my prayers when I attended a Veterans Day brunch in Orange County. I was running late for the event, being a nasty civilian, and I was getting back on the freeway after getting an energy drink and a coffee to help wake me up a bit. Once I was back on the freeway, I noticed I had a message from one of my cousins, and she had texted, "I don't know why I feel compelled to tell you this, but something great will happen to you today."

It was raining, so when I stopped again, I thanked her and just continued on with my drive. I was worried throughout the whole drive thinking of every possible scenario to include, coming across a massive accident and saving a life or a few to just inspiring a wounded warrior at this brunch. I tried to shake it, but once that was planted in my mind, I couldn't stop thinking about it. Well, I forgot about it once I started seeing some friends at the event and meeting new people.

A short while after I had been at the brunch, I was ushered to a table where I had been introduced to a familiar face, and we began talking about mutual interests, and the small talk had led into this amazing baseball legend inviting me out for a possible shot at baseball . . .

15.

TIME FOR NEW CHANGE

The origin of baseball can be traced back to the summer of 1839 in Cooperstown, New York. Although Abner Doubleday invented baseball in 1839, the first game that was actually recorded was on June 19, 1846, when the "New York Nine" smashed the Knickerbockers in a short four-inning game and a score of twenty-three to one. This was the beginning of millions of dreams and fantasies and the game commonly known as "America's Pastime."

One hundred fifty-two years after the birth of baseball, there was a boy, who was just a few short months shy of his sixth birthday, at Cleveland Municipal Stadium becoming one of the millions who'd fantasize about playing professional baseball. The summer of 1991 was my first game that I can remember, and even though I don't recall too much from the game, I can recall the instant love for the game.

Over the next two-plus decades, I gazed on as the emotional rollercoaster as a Tribe fan carried its ongoing course of my love for the game.

October is a month that brings happiness to many throughout the world. This is the first full month of fall. Families are beginning to arrange their holiday plans with their loved ones, football is fully underway, and baseball is dwindling down into who will claim the title of World Champions. Look back and think of your past Octobers and remember the feel of a cold chill in the air, the leaves starting to change colors and slowly fall with that cool breeze.

Think back to visiting those pumpkin patches as you and your loved ones sought out the pumpkin of your liking for that super scary carving you were about to do. Remember the sound of your doorbell as the little trick-or-treaters came to your door in their vast array of costumes from their favorite movies. Perhaps you just wanted to squeeze in some fishing before winter set in and made it nearly impossible to go out and throw the lure out again.

Now envision a young lad that just turned twenty-seven and recently underwent one of his surgeries that pushed him well over fifty times in the operating room and facing a medical retirement from his injuries sustained while serving in combat. This was just another crazy step into the unknown for me, but I was willing to face the path ahead.

My first full fall month of 2012 was one that was of remembrance. I just received my disability rating from the Department of Defense and from the Department of Veterans Affairs. Once I signed and accepted my ratings, I had so many days until my end of active service (also known as EAS). During this time, I was enjoying my peaceful morning drive into the medical holding unit that I was assigned to in the San Diego region as I transitioned out.

Throughout my short remaining time in the Navy, I spent a fairly large portion of my time driving from one base to another, working on my transfer back into the civilian sector. Many of these trips led to further complicate things as I was in transition. I had to go under the knife to have a revision done to the nerve stimulator that the pain clinic at Naval Medical Center San Diego had placed in my left leg just a year prior.

This really threw a wrench in the system because most of the time if you required a surgery while on a medical board, you had to wait another set amount of time before you could get out. So not only was I fighting to get my surgery, I was fighting to stay on track to get out on the date that I signed for. I eventually signed a deal stating that unless I ended up losing my leg higher up then I would not strike to add an addendum to my record.

I was convalescing from the revision on my nerve stimulator, and although not outwardly expressing it, I was stressfully pondering as to what may lay ahead of me. I just had to keep telling myself to have the faith that everything would work itself out. Saying that to myself 600,754 times a day didn't equate to formulating actual plans and setting them into motion. Thus returning back to the stressful pondering.

While I was on active duty just years before and I thought for sure that I was set to serve this great nation for at least a full twenty years, I had tried to take online and night classes. That seemed to be one of the greatest failures I had while trying to advance my naval career in all aspects. The Navy encourages their sailors, of all ranks, to seek higher education. For those in the enlisted ranks, you were awarded extra points on your advancement exams, as well as extra notice in your evaluation reports from your commands.

As you'd recall from earlier, this failure in pursuit of me advancing myself within the ranks of the Navy was due to the fact that I had to exhaust a massive amount of my time and energy trying to prove to the various commands, and even my peers, that I could not only hack it with them but excel as an excellent sailor. Most of my days, I would spend working long hours, sometimes up to eighteen hours in one working day.

While I was sitting there in my comfy olive drab recliner exploring the possible jobs that I was qualified for, I was really stressed knowing that I was really only trained for one thing and there was a very little need, if any, for combat trauma. Again, as you'd recall from earlier, my commands wouldn't even authorize me to go to a C-School (an advanced or technical school for the field that you are already in, i.e. respiratory technician, x-ray technician, bio med tech . . . etc.)

Well, I wasn't one to sit around boo-hooing about what could have been and how that would change things now. So I began developing a plan, even if it meant starting with step one all over again. On October 29, 2012, that was what had to happen.

Although I was to be placed on the temporary disabled retirement list, or TDRL, I knew my chances of being called back to duty were very slim. TDRL was designed to allow a service member up to five years to recover and/or rehabilitate themselves in a way that being on active duty really couldn't allow for. During this time, I knew that I had to work on getting the care that I had put off so I could get myself ready for the next chapter in my life, regardless of what was in that chapter.

I first began my pursuit of a college degree May 2011 by doing accelerated online courses through an accredited university. This proved to be difficult at times, but I was determined to not only advance myself both personally and professionally, but was still hellbent on proving myself to my command and peers within my ranks. This didn't last long, but at least I got a jump start and acquired ten-and-a-half semester credits during my short stint back at division. During my arrival at division and my departure from the Navy, I had led various departments within my respective commands and took college courses, all the while undergoing three major surgeries.

Kicking off my college career was the boost that I needed just knowing that the reality of having degree was a vital aspect to survival either while still in service or out in the civilian sector. My dad once told me that even the "average" jobs on the civilian side that wouldn't have required more than a GED or high school diploma now "recommend" a college degree of some sort. Then he would tell me, "Danny, kid, you have to read every day and get your college done so you're not a dummy like your mean old dad."

Knowing that I had some sort of game plan, I reluctantly began accepting that my next chapter was underway. I say reluctantly for a reason, too, so stay with me on this one. As I was processing out,

I would talk to Dad and my seniors every day about the process and what to expect both mentally and in the realms of employment and college. They would tell me that I would come to accept the transition but hate it at the same time. I was also told that the transition from doing eight years of service to a college classroom would be a difficult one. This was because the discipline, values, and mindset were different than the kids who were recent high school graduates. I took that advice to heart and decided to avoid that transition by going to school online through accelerated courses.

October 29, 2012 was what I had deemed my half-freedom day. I say half-freedom day due to the fact that I was placed on TDRL and my medical was to be under review for up to the next five years, and during that time, the Navy could call me back to continue my contract. In no way was I upset by the situation, seeing as I signed the forms accepting these terms and just the simple fact that I had always wanted to stay in and serve to my fullest abilities. I did, however, feel like only half of a civilian.

If you recall from earlier, I had broken out of the hospital after my second jaw surgery and attended an event in the Los Angeles area as a guest of honor with Justin. When Veterans Day of 2012 came around, I was invited to another one of those amazing events. I honestly had been feeling kind of down and bummed about the slow transition and seriously considered not going to the event.

Even though I had these feelings, I figured I couldn't back out of a commitment. Once I give my word, you then have my word. That was a day that I could never forget even if I tried. It was a breakfast/brunch event instead of the happy hour/dinner-style event that I had attended over Memorial Day. The event was held in Orange County this time instead of Los Angeles. So that made the drive more bearable.

It was an overcast day with what Southern California folk like to call rain, so in other parts of the country's terminology, a light drizzle.

Nonetheless, it was a slippery road for those who don't understand Southern California rain and road conditions. I left the condo with a mix of thoughts and feelings on how the day was to be projected out, and I remember getting in the truck and calling one of my family members. During the initial portion of that conversation, I had told her that I had this weird feeling that I couldn't shake. It wasn't a bad feeling, like one of the ones we would get overseas, but one I couldn't properly put my finger on, even one of the partially amputated ones.

She told me to be safe on the roads, stick with my mission, and believe that great things were to happen. I agreed and told her I would be as safe as possible. I hung up and kept jamming out while going over every possible scenario in my head to better prepare myself for what could be in store for me that day. A quick side note: for those who don't know me, every time I am in a vehicle or getting ready to go somewhere, it is always a jam session and practically a full-blown concert. I know it is funny, but I love music and playing the drums. So, when at all possible, I am drumming on my steering wheel or air drumming like none other. I may look like a completely crazy dude driving down the road while drumming on the steering wheel and pedals while singing as loud as I can to whatever I fancy in those drives.

Due to the rain and traffic conditions, I arrived ten to fifteen minutes prior to the event start time. In military terms, this was either late or on time, depending on who you asked and where they stood in the ranking structure. I sent my family a text to let them know I had arrived safely, and then I texted my friends at the event to let them know I had arrived and would be in shortly.

I went in and found my friends, and they had greeted me with some funny comments about me driving like a retired civilian like when I was to be back at the nursing home for bingo. They then took me down to the table where I was to be at and then took me over to another table to meet someone who needed no introduction. I went over to the table speechless, and my nerves were as wrecked as could be.

Before I could even process what was taking place and what the feeling I had all morning on my drive was, I was being introduced to Dodgers legend Tommy Lasorda. Could this be? Was I being introduced to Tommy Lasorda? This had to be a dream. When would someone wake me up? Why was nobody waking me up? This had to be a dream! There was no way that small town Doc Jacobs was being introduced to Tommy Lasorda!

It's true. It wasn't a dream. I walked up, and Justin introduced me as "Doc Jacobs, a wounded warrior baseball player."

Mr. Lasorda asked if I could hit a baseball, and he meant *hit* a baseball. I told him, "Yes, sir, I can."

He responded with another question. "What's the fastest you've ever hit?"

I said, "It's been a few years since I've hit a real fastball, but I hit off a guy throwing ninety-two miles per hour in high school, and even then I only fouled a few off."

He then said, "Here's my card. I want you to come hit some with the team."

Holy shit! Tommy Lasorda, the Dodger legend, had just invited me to come hit with the team! I had to compose myself in a very professional manner. Luckily for me, the event was just about to start, so they had started ushering everyone to their seats. I had excused myself and gone to the "restroom." Instead, I walked at a "brisk pace" to go outside and call my dad. I thought for sure he wouldn't believe me, so I took a picture of the card just before I called so I could send it to him as we talked.

Sure enough, he was in amazement and near disbelief, as I was. So I sent him the picture of the card, and he was beyond thrilled for me. I told him that I would call him later and that I had to go back in. The rest of the event was amazing, and I was truly grateful to see all of the businesses and celebrities showing their gratitude for the troops of the past, present, and future. At the end of the event, I was more composed and collected, so I went over to Mr. Lasorda and thanked him for such a gracious offer and told him that I wouldn't let him down. He told me, "I know you won't."

Soon after the event, on my drive back to north San Diego County, I was as giddy as before. I think I called every close family member and friend that I could and told them about it. Most of their responses were along the lines of, "Get the eff out of here!" or, "No effing way!"

Those amazing friends that were at the event had immediately begun working on getting me back into some professional-style training. I soon began working with a hitting coach while I was strengthening and conditioning on my own. From Veterans Day weekend until the tryout, I worked on my training.

During this time, I was in a real bad place because for some reason when you transfer out of the military's pay system and into the Department of Veterans Affairs pay system, they decide that you only get half of your pay for a specified amount of time. Luckily, we'd saved enough to cover the bills, but the pay being cut in half around the holidays and then finding out that my daughter was to be born in August was even more stressful. This made me really question my decision to get out, but I figured everything had happened for a reason up to that point, and now Tommy Lasorda had my word and I wasn't going to let him down.

I am beyond grateful and blessed to have had a hitting coach that took time to help analyze my situation and how that effected my future potential plate appearances. He took me in the cage and told me to wipe my batting hard drive clean, because it was time to upgrade to new software. So we would work an hour or so per session, and it wasn't long before I was crushing the ball and my leg wasn't inhibiting my hitting.

Unfortunately, this awesome coach was at least two hours of driving time away, and that put a huge damper on my finances. I was on a mission, though, and complaining wasn't it. I scheduled the sessions so I could get enough training in and not be over budget. I would also take what I learned into the local cages to get some cuts in there.

I received word that the tryout was to be held on February 28, 2013, at the Dodgers' spring training facility at the Camelback Ranch Sports Complex. This was a true blessing for me because exactly seven years before, I had arrived at National Naval Medical Center Bethesda in Maryland, where I coded in the elevator on my way up to the ICU. In a miraculous turn of events, I went from fighting for my life to fighting for a spot on the Dodgers' roster.

I was fortunate enough to have the support of the same organization that made such a meeting occur to assist me with my travels out to the tryout. I will forever be indebted to them for making everything possible. I was to fly out the day before the tryout and fly back the day after.

In the months leading up to the tryout, I had to ramp up my training and prepare to possibly fill in a roster spot on a minor league team. My training during that time consisted of a variety of things ranging from long runs to building cardio to cage time in the Long Beach area with some great friends and mentors. I had also changed my diet to accommodate my new training style.

One of the biggest issues with training to prepare oneself for the pros is finding the perfect physical build. Being too bulky meant you could affect your speed, and if you're too scrawny, then you could affect your potential for power. Now, don't get me wrong, I have seen some of the muscular power hitters fly around the bases and the smaller ballplayers crush four hundred fifteen–foot home runs.

As an amputee, however, I had to find and manage the perfect balance to be fast yet strong enough to rip the cover off the ball. This style of training was all new to me because my training in the years leading up to it consisted of mostly endurance instead of short burst energy. Needless to say, it was quite the shocking experience to my body.

One of the biggest and most difficult hurdles was figuring out a new batting stance. Seeing as I was a left-handed hitter and my back leg was my prosthetic side, we had to be inventive with it. Luckily, my hitting coach at the time was very creative, and within a few sessions, I was getting some good pop on the ball. Besides trying to configure a new stance that would effectively help me in the box, the hardest thing I had to deal with was not knowing when the tryout was set for. This always put a damper on a trainer's plans for their athlete, because they had no timeline to work with on preparing the athlete for such a big occasion.

Once the day was set in stone, it became a media frenzy. I was not as set on that as I was more focused on trying to mentally prepare myself for what may be ahead of me and how I should prepare for those moments. Justin had described to me what he encountered as he was playing college ball and when he had his shots with the pros before being signed. So, in a way, I had something to prepare with. Having some knowledge, I did the best I could with what I had and in the amount of time that was given.

Soon after I found out the tryout date, I was on my way to Phoenix with one of my great mentors. Just prior to our departure, he had given me a fair warning of how much media might be there. Besides a few interviews for military news sources and a documentary for a group out of New Zealand, I hadn't had too much experience with the mass amount of cameras, recording devices, and notepads. My mentor had tons of experience and had planned on giving me a lengthy course to better my media skills.

Once we landed in Phoenix and got over to the hotel, we linked up for this preparation class. Honestly, those hours seemed like an eternity as he grilled me with questions and how I should answer them. Without him preparing me for the interviews that would soon follow, I would have been eaten alive and made to look like an ignorant fool on camera. Soon after the grilling was over, we went to get a good healthy meal in us as we prepared for the next few days.

I will never forget what he said to me as we were at dinner that night. He told me, "Doc, when you wake up tomorrow, I want you to take a moment to take in all of the senses and not worry about the hours that lie ahead. Take a second to listen to the sounds that surround you, the smell of the hotel room, the taste of the coffee, the feel of flipping the sheets off of you to begin such a magical day. Then when you step onto that field, I want you feel your cleats as they dig into the grass, feel the cool morning breeze as you catch the ball in your glove while you warm up, focus on the glorious sound of the ball connecting with the leather glove, smell that leathery glove as you breathe in the morning air filled with the scent of freshly cut grass."

We said our goodnights and headed to bed to get a good night's worth of sleep, or so we hoped. It was difficult for me to sleep as I was excited and anxious to get on the field and see what I could do to impress the scouts and, of course, to not disappoint Tommy Lasorda. I slept a few hours and woke up hoping to get as much coffee in me as possible. We had planned on meeting a few hours beforehand so we could get some healthy chow in us before a grueling day. Soon after we ate and reviewed what I had learned the previous day about how to handle the media, we headed to Camelback Ranch to sign in and get started.

I can honestly say that once I saw the news crews, I began to become a bit nervous. I was able to get some stretching in prior to the interviews kicking off. It was actually fairly difficult to get warm-ups in as I was being pulled to do this interview and pictures for that media group. I honestly didn't mind, though, because I had previously agreed to it and figured I would be all right with even a little warm-up. Shortly after everyone warmed up and had completed their sixty-yard sprint, we had begun doing our positional drills. I was going for a spot at second base; it seemed about ten others were, as well. Once the outfielders were done, the positional players began our drills. Third basemen, shortstops, and second basemen had to do our drills from the shortstop position. Once we were done, the first basemen had their run with the drills. After the positional players had their turns, we worked our way into the initial portion of the hitting.

During the first round of hitting, we were split up into hitting groups, and they brought out the machine. One only had so many chances to impress the scouts with their abilities. If your hitting group wasn't up, then you were out in the field shagging. I believe my group shagged for a couple rounds then we got called in. I did my routine warm-ups and took this time to hone in on my stretching. I was also focusing on the recent hitting lessons that I had just weeks prior.

When I came up to the plate, I was a bit nervous, but I kept telling myself to make it as memorable as possible and to just soak in the experience. This helped me relax and focus on crushing the ball. I did so, and the ball was really popping off of my bat. The sound of the connection of that sweet spot meeting that five-ounce ball was such a sweet sound. I loved hearing that crack echo throughout the dewy morning at Camelback Ranch.

I did get a few extra pitches as some of my line drives seemed to gather the attention of the scouts. That was such an amazing feeling, seeing as I was worried about switching up my stance and swing the weeks leading up to the tryout. At this point, I had hoped it'd be enough to get into the second round for another look from the scouts.

I finished my hitting and eagerly went back into the field to get more chances at a wicked hopper off a lefty's bat in preparation for the potential second round. During the last phase of waiting to see who made the cut and who hadn't, I noticed a gentleman asking around for a bat to use as he forgot to bring his. I then noticed, and this pissed me off, that not one person was willing to lend him a bat to use. All of these baseball players trying out for a spot on a team and not one of them could be a team player and lend him a bat for five or more pitches. I didn't hesitate and told him where my bag was and that he could use whatever he needed out of it.

At the end of the first round, we all hustled and helped to get the field cleaned up and get the scouts ready for the second round.

I, however, was quickly pulled and taken by golf cart over the spring training field, where a game between the Angels and the Dodgers was ready to take place. I was brought over as the guest of honor to throw out the ceremonial first pitch.

It was truly an honor to do so, not only because I was trying out for the Dodgers on a field behind the stadium but because I felt like I was representing the Navy/Marine Corps and the wounded veterans throughout the nation on that day.

I walked out to the mound shortly after the national anthem, and as I stood there waiting to throw out the ceremonial first pitch, the announcer read my bio, during which the crowd was on their feet applauding and cheering. Now, mind you, I am not really one who likes the spotlight, but I will do it for the greater cause and for the American people, as well as the world, to know that even though we may have been wounded and disfigured, we did not lose heart and our will to fight. I gladly shook hands with Tommy Lasorda and Mike Scioscia.

I was nervous on the drive back to the field that I had spent the majority of the morning trying to impress the scouts and land a spot on the Dodgers minor league roster somewhere. I was expecting to go back and have my bag outside the dugout and the scouts saying thanks but no thanks. I happened to get just the opposite.

I arrived back thinking to be kicked to the curb and told to not come back, but I was told to get my glove and get back out on the field. I did as such and jumped out behind the guys already at second base, hoping to get a play in during this second round. This round was known as the simulated game. During this round, the pitchers and catchers came in an effort to show their skills for the scouts. We were split into hitting groups for this round as well.

After a few pitchers rotated through and I wasn't getting much playing time, I looked to my left and noticed that there was no first baseman. I jumped over there to man the fort with my little infield glove from my high school days at third base. I knew the Dodgers had an excellent first baseman and was still unsure why no one was over at first base during the second round. Not for me to question. So I just hopped on over and filled the role. I felt as though I did exceptionally well as I fielded a grounder cleanly and took some throws from home plate and the mound in some pick-off attempts. Soon after, a scout asked me where my first baseman's glove was and why I was using my infielder's glove. I told him that I had never played a day at first base in my life. He looked at me with a severely puzzled look on his face and said, "Son, go get yourself a first basemen's glove and come back because you look like a natural over at first, and I would have guessed that you had many years of experience in the right corner."

I thanked him and went back to my mentor to relay what he had just told me. He was pretty excited about it but told me to not get too excited and bigheaded as I still had to hit. As that time approached, I began to get a little nervous, not because someone was throwing mid-nineties at me, but because I hadn't seen live pitching outside the cages since I had been working with my new hitting coach. Naturally, I began to overthink it all and started to let the thoughts and scenarios play out in my head before I even glanced at a pitch from this hard-throwing righty.

Right when I thought I had studied the pitcher on the mound enough to know what he was throwing, the scouts switched it all up and brought in a new pitcher and catcher. I wasn't on deck at the time, but I was in the hole, which is a term for the third batter, not the batter at the plate or in the "on deck circle" but the guy following those two. So I was able to see some of his stuff. Boy, was he throwing some heat. It seemed like a split second before it was my time to step into the lefty's batter box.

Throughout this whole time, I kept telling myself to not fall back into old habits and stay focused, as he was trying to impress the scouts just as much as I was. It was my mission to knock him off his high horse, even though I knew his stuff was good and I respected his game. I did just that. He was throwing some high heat, and I kept fouling the ball off. We must have gone through about eight fastballs before he finally got me with a curve that caught the outside part of the plate. I don't know why I wasn't thinking off speed, but it was a good pitch, and he rang me up. I looked out at the mound and gave him a smile and nod in approval.

After being wrung up on a sweet curve ball, I grabbed my glove and got back out into my fielding mentality and went right back to first base and finished up my tryout with a relatively quiet portion there. Thus concluded my tryout with the Dodgers organization.

Although the baseball part was over, the day was not. We gathered around the scouts as they talked about the day and said they had our information and would call if they felt they may need any of us. We all thanked them for having us and showed our gratitude individually. This was far from the end of my day, even though physically I had wished it was over. Mentally, though, I was rocking a high like I could never imagine duplicating. I was beyond cloud nine with my tryouts, even though I was shown some of my weaknesses.

I was sunburnt, worn out, and moving on to the next evolution, an interview with *NBC Nightly News.* This interview was an on-the-field meeting with the cameraman and the reporter. Although I had spent the morning and bits of the afternoon with other news sources, this was the big kahuna. While the kind folks with NBC were getting set up and deciding which location would be best for the interview, I found out I was invited to dinner with Tommy Lasorda and his staff. In my head, I was bouncing all over the place with excitement, as this was something that every baseball fan couldn't even fathom.

Once the interview had started, we did many takes with many different angles. As this was my first time doing a major interview, especially on camera, I had to remember what my mentor had told me about keeping to the same answer, same tone, and same composure. This proved to be difficult, as I was not only excited about how the day had panned out but I was more enthusiastic about my upcoming dinner with Tommy Lasorda.

We had spent a good hour or so filming the whole interview, and I was fairly impressed that even though we had spent that much time on the field filming and doing different takes that the airtime was barely a few minutes. I did like how NBC used some of the footage as a teaser for the night it aired and saved the actual interview for one of the last. For one of my first major media interviews, I was really impressed by the outcome and the outpour of support.

Going through all this at the age of twenty-seven, right out of the military, no college playing time, and not having an agent made it seem like such a crazy, uphill battle. I am not talking about a little hill by the beach that you'd climb up to get back to your car but more of like Half Dome in Yosemite with the snow falling on you. However, having a mentor (and a public relations) guy, a hitting coach, and a former professional baseball player as your friend and mentor felt like having breaks of sun with the snow as you're battling the uphill battle.

After the filming was over, my mentor and I watched the grounds crew clean up and prepare the beautiful diamond behind the stadium. I just had to take in the last bit of memories from that experience. It was very pleasant to smell the water hitting the sunbeaten and cleated-up dirt as the Arizona sun was falling further to the western aspect of the desert. It was unique to watch and have that inner child going berserk over what had happened throughout the day, and to think it wasn't even close to being over.

My mentor and I had decided on a game plan as we sat and watched the grounds crew do their magic. We were going to extend our time at the hotel near the stadium and then get ready for such an amazing opportunity that was just ahead of us. He told me to be quick with my getting ready as we couldn't be late for our dinner with Mr. Lasorda, as that could leave a bad impression. We had been ready and waiting for the call to tell us that they had arrived. We played it off as though we had just got there so we didn't seem too eager as well.

We linked up with Tommy Lasorda and his amazing staff. We walked into a sushi place and sat down. I sat next to Mr. Lasorda, where he began to grill me about my tryout after we had ordered our food. I was a bit nervous to be sitting and having dinner with the Dodgers' legend and for him to be asking me about my tryout. I didn't want to sound too confident, but I wanted to be honest and not downplay it.

When he asked how I thought I did and I told him I believed I did fairly well, he responded with, "Yeah, we will see when my head scout gets here." Then he just chuckled and asked me again. I told him, again, that it went fairly well. I wasn't sure if he was testing me or if he was seeing if I would change my answer to embellish or downplay my workout.

We chuckled and ordered our massive amounts of food to compensate our busy and stressful day in that hot Arizona sun; even though it was February 28th, it was still hot. As we sat there with the great Dodger's legend, I sat in awe listening to him speak, share stories, and hear his staff talk and share their stories. I was truly living in every boy's baseball dream.

I was startled by one of Mr. Lasorda's staff members when he struck up a conversation with me. We began talking about how long I had played baseball, what I did in the service, how many tours I did, how I got my injuries, etc. He then asked me a question I will never forget. In that dim, cool room at this sushi restaurant by Camelback Ranch, he asked, "Who were some of your favorite players to watch when you were growing up?"

"Omar Vizquel, John McDonald, Jim Thome, Kenny Lofton." And as soon as I said Kenny Lofton, he interrupted me and asked me if I would like to talk to him.

I blinked a few times in disbelief that this dream just kept getting better. I thought to myself, just briefly, before a quick response, *I am having sushi with Tommy Lasorda and I am about to talk with Kenny Lofton on the phone?*

"Ummm, yes, sir. That would be incredible," I said.

Before I could really grasp the moment, he handed me the phone and said, "Here, talk to Kenny."

I was so nervous and starstruck that I do believe I said, "Mr. Lofton, I am a true inspiration of yours. I mean you are a true inspiration to me. Watching you scale the wall out in center field at 'the Jake,' stealing home, and slapping doubles down the line or in the gaps made me want to play baseball just like you."

Although I couldn't recall the rest of the conversation, it was so incredible. I thought to myself then and there that even if I didn't get a call from the Dodgers with an offer, many dreams had become a reality for me and I would be forever grateful to Tommy Lasorda and the Dodgers.

It seemed like the whole dinner lasted about five minutes before we were out the door saying farewell. My mentor and I went back to the car and then drove back to the hotel in complete disbelief at the whole day of events. In celebration, we went out by the pool that was closing within the next fifteen minutes and lit up two celebratory cigars and sat on the curb by the pool in that warm Arizona evening air.

We just looked up at the stars and occasionally passing aircraft and reflected on the recent events. We vowed to not let this be just a one-time pursuit of such an incredible dream. We began spitballing ideas and plans for training, schedules, possible coaches, and how to approach teams. We then discussed the potential of future interviews once the *NBC Nightly News* interview aired and how to approach those.

I was shocked that the tryout was over, yet there was still more to do, more to plan for, and—my favorite part—all of the training. We finished up the cigars and discussed our travel plans for the next day then headed off to bed. Even though we were in our rooms resting for the night and shaking off the events of the day, I couldn't sleep. I laid there thinking of every moment of the day. What I did, what I didn't do, what I could have done differently, what I would do differently, how I could have better prepared, what I felt my weaknesses were, if I had any weaknesses, what my strong aspects were, and so on.

I finally dozed off and headed back to Orange County uneventfully yet still going through everything in my head. The biggest thing that was eating away at me was not waiting for a possible call from the Dodgers but was wondering what they saw in me and what they felt I needed to work on. Then I tried to come to terms with the possibility that I could never know. So I had hoped to see my tryout from a different perspective, *NBC Nightly News'* video footage.

Once my *NBC Nightly News* footage hit the airwaves, it blew up into a big mainstream story. I had media outlets from all over the nation, including NBC and ESPN, contacting the Dodgers front office, my mentor, and even my social media accounts. I had interviews with ESPN and Fox News and was even featured on Perez Hilton. This kept me busy and focused on the media aspect and not pondering what could have been or what would be. I just flashed my smile and remained as positive as possible even though my mind was racing a million miles per hour.

I know this was something that I couldn't change because what was done was done. However, I was a guy that strove for perfection and had to know what I could work on. Luckily, my mentor filmed a fair amount of it, and we were able to go back and review it and take it to the hitting coach and my other coach/mentor. In between media events, I was driving to Orange County for meetings and practices.

One of the biggest things that I thought was funny were the haters. And by haters, I mean folks who had no idea about the amount of training that I put into building up for the tryouts and then what the actual tryout entailed. These folks are what now are deemed "keyboard warriors," someone who talks trash from the safety of their personal space but who would never have the fortitude to say the same thing in person.

When I first started reading their harsh comments, I wanted to respond with equally harsh comments in return but knew I needed to maintain professionalism and take the high road. So, in turn, I would click "like" on their comments or simply respond with, "Thank you for your support," or even, "I appreciate your advice." I am pretty sure that didn't really stop them from making further comments, but I just wanted them to know I actually paid attention and really did actually appreciate their support, those that did actually support my pursuit of the pros and other quests.

16.

POST-DODGERS' TRYOUTS AND CONTINUING TRANSITION

M ost folks typically get bummed out when they do something outside of their comfort zone, throw themselves out there for others to have a field day of judgment, and then not get the job or signed by a team. I must admit that I was a little bummed out by not being signed, but I know that scouts have certain skills they look for in a ballplayer and certain spots to fill. I know that as a huge baseball fan and knowing that each team is doing the best with what they have to assemble a team for the coaching staff so they can battle and bring home the Fall Classic title.

As I began to review the films and my times, I understood some of the things that I needed to work on and things that I needed to cut out altogether. This was a tough thing to sit down and do, but I needed to be honest with myself and realize what was working and what wasn't. I sought some advice from some close friends, especially those that had made it to the show. There was a sense of pride in me that wanted to do it on my own, but I knew that I had to listen to others and seek an outside opinion.

One of the toughest things that I have ever had to do was to be honest with myself about things. Most say that this is a result from "just being a man" or from "being a military man." I would say that a good chunk of it stems from just being stubborn and knowing that I am in great shape and I can do this and that. Throughout most of my recovery, I stuck to what I knew, and I did most of my own physical therapy and saw good results.

Pursuing the pros, though, that was something that I needed to tell my prideful self to shut its damn cake hole and let some advice in. One of the first things that I cut out was the driving to Long Beach to go see the gentleman that was helping me out with my hitting. That freed up so much time and allowed for me to hit various workouts and find a local batting cage to go to.

My tryouts generated a ton of attention, mostly good and some bad, as I previously explained with the haters. One of the great things that came from it all was one Coach Lou. I was introduced to Coach Lou a few months after my tryouts, but let's work into that timeframe.

I was approached by a former Marine Corps officer who asked if I would like to play on his baseball team that consisted of service members with Purple Hearts. I was really excited about this opportunity. Of course I was all about playing baseball with my Marine brethren! I was thinking, *Man! What an opportunity! Where the heck has this been for the past few years?*

Coach Lou was ever so graciously volunteering his time to coach our team. Once I was introduced to the team and the staff, I was comfortable and ready to play, but we had to overcome some big issues. There was one big hurdle for the team, and it was that Coach Lou taught out of his facility in Riverside County and most of us athletes were driving in from all over Southern California. This was no fault to Coach Lou but just rough for the athletes. One other big issue was that the games were not always in Riverside County but in Orange County. It was also unfortunate, and again no fault to Coach, that if we missed a practice due to work or other scheduling issues, we would sit the next games.

To prevent discouragement from the other players, I would work with them directly and report to Coach Lou with video evidence. I would also find out if finances were an issue with the guys and try to buy them gas cards to offset the cost so they could still make practice and play in the games. This was huge for them and their families to see them playing sports through their injuries. I quickly picked up the role as Team Captain and continued to work with my teammates as we attempted to bring this team to have a bigger presence.

Any athlete, entrepreneur, CEO, military leader, or politician knows that you have a set event and date to build and train for. This challenge held true for our team and eventually became the downfall of the organization. This was not something Coach and I could control as we tried vigorously to build communications with those running the events and administration side. Coach and I were told of "possible games" and of potential timeframes, but nothing was ever set in stone. So Coach built his training plans the best he could, and I would do my best to rally the troops.

Coach and I did our best to work together to build to best team we could with what little supplies and information we had. Coach would integrate us in with his college students during weekend tournaments in order to give us some real playing time. This allowed for the other athletes to get some big confidence boosts that they needed. This was Coach's way of being able to see how much we had retained and actually used in the games.

Coach had a great way to integrate us with his college athletes, whether it was at practices where they would help go over drills, plays, or scenarios or when we would work with them in games. Coach Lou was not only a great coach to us, he was a great mentor. We grew to trust in Coach and could eventually talk to him about things off the field.

Throughout the initial phases and ironing out some things within the baseball organization, we kept training and practicing.

This only got better when we caught word that we might play at Angels Stadium after a Sunday home game. This really excited the team because we would be playing against a team of other wounded vets from a different part of the country. We had been playing in summer wood bat leagues and local adult leagues and scrimmaging against ourselves, but to play at Angels Stadium was huge.

This dream became a reality in mid-May 2013. We all arrived at the stadium early to stage our gear and go enjoy some of the game before going back down to prepare for our game. During the game, I was pulled to go up to chat with the White Sox radio announcers about the event that day, my personal military stuff, and my Dodgers tryouts.

We chatted a bit about my military stuff and then got on the topic of the Dodgers tryout. They asked why I hadn't stayed and tried out with them, as they share a spring training facility with the Dodgers. I told them that it was out of respect for Tommy Lasorda and the Dodgers that I was making that trip specifically for them. They asked why I hadn't reached out to the White Sox after. I told them that I simply didn't think about it but would reach out as soon as I could.

After my half of an inning with the White Sox announcers, I went to rejoin the team to go down and gear up. We spent the majority of the time stretching, taping ankles and wrists, warming up, and doing meetings about positions and lineups. Once the Angels and White Sox game was over, we took the field. This was fun because most people leaving the stadium were caught off guard when another game started to take place. I think this piqued their curiosity but didn't really keep them around.

The game was fairly short due to the time of day but was fun and interesting while it lasted. I was holding a runner on at first and was in a squatting position ready to tag the runner should our pitcher attempt a quick pick off. As the pitcher moved toward the plate, I pushed off on my left leg (prosthetic side), as I have many times, and I heard and felt an extremely loud pop. This sound could have been heard from any seat in the stadium.

In a crazy sense, I knew exactly what had happened. I had snapped and shattered my prosthetic leg at the strongest part, where the two bolts connected the pylon to the carbon fiber blades that made up the foot. I was quite impressed with my level of intensity but super bummed that I couldn't play the remainder of the game. I knew this as I hopped from first base to the third base dugout unassisted. I didn't bring a spare leg because I never thought in a million years that I would shatter a leg. In all the years as an amputee, leading up to that point, I had cracked many prosthetics but never shattered one. I had finished twenty-mile hikes, in full combat gear, on a cracked prosthetic but never shattered one.

When I scheduled my appointment with my prosthetist, he was in pure disbelief. When I brought it in as proof, he told me one thing: "Doc, in my decades of work in this field, I have *never* seen *anyone* do this to a prosthetic." I later found out that he was so impressed that when he was supposed to send it back to the manufacture for the warranty, he outright bought the prosthetic.

Although the Major League Baseball season continued on into the late summer, I didn't hear anything back from the Los Angeles Dodgers. I did finish with the summer league with Coach's team and continued to do work with my hitting coach while working on strength and conditioning.

In June 2013, I kept my promise to the US Navy and continued to get the care that I had neglected to get while remaining on active duty. I went in the operating room for a lengthy procedure to have a hammertoe, or claw toe deformity, corrected on my second toe. I went into the surgery knowing the risks of coming out of the operating room with that toe being amputated.

This one made me a little emotional because if I'd lost my second toe, I would have had my big toe and my third toe left. My third was another hammertoe, and I was staring down another surgery for that toe as well. The emotional attachment to the second toe was simple. If I lost that toe, I was unsure of the future of my foot. The structure and future of my foot loomed, and still looms, over every procedure on my foot.

Another emotional part to this surgery was the recovery time. This was one where I couldn't half-ass my recovery and screw it up. Otherwise, I could cause further damage to the toe or foot or even get some serious infection and then end up losing my right leg as well.

The ortho foot and ankle surgeon that took care of my foot was one of the best surgeons and very passionate about her work. This made me trust her even more. Many other ortho surgeons sang praises, and they still do, about her. She was so passionate and caring that I took her word as pure gold. When I first came to her with mid-foot tightness and pain, she ordered a foot orthotic and taught me some ways to ease up the plantar fascia before we discussed, in depth, the surgical options.

I scheduled a follow up a while later and came in complaining of mid-foot tightness and pain again. She came into the room, and we started discussing things. To my surprise, she looked at my shoe on the exam table by my side and made one quick motion. She picked up my shoe and started hitting me, half-playfully and half-seriously, with it while saying, "Maybe you wouldn't have such mid-foot tightness and pain if you actually wore your damn orthotic that I prescribed to you!"

I acknowledged my fault real quick and told her I would go pick it up and schedule an appointment for a follow up after giving that and the more conservative treatment options a go for a while longer. I combined the orthotic and the other treatment options, but they weren't really working out that well.

My second and third toe were pretty fixated in a retracted state. They had been slowly retracting over the years since my injury date. This was due to not being able to move my toes like before. In turn, they naturally retracted into a claw form. Thus the term "claw toe deformity."

She understood my emotions and ensured me that she would do whatever it took to save my toe and my leg. She assured me of this during my appointments, during my pre-operative meeting with her, and even in the operating room before being put under. This was comforting, but she did inform me of the pain that would be ahead of me post-surgery. She explained that my toe was rigid and had been stuck in the same spot for years. She said she would be cutting into one or more joint spaces and cutting the joints out while dealing with other things with the toe and midfoot.

I opted to have the block team numb my leg up to make it easier on her during surgery and on myself for a day or two post-surgery. Once the block was set and my leg was fairly numb, we went back, and she was sitting in her spot waiting with all of the x-rays and equipment, ready to rock. When I transferred onto the operating room table and scooted into the spot that she needed me at, she lightly grabbed my foot and told me that she was the best and she would take good care of me. I felt comfortable with that and then prayed while being prepped for anesthesia and surgery. She held onto my foot while I prayed and then gave the anesthesiologist the nod that I was done praying and ready to rock and roll. Soon after, I was out and then waking up in the PACU.

I woke up with a numb leg and all three toes. This was a sigh of relief. I did a quick recovery in the post-surgery ward. That typically entailed being able to eat something, drink some fluids, pee, and to do a few laps around the ward. For this surgery, I would have to show the staff that I could crutch on my prosthetic side. Doing so was nearly second nature to me at this point, so I burned a couple laps around the ward on my crutches and prosthetic. It probably took them longer to print my discharge instructions than it did for me to cruise around the ward. I was then wheeled down to the flagpole area to load up and head home to begin my recovery.

As I dosed off, wondering how the pain and the recovery would be really boggled my mind. This was new territory for me because I was typically given up to thirty days to recover before being back in uniform and back at work. Having all this time to recover seemed absurd to me, but I knew with this big of a surgery and the implications of one mistake, I had to play it just right, especially having a surgeon as passionate as my ortho foot and ankle surgeon.

As I awoke from the previous day's surgery, I immediately realized that I forgot to set an alarm to take medicine before the block was due to wear off. As I was coming to, I knew that the block was wearing off and that the medicine I was to take was the extended release and thus wouldn't be kicking in right away. I took my medicine and tried to stay as still as possible until it could work its magic.

I spent the next few days allowing things to settle and heal the best they could. Even though I was really itching to get back into workouts, driving, or doing anything independently, I knew that keeping my foot elevated and iced was best. I was unsure how much laying around I could do. After about three days, I felt lost and couldn't take being held up and not being productive.

In true Doc Jacobs fashion, I found something to do to escape my mind. I asked Baskee if he wanted to see REO Speedwagon at the San Diego County Fair with me. He was thrilled and gladly accepted. He said because I bought the tickets that he'd buy the drinks. I agreed, and just a mere five days out of my hammertoe correction, we met up at the San Diego County Fair.

I am unsure as to why he was as shocked as he was to see me on my prosthetic crutching and a cast on my right leg. I had previously linked up with him post-surgery to help him move. He seriously laughs every time, and he now asks if I am recovering from a surgery every time we link up.

It was a bit dangerous to my toe and wellbeing to be out crutching around. I say that but not in a sense of instability or just being in pain or being at a higher risk of infection. I had a metal wire hook hanging out of the end of my second toe. This could have easily been jammed further in my toe or foot or snagged and yanked out. Being out and about with an excellent friend while seeing a great band was worth the risk to me.

We made our way through the crowds, and I crutched past so many people in hopes of making them feel bad that a one-legged dude just crutched faster than they were walking as they slowly chugged along. While crutching past these seemingly snail-like people, I actually felt like I was getting a decent workout in. I was killing my upper body, and the pace I was going seemed great. The night went seemingly well, and we created more funny memories of our times together.

At some point after my tryout with the Dodgers, an incredible gentleman offered something to the organization that I helped form and was the West Coast Director for. He offered to take a group of veterans out for a deep sea fishing trip, which we later dubbed "Operation Big Hairy Tuna." The timeframe for this multi-day trip down the Baja, California, coast and back was during my recovery from my second toe surgery. I was offered, multiple times, to sit that one out and heal up. I declined every time, mostly because my spot was already paid for and donated but also, as the West Coast director, I felt that I needed to be out there in case of any issues.

This trip began at night and on such an incredibly big boat. It had a dining area, a chef, staterooms, showers, Wi-Fi, you name it. As we hit the open sea, we began to roll around. This was a bit challenging for my stability with the crutches. After a short while, I tossed the crutches in my room and mainly just kept the balance on my heel. I thought for sure this wouldn't be good for the healing, but I was even more sure that falling and stubbing my toe and having a metal k-wire jammed further into my foot while on a deep sea fishing trip, dozens of miles away from the shore, wasn't good, either.

When we got back and we all went our separate ways, I dreaded the follow up and the surgeon seeing the overly used cast. I mainly feared her finding out because a cast would hurt a hell of a lot more than my shoe. I truly lucked out and was sent to the cast room to have it removed before crutching to get post-operative x-rays. Thus she never saw the cast, and to this day, she doesn't know.

Having said all of that, we got on a serious discussion about me feeling like my k-wire was being pushed out of my body. She said that rarely happens and it was probably my mind thinking too much about my toe. She said it's like having a headache, and if you thought about your headache, it hurt more. I got that to a certain degree, but I told her I could feel my body pushing the k-wire out of my toe. She clipped it at a certain spot and told me to schedule a follow up.

I scheduled the follow up and came back to tell her the same thing. She was in shock when she looked at my toe and noticed the k-wire was further out of my toe. She had clipped it and noted the hook being only so far from the end of the toe. When I came back for the follow up, the k-wire was nearly completely out of my toe. She simply just grabbed it and barely pulled then the wire was completely out. She laughed and walked away in disbelief.

My recovery time from that point on was smooth, and it really had to be. Come August, I was entering fatherhood and had no option but to deal with the pain and be at the ready when my little angel needed anything. As I have come to learn since August 2013, this didn't end at a certain point in time during parenthood. In fact, it had made me think completely differently about everyone and everything in the world. Being a father, I quickly learned what the world really centered around, and how I was there to help grow, mold, educate, and facilitate all the aforementioned aspects of being a parent.

My Marines had always called me "the Mom of the Platoon," and this is still true, but being an actual parent really created heightened senses and many different feelings. This all impacted (and still does) my surgeries, my training, my education, my writing, my tryouts, my meetings, and many other things. Life goes from being about an individual into a team role again. It is odd because I found myself as the commanding officer, the punisher, the lawyer, the bank, the mentor, the teacher, the friend, the medical advisor, the shoulder, the punching bag, the cook, the janitor, and the driver. All of it is fun, and ensuring the overall health, happiness, and wellbeing of a child all that matters.

October 2013 rolled around, and I was still working on taking care of the medical things that I needed to. I was on a time crunch because I was entering one year of being placed on TDRL (Temporary Disabled Retirement List). I was six months away from my first of a maximum of three evaluation boards. One issue that I had while being on TDRL and still maintaining Navy physical fitness standards was I didn't had enough padding on my body for the nerve stimulator pack that was sitting in my upper thigh (near my bony hip bone). It was migrating to the surface and had to be taken out and sutured deeper into the muscle tissue. This recovery was one that wasn't too bad in comparison to some others. I healed relatively quick and got back into training.

Although I had no professional tryouts lined up, I was playing on the team with my fellow wounded veterans and playing in a local adult league in San Diego. This was some fun times for training, because I was maintaining the Navy standards while training for the short burst energy style of training for baseball.

During a game in November 2013, I was at the plate and had a pitcher's count against me, one to two. I knew the next pitch would be a fastball. I sat back with wrists locked and drove the ball . . . straight into my right foot. I hobbled around and refused to leave the plate. I ended the at-bat with a walk and hopped all the way to first base and signaled for a pinch runner. I hopped off the field and drove straight to the Naval Medical Center San Diego emergency room before taking my cleat off. Throughout the drive, I used my prosthetic and cruise control to control the speed and braking. When I took off my cleat, it looked like I had a baseball wedged under my skin.

I was sure that the plates on my first and second metatarsals were broken as well as many bones. When you looked at the picture, would you have guessed that as well? To my surprise, and many others, nothing was broken. The ortho surgeon said that the plates absorbed the brunt of it and more than likely saved my bones from many fractures. I was stunned that my foot wasn't broken considering the baseball-sized bruise/contusion on it. To this day, I am grateful for those plates saving me so much trouble. You can bet your last dollar that I was online shopping around for a batter's leg guard. I ordered it and still use it to this day. Of course, I have yet to hit one off of the batter's leg guard.

As 2014 neared, I could tell the year was going to be wild ride. I was just unsure of what direction it would take. Many scenarios of how the year would pan out flooded my mind. With each scenario, I tried to figure out every possible outcome. I know that I am not the only one in the billions of people that this happens to, but it happens with every scenario. In the professional off-season of 2013-2014, I took some advice from the White Sox announcer and wrote to the White Sox requesting an open tryout.

In true professionalism, I received an email back from the Chicago White Sox on January 13, 2014. This email energized me and really kicked off my 2014 into the direction that I wanted it to head into. I knew that my evaluation with the Navy was between January and my potential summer of 2014 tryout. I knew anything was possible in either scenario but had to train and prepare for both possibilities.

I was still playing on the team with my fellow combat wounded and the local adult baseball league, training at the local cages while working with various instructors, training to run my first half marathon, training for sitting volleyball, and training for a possible return to the Navy. All of these different styles of training were great on my body and my mind, but I felt like I was being pulled into a million different directions.

To add to all of my craziness, I had just started full time at National University to pursue a degree. I figured that no matter where I was bound to end up, I needed to be educated, healthy, and diversified in many walks. I knew that I would at least have to have an associate's degree to make myself more desirable in the civilian sector or if I were to go back into the Navy. Between December 2013 and October 2015, I took fourteen classes to finish my requirements for my associate's degree. These classes were compressed into four-week courses. I knew that my evaluation was coming up in April 2014 and that I had to keep showing improvements in all aspects.

During all of my training for the various sports and events, I kept running into an issue from a previous surgery. This issue technically stemmed back to the day that I was injured. This one was located on my left hand. As a result of the IED, my left ring finger at the DIP, or distal interphalangeal, joint had the flexor tendon severed. This resulted in my not being able to bend or extend it. This began to be an option as it seemed to be floppy and in the way. As you recall, I had it fused to solve the flexor tendon and arthritis issues. As I became more involved in sports and my daily activities were different than those in the Navy, I had to figure something else out. It was becoming problematic for sitting volleyball, baseball, typing with school, fatherhood, home projects, gym workouts, and indoor rock climbing, as well as many other things.

After doing a ton of rock climbing, infield drills, and time in the cages, I realized that it was more problematic than I had previously realized. While rock climbing, my finger would get caught between the wall and the holds while falling. There were a few times when I could hear and feel a popping sensation and sound. While doing infield drills, the finger wouldn't bend when I would try to close the glove, and the ball would hit the tip of the finger and cause discomfort. When I would be at the plate, my finger would hang under the bat and get hit while working on bunting drills.

Obviously, this didn't stop me from training and bettering myself within the sport and as an athlete, but I knew that something had to be done and that downtime was the time. I knew the only option and just needed to get it done and over with. I got in with my primary care physician at the San Diego VA to get the ball rolling.

I sat down with her and told her what was wrong and what I needed done. She agreed and ordered the x-rays and put in the consult for me to be seen by an orthopedic hand surgeon. I was seen and evaluated fairly soon after and was on the surgery books. When I asked the doctor about his experience, he looked at me and laughed then said, "Son, I have been cutting off fingers since Vietnam. I will have you in and out of the OR in less than forty-five minutes." This actually gave me a sense of comfort, and I was actually pumped to get it done and over with.

I asked about the recovery time and if I could be awake but have light meds for the surgery. He told me that I could be awake for the procedure if that's what I wished. I asked for a local nerve block and to be consciously sedated. I mainly do this for my surgeries as I have issues with general anesthesia. So to prevent myself from getting a painful headache that typically lasts days with some serious nausea, I decided to be awake and to hear the whole thing.

Before I knew it, I was checked in to the pre-surgery area at the San Diego VA for my first surgery at any Veterans Affairs hospital. This honestly made me nervous as I had heard, and read, so many horror stories about surgeries going wrong at the VA hospitals and outpatient clinics. I then told myself to stop thinking so negatively because one didn't hear or read about all of the successful surgeries that happened *every day* at the VA hospitals throughout the nation day in and day out.

I checked in and waited for a short time before being taken back to a bed so I could change into some of the finest hospital attire. Soon after donning the sexy hospital gown and robe, I was taken back to the area to get my local anesthesia or the nerve block that would be numbing the affected area.

For the local block, they give the option of medicine to keep you comfortable while the anesthesia team uses the ultrasound machine to guide the needle and medicine into the appropriate nerves. Once complete, they come back within a certain amount of time to check on the status of the block before taking you back into the operating room.

They gave me some medicine to get me comfortable before facing my hand palm up and using the ultrasound wand. Before I knew it, I felt a needle go into the middle of my hand. Even with the medicine, that hurt like hell! The anesthesiologist was great, though, and was done fairly soon after I felt that needle pierce the center of my hand. Within fifteen minutes, my hand was numbed up, and I was ready to rock and roll for surgery.

When the operating room and the staff were ready, I was wheeled out of the holding area and rolled into the operating room. I transferred to the operating table and was ready for the "time out" while they hooked all of the leads and monitors up to me. I was laying there facing the door in the operating room on the most southern end of the building and was enjoying the view. Once the "time out" was complete, I began to pray and get as mentally prepared as I could for being lightly sedated while having my finger partially amputated.

I must say that having my left middle finger split apart and then ripping off the left index finger, as it was dangling by tendons and ligaments, in a combat setting was completely different than building up for an amputation. I say that because of the chaos, adrenaline, and having a job to do right after that kept my mind busy and kept me distracted. I do remember being on the medivac helicopter and knowing, as the adrenaline was wearing off, that my fingers began to hurt like hell.

I am a Christian man, and although I don't push my religion or my beliefs on anyone, I still like to pray before any surgery. Coming from the medical field, I know and understand that people die on operating tables. So right before the anesthesiologist pushes any meds, I like to ask for the surgeon's hands to be steady and for peace and patience in the operating room as I get right just as I am about to enter an altered state of mind or being put under.

I finished up my prayers and then looked at the anesthesiologist to let them know that I was, personally, as ready as could be. The lady looked at me with a weird expression, though, and I told her that I was ready for the medications whenever the surgeon was ready to start. She seemed confused and annoyed. She thought that I didn't want any medications at all. I proceeded to tell her that I would like to be as lightly sedated and comfortable as possible as I was unsure how deep the block was and unsure if I would feel anything at all. She finally understood and pushed some medications to keep me lightly comfortable.

A whole thirty-four minutes after the surgeon started the amputation, I was sutured and bandage up and on my way to the recovery room. I was in there for a short time before being on my way home. I was instructed that once the block wore off, I could be in a great deal of pain and if that pain was intolerable to return to the ER for pain control. We shall just say that I was not going to be doing that. I had been to the ER at the VA before and had experienced eight- to ten-hour waits for things from a fractured sinus cavity to severe phantom pain that wouldn't let me sleep for days.

The recovery went about in true Doc Jacobs fashion. I would spend the first day or so with my hand elevated and taking my medication as directed. I mainly did so due to the fact that when the local anesthetics wore off, I truly felt the pain from the most recent amputation. I knew that more swelling meant that there was increased pain. I was doing what I knew would work to keep me from the ER and/or from going in for stronger medications. I kept my hand elevated, took ibuprofen every six hours, took my low-dose pain medication, iced my hand, and stayed hydrated. For those who don't know, I was going stir crazy and trying to stay entertained. Having my hand bandaged and in pain meant holding my phone and texting with my right while keeping my left in place, which made entertainment more difficult. After about seventy-two hours, I decided that I would bear the pain and find something to do.

I found a way to entertain myself. That was to jump back into training and to get back into practicing with the wounded veterans and service members. I vividly recall driving up to Riverside County for practice, and the slight vibration of the steering wheel bothered my finger. This was not going to stop me from practicing and being with the team. When I arrived, I put a batting glove on right away to not draw attention to my hand, which still had sutures in the amputation site of my left ring finger. I opted to bat with the first group while others shagged and did their drills.

For the baseball players reading this, you already know the sting of hitting the ball on an inside pitch on your hands. This sting was amplified tenfold (easily), with a fresh finger amputation. Once our group completed our at-bats and helped clean up the field for the next group, we went in to switch out to the field. I slowly took my batting glove off while blood dripped down my hand and onto the field. The Navy physical therapy nurse that was with our team noticed and came over to give me her piece of mind about it all. She was very adamant about me going to an ER to be seen and attended to. I reassured her that I'd be fine and slid my bloody left hand into my first baseman's glove and sprinted to first base to field and run drills.

The pain of the ball meeting the glove from a hard-throwing pitcher or catcher doing pickoff drills or the snap of the ball meeting my glove from an infielder or a hard chopper to me was painful and caused more bleeding. When the Navy physical therapy nurse approached me again, I could see some medical anger in her, and I told her before she said anything that if I couldn't get the bleeding to stop that I would go the nearest VA ER. I think we knew this was some bullshit, but I knew she needed my acknowledgement and agreement of the problem. I went out of her field of view and painfully pulled my hand out of leather glove and let the blood drain.

I cleaned out the blood and wrapped my finger with gauze and silk tape. We held our team meeting and cleaned up the field. I drove the hour and a half back down to San Diego uneventfully. This style of therapy continued until the sutures were out and the pain eventually went away. The ortho hand surgeon kept insisting on me going into occupational therapy at the La Jolla VA. I kept declining and told him that I was a corpsman and had already desensitized amputated fingers before, thus kind of already having some knowledge and personal experience. I am not saying I know more than the great folks in the occupational therapy field; I just didn't want to clog the system and hog any appointments that someone else could use.

My partial finger amputation was on March 31, 2014. Even though I was being a nutjob and jumping back into training, I took April off from school. For some reason, taking World Civilization I seemed like a lot of online class chats and papers. I needed to focus on getting my hand better and the re-approach the whole typing aspect. Oddly enough, I recovered and reconfigured my methods of typing. Even as I type this, I sit in the cool darkness of my room listening to some classic eighties' jams and need no assistance, even from a backlit keyboard.

I am glad that I took April off from school anyway because my evaluation appointments with the Navy happened to take place during that timeframe. To my surprise, the appointments went fairly well, and each doctor made their recommendations in their reports to the Medical Boards Department. I was told that I would hear back within a certain amount of time. This seemed to be a bit odd to me that I wasn't privy to most of the recommendations. The orthopedic surgeon told me, straight up, that he was recommending me to be placed on PDRL (Permanent Disability Retirement List). This seemed fair enough to me, as I had just had a finger partially amputated.

The Navy psych doctor just kept telling me that I was a more functioning member of society than most. She kept mentioning how impressive this was seeing as I experienced so much trauma and was in such great shape in all aspects of life. I told her that I found what worked for me, and I had a great inner circle of support. This worried me a bit, though, because that seemed to be two conflicting reports, and a decision would have to be made in favor of one recommendation or the other. Although the Navy psych doctor never told me her recommendation, I assumed she was in favor of my return to uniform and duties.

This left me in a mental limbo because I had to ramp up my training for the upcoming White Sox tryout and had to still train for a possible return to the Navy and thus having to run a PRT (Physical Readiness Test) upon being recalled. I left with the mindset of having to train for both. This training mindset was fine by me. I would go for a three-mile run and then drive to the batting cages to get time in with my hitting coach.

As the summer of 2014 drew closer, I was ramping up my training and expecting to hear from the White Sox at any time. Not knowing a date in the months leading up to the tryout messed with any sort of training regimen. For those that are marathoners or have done any sort of intense training for an event, you know how important a training schedule is, along with a timeline to accompany said training schedule. Mind you, I am not faulting the White Sox by any means. I am just noting that it is difficult to train and build up for a shot at the pros and especially to train without knowing a timeline.

I don't remember what day the White Sox scout called me, but I know that I was doing homework, so more than likely in May 2014. I do remember answering the call and holding that same excitement in as when I met Tommy Lasorda. Even though I tried to retain my excitement and maintain a level of professionalism, I am sure that the scout could tell that I was like a Little Leaguer that dreamed of this sort of phone call. For those Little Leaguers out there reading this, I had that same level of excitement that I dreamed of while walking into the batter's box during a Little League game.

When I got off the phone, I began jumping up and down, and when I realized that the excitement was too much for jumping and shouting, I began punching the couch pillows until my dog, my sweet Romeo (a one hundred pound English Golden Retriever) jumped on the couch and joined in on the fight. We probably wrestled and fought for a good half hour.

Knowing that I had a set day for my tryout, I notified my new hitting coach, and we began to work on a schedule for some training. This really helped my mentality because I had a goal and I could then place a vision with that goal. While I was out running my distance runs, I wasn't thinking of the Navy anymore; I was thinking of the tryout and everything it would entail. I was thinking of everything from my Dodgers tryout and what I knew I needed to tune up on or all-out fix. I was thinking of the weather and how that would impact everything. I was thinking of the travels and how the time change would impact things. I was thinking of getting a room at a hotel with a pool and gym to stretch. I was thinking about my dieting for my training and travels leading up to the tryout.

Throughout all of this thinking on my distance runs and late at night while researching all of what I was preparing for, I kept envisioning myself making the roster and getting a chance to prove myself. I recall planning my runs around Lake Hodges during the heat of the day and would think, with every stride, about the tryouts and being in the locker room then running out through the dugout and onto the field. I know this sounds crazy, but I have always had the mindset of envisioning myself in whatever scenario I want to be in, and if I truly believe it can happen, then I keep pursuing that dream and make it into a reality.

I booked my flights and was bound for Birmingham, Alabama, via LAX and Houston. I left a little wiggle room in case of any delays or anything crazy. I am grateful that I allowed this sort of leeway for this trip, as I do most trips but especially this one. I was to fly out of Carlsbad, California, on a twin engine EMB-120 to LAX and then transfer from there. The security lines didn't open up until thirty minutes before departure, but I still arrived there early and checked in. I noticed that there was a group of Marines that were in the terminal, and they had a bunch of gear with them. I didn't know exactly where they were going and didn't ask. We gave one another the bro nod and went about our way.

When the security line opened up and I went through, I went and spoke with the gate agent. I told them that if they needed any volunteers to take a different flight, I would be glad to in order to ensure the Marines weren't split up or their gear didn't get split up, either. They noted my suggestion, and sure enough, just before boarding, they asked me to go up to the podium. They said they could get me on a flight out of LAX, but I'd have to take a taxi or something (that they would cover) and they offered compensation for the inconvenience. I told them that it wasn't an inconvenience and I was honored to be rerouted for them.

I loaded my bat bag and backpack into the cab and headed to LAX. Let me tell you that a taxicab from Carlsbad to LAX is hundreds of dollars. Also, let me tell you that you are in for a ride of your life in a taxicab on I-5 and the 405 from Carlsbad all the way to LAX. I was welcoming turbulence and uncomfortable airplane seats at the end of the cab ride.

I arrived and got checked into United Airlines at LAX and began trying to find my flight in United's many connecting terminals in LAX. From that point on, my trip to Birmingham was smooth and uneventful. Throughout my two flights, LAX-IAH and IAH-BHM, I was going over every possible scenario and possible outcomes for each scenario.

When I arrived in Birmingham, Alabama, and gathered my gear from the baggage claim area, I walked out into a late afternoon wave of heat and humidity. This heat and humidity combo hadn't hit me like that since my Field Medical Service School days in Camp Lejeune, North Carolina, in April to July 2005. The air was heavy, and I was about to welcome the air-conditioned cab ride to the hotel. That evening, I began to stretch and loosen up from my adventurous travels to Birmingham. Soon after, my buddy was getting into town, and I made my way to his part of town to grab dinner with him and review the plan for the next day.

We sat and enjoyed a fairly quiet restaurant as we discussed when to arrive at the stadium, the media, and mock interviews. The whole time, I kept envisioning my next day and getting the call for another look or even a contract. I was even ready to sign a league minimum deal and to even stay in Birmingham to play there in the muggy heat. Throughout the whole dinner, I probably had about five tall southern iced teas. They were as delicious as the folks had raved about.

We decided to call it at a certain point, and I walked back to my hotel. During that walk, I got caught up in a typical southern storm that probably developed throughout the day due to the June elements. I stood under a bridge and waited for it to die down a bit before continuing on.

Just like the night before my Dodgers tryout, I was so excited that it was hard to not only fall asleep but to stay asleep. I decided after my umpteenth time of waking up before the alarm clock that I would get up to shower and begin stretching, loosening up, and getting pumped while listening to some heavy metal. I was expecting it to be a full day like the Dodgers tryout, but my mentor told me that every team does things differently, and it depends on what they are needing within their system.

When I met my buddy downstairs, we headed to get some food and coffee by the stadium. We reviewed everything again before parking and heading into the stadium. Just being there and having my name on the list, I felt like a kid opening presents on Christmas. We were all told to gather in the sections behind home plate while we awaited instructions.

When the scouts showed up, they briefed us on the plan for the day. That plan was to be fast yet efficient as possible and for two reasons: one being the heat and storms rolling through in the afternoon, two being that the grounds crew had to do their thing to prepare the field for their next game. We were then told to head down to the dugout to stage our gear and begin warming up.

Soon after, we began doing our timed sixty-yard sprints. After a short break, we broke into our positions to do our workouts. Next was the batting workouts. They definitely did things differently than during my tryout with the Dodgers, and here was why: we had different weather elements, the group was smaller, and this was by invite. This allowed for more time during our batting workouts. It was live pitching, too, which was better for timing than off of a machine. I had been working with a new coach in between my Dodgers tryout and this one. I noticed my hitting improved so much. I am not saying that my first hitting coach was wrong; this just allowed me to take two coaching ways and mesh them into something that worked for my stance and swing.

One of the scouts pulled me to the side after my first round at the plate. He told me that I was pulling the ball because my front shoulder was too tense and making me be out in front of the ball instead of where I would be when my hands and eyes made the contact. I took this advice back to the plate, and that little bit helped me out so much. He told me to work on it some more and give it another go at another time. This had me excited. In that moment, I showed them my hunger for knowledge and my willingness to be coached and mentored.

I went into the outfield and shagged fly balls like I was Kenny Lofton in a playoff game giving my all for the team. I knew that every move that we made while we were on and around the field was being watched and judged. I was sure that the scouts were watching our every bit of effort or lack thereof. I hustled and ran my ass off throughout the whole day. At the end of it all, I noticed the cameras were being set up by the dugout. I waited until we were done and officially dismissed by the scouts before allowing any distractions into the mix of things. I also wanted to give the media crews my full undivided attention, and I knew how things turned out in Phoenix during my Dodgers tryout with the media being a distraction.

We were done and back at the hotel by one p.m. I was exhausted from sprinting during my every move throughout that mid-June muggy morning. I went to shower, hydrate, and rest up for a bit. I was set to leave the next day at ten thirty-five a.m. and was bound to enjoy some more southern-style sweet tea and southern-style food. I went to eat dinner again and enjoyed another five or so sweet teas.

The next day, I was already working on a plan to work on my new advice. Taking this new advice to my hitting coach and implementing it would take some time, but it would be great for future reference, especially knowing how much of a difference it made within the next ten to fifteen pitches. I told my new hitting coach, and he got the batting tee out, and we began from square one again. We worked on everything from what hand did what and when. Then we went on to stance and the importance of many things. Once we combined those, we worked on the importance of keeping the front shoulder relaxed, the hands relaxed yet firm, and a flat bat to prevent wrapping around during the windup and thus dipping my back shoulder.

We worked on this many times per week. I implemented it in my many forms of live play. All this took time, and during that time, my timing was off, but I eventually had a system down. I just had to keep telling myself to be patient and trust in the advice and the coaching that I was blessed with. Patience is tough for some, especially those of us that demand perfection of ourselves. One of my coaches told me something that will stick in my head until I am long gone. He told me, "Doc, we play a game where we are viewed as legends when we get it right three out of ten times." I really thought about this, and it really sat heavily, but I wanted more than that. So I kept at it.

While training for baseball and sitting volleyball, I decided to step up my game and add another training aspect to things and began training for my first ever half marathon. I had decided that I wanted to venture out of the handcycle and run a half marathon. In summer 2014, I began training for the Detroit International Half Marathon, scheduled for October 19, 2014. Throughout all of my training, I was in such great shape that I figured, why not? Just add something else to my list of craziness. In the summer months, I was running up to eight miles per run around Lake Hodges in north San

Diego County. This was some great training. It was close to where I was living and some sandy trails. In all honesty, I had no real idea how to train for a half marathon, so I just ran up to eight miles and figured I would be good.

October rolled around, and I flew out to Detroit to meet up with the wonderful folks of Achilles. I was truly blessed and blown away by the incredible folks of General Motors and felt like I was a member of their family from the first moment. It was definitely a different feeling to be on the runners' side of the marathon weekend. I was actually more able to help those who were handcycling as opposed to me being focused on my handcycle and all the worries and planning that went into it.

The morning finally rolled around for my first half marathon. The temperature before the start of the race was thirty-seven degrees, and I was not dressed accordingly. Partially because I had been training in San Diego, which the same morning was a whole thirty-one degrees warmer than Detroit. The other part of being underdressed for thirty-seven degrees was having been "no-ballsed" to run the half marathon in silkies or, as it was known throughout some of the military, "Ranger Panties." When one was summonsed to a "no-balls," one must accept or be publicly shamed by said challenger.

I was wearing low-cut socks, thin running shoes (scarlet and grey in color), silkies, and a very thin breathable Achilles Freedom Team race jersey at the start. I wore this the whole 13.1 miles. One thing that I learned the hard way was to train for the terrain. I was running sandy trails for training, but the whole 13.1 miles was asphalt or cement. This was a shock to my joints and the rest of my body. Although the terrain issues occurred, Bruce and I still finished with a respectable 2:33:52.

After the extreme soreness from running my first ever half marathon wore off, I was back in the operating room for another orthopedic procedure. This one seemed simple in discussion but turned out to be a little more difficult. The surgeon had to remove some soft tissue and other things to access the screws that were placed years earlier during a calcaneal osteotomy. The recovery was relatively easy in comparison to other orthopedic surgeries that I have had. I think part of it was the fact that I received word from the Detroit Tigers. I was invited to the tryout they were hosting in Lakeland, Florida, their incredible spring training location.

I began working with a great organization to begin the logistics of getting out to the tryout while working on ramping up training again. When I got the date locked down, I began a plan of logistics and training. A great organization, Challenged Athletes Foundation, helped out with funding the airfare to and from the tryout with the Tigers. This helped out a ton and offset the costs that I was enduring due to all of the training, other logistics, and other finances I had to worry about.

On March 7, 2015, I was embarking on a journey to Lakeland, Florida, via Orlando. When I arrived at the Orlando International Airport, I went to gather my bat bag and the rental car. I stayed in Orlando that night and then ventured out to Lakeland to stay at a hotel nearby the Tigers' spring training facility. I headed over to the stadium on March 8th to catch their game against the Astros. Sitting on the first base side, I could see the first base coach and longtime great, Omar Vizquel. I was in awe and starstruck by him just as I was as a kid watching him play with the Cleveland Indians. It was truly an honor to be there at their stadium and to know I would be at their facility the next morning for a tryout.

After the game, I headed back in hopes of getting a few hours of sleep before waking and arriving early at the facility on March 9th. As anyone who has had any dreams, and a shot, at the pros knows, it is hard to sleep going into the tryouts. As you are all aware by this point, I went over every possible scenario and outcome. Finally, I drifted off to sleep and awoke hours before I was set to arrive at check-in. I did some static stretching and some foam rolling in my room. I was using some stretches that I learned while playing on the

A2 team for the Paralympic Volleyball Team.

The time finally came when I began my journey to the Detroit Tigers' spring training facility. When I arrived at the check-in table, it was a cool sixty-three degrees, overcast, and eighty-eight percent humidity. I thought, *I shouldn't even compare the weather to San Diego because it was virtually the same weather.* I was in the zone and ready to stretch and give it another shot.

We all lined up along the fence and were doing our own dynamic stretches and warmups. Soon after we began our individual warmups, we were huddled around the Tigers staff as they began going over the plan for the morning. They told us that the morning would be a quick one due to there being a home game at one p.m. and their need to use the facilities and the staff needing to get back to their respective duties. They then called out to see who had prior professional or minor league experience. They took their names and categorized them accordingly.

We then did some quick stretching and were broken up into our respective positions. At first base, we fielded our grounders and threw either first to home or first to third. The field was incredibly smooth, and the grounders seemed like they were just churned in butter, they were so smooth. It felt great to be back on a well-groomed professional-level field. I believe we got a total of five grounders. I can't remember if it was three throws to third base or just two. My throws were where the third baseman had his glove. When the other position players did their grounders and throws to first base, we rotated through our line and tried to help the other position players when their throws were off the mark.

We didn't have time to get through the good-sized group for the sixty-yard run. Once the fielding was done, we shagged the balls and helped the staff transition into the hitting portion of the tryout. We rotated in and out of the batting order by groups of five or so. I stayed at first base to get some extra grounders, line drives, and throws from others. While rotating at first base, one of the coaches pulled me to the side and asked if I was military or a veteran. I told him that I was a veteran. He said he noticed my leg even though I was wearing the high socks. I laughed and told him I tried to hide the fact that I was an amputee because I didn't want special attention or consideration. He shook my hand and with a tear in his eye thanked me for that. He appreciated that I was there trying on my own skills and not seeking a deal because of appearance.

I got back into the rotation and soon got my turn at the plate. I utilized what I been working on with my hitting coach. I felt like I did well but was still pulling the ball to right center and right field. Due to the time constraints, we were limited to our pitches, so there wasn't much time to impress the scouts.

When I was done hitting and getting my gear all situated in the third base dugout, a gentleman approached asking if he could do an interview. Apparently, he too noticed my leg and wanted to get a quick interview in. I gladly agreed, even though I was not there under those circumstances. I sang praises to the Tigers for having me and all the great folks out there living their dreams. I was truly another incredible experience as a twenty-nine-year-old still pursuing my dreams no matter what adversity came my way.

I didn't stick around for the one p.m. game because I had to leave out of Orlando bright and early the next morning for a six forty-five a.m. departure. I actually ended up sleeping longer than anticipated, but luckily, I returned the rental the night before and just took the hotel shuttle. I made the Orlando to San Francisco flight as they were doing the final boarding call. I don't think the folks in my row appreciated that, as I was on the window seat. I threw my bag under the seat in front of me, put on my headphones and my hoodie, and slept the flight. There was no reviewing the previous day as I saved that for the short hour-long flight from San Francisco to San Diego.

The next few months were super busy and emotional. I was invited to be the guest of honor and guest speaker at two Navy commands in the Pacific Northwest. This was truly an honor, and I accepted without hesitation. They asked how much I charged for my speaking and time. I said, "Just pay the flights and hotel stay. Save the rest of the money to make the Corpsman Ball even better. I am just honored to be there." This shocked them as they anticipated thousands of dollars to come out of my mouth, but in all honesty, I am still truly honored to have been a part of it.

That was scheduled for June, and so was a much-needed Hawaii trip. Events that fell around those times caused much hurt. On May 28th, I received a phone call that was one I never thought I would get. BamBam called, and as I looked at my phone, I knew it wasn't good news. His voice and what he said sent me into a mental spiral. Even as I sit here typing this, I have full body chills and tears in my eyes. He called to tell me that an incredible mutual friend had died. I thought this was impossible because of the pure beastly size of our friend and his larger-than-life persona. All that knew him thought of him as the one to outlive us all.

I got on my app and booked flights for the next day to New York City to be there with his amazing family and our friends. The morning of the 30th, while at my friend's house, I got word that Romeo wasn't eating his morning breakfast. I said he needed to go to the vet because something was wrong. Romeo would eat anything and anytime, so this was abnormal. Within hours, the news came of Romeo's passing. I didn't want to make a scene, so I walked outside and started hyperventilating. This was the only time I had ever done that. I immediately had visions of smashing my head against a big tree and started walking toward one to do so.

I was stopped by some folks, but this didn't stop the pain nor my will to leave this cruel world. *How could I go home to process the loss of an amazing friend to an empty pillow and no best friend to nearly tackle me when I walked through the door?* Romeo was a giant shithead, but he had that pure, unconditional love. He understood my every emotion, and looking at his blanket and pillow when I got home didn't make things any better. This literally tore me apart, and it still has me torn. For eight solid years, he impacted my life and helped me get through some rough times in my life. He understood me in such a way that he would lay his big furry body on mine until I would find a calm and tell him it was okay. He slept wrapped around my head and would wake me up out of nightmares by licking my forehead until I found that calm.

To go home and see his empty blanket and pillow seemed impossible to do. Luckily, there was this prescheduled Hawaii trip to offer a bit of a break. It didn't help that sort of processing, but it was a good distraction, though it just prolonged the inevitable. Being in Hawaii working out and enjoying the beauty that the main island offered was a great distraction, but my heart was still shattered knowing that I had to face life without my healing helper.

I had another way to help me stay distracted throughout my recent losses and one that was good for my mission. I was set to have another tryout with the White Sox on June 17, 2015. Soon after my tryout with the Detroit Tigers, I had a friend connect me with a great trainer in Carlsbad, California. When I first showed up for training, I was blown away by the owner (and main trainer), the other trainers, the facility, and the quality of athletes that trained there.

I had begun training under a former NFL wide receiver and with some incredible professional athletes. They welcomed me with open arms, and I just jumped into their training. In doing so, I got in such great shape and made great friends, but most importantly, I became so much faster and had so much more confidence. This would soon come into play during another hot and humid June tryout, so I hoped.

On June 15, 2015, I boarded a flight from San Diego to Chicago's O'Hare International then on to Birmingham, Alabama. When the aircraft was in the holding pattern to land, we kept circling around. The weather was fairly bad, and we were bouncing around a bit, but it was still manageable. We were then told that we might have to go to Milwaukee due to running low on fuel. We ended up landing in Chicago, but due to the weather being so bad, the smaller aircrafts were not allowed to take off or land. This was concerning for my schedule, because now I was to stay the night and possibly miss my tryout because I would then be placed on standby for the next day's flights.

All the hotels within a thirty-minute radius were completely booked up, so I paid for a ride share with a group of folks in the same situation, and we went forty-five minutes out of the city to then be up early in hopes of catching our respective flights. I was just glad I gave myself a day buffer on the front end of this trip. I did so having had such luck with the Chicago weather throughout many summers and winters before.

On June 16th, I arrived bright and early with my standby paper in hand. I ended up on the 12:22 p.m. flight departing Chicago and arriving into Birmingham at 2:08 p.m. While boarding the flight, I sent out some very important texts to let some folks know that I was on board and on my way. You may be thinking that I sound a little pompous or arrogant by sounding selfish about my flights or my important texts. I made mention of all of that due to the importance of my being in Birmingham because an ESPN crew was going to be recording this tryout and airing it on July 4th, and I had to be there on June 17th.

Sitting in my seat and flying down to Birmingham, I felt at peace knowing that one of the key issues of the episode was covered, me showing up. As I was on the plane with headphones blaring some heavy music, I was going over my training, including my new strength, speed, agility, and conditioning. It was go-time in my head. I just had to configure having the biggest of spotlights, ESPN, on me while trying to get into my "go-time" mindset. I knew I just had to trust my training, my coaches, my mentors, the White Sox folks, and the folks from ESPN.

The morning of June 17th came, and I was in my rental, pulling up to the beautiful home of the Birmingham Barons. I quickly met the director of the ESPN crew, who was such a great dude, and I am blessed to still know him and his crew. They put a microphone on me, and we did a couple shots before the whole sign-in and briefing. They said they would hang back and get footage that they would need without being a bother to my actual tryout or others giving their all in their pursuit of their dreams.

I feel like my second go around with the great White Sox organization was way better than the first. I was faster, stronger, and had way more agility and insight to the process. My training with my new conditioning coach was paying off. I felt like my legs were stronger, and I had more power from that when I was at the plate. I knew my speed and technique had improved tenfold as well. I was still hitting pull, but my goodness, I was making great contact. I felt like my new set of stretches helped my throwing and gave me more velocity.

By working with such great coaches, trainers, and mentors, I had built a level of confidence that I had yet to experience since my injuries. I have had many great friends and family that have been supportive of me throughout the whole process, but to put that support to work and see the results felt like a whole different level, and for it to be captured on camera amplified the lasting memories.

Soon after the tryout ended, I thanked the incredible folks with the White Sox for having me and especially for having ESPN to capture the motivation that we all hoped would inspire as many as possible throughout the lifespan of television and the Internet. I headed back to the hotel to shower and prepare for my adventure back to San Diego. When I arrived back at the room, the United Airlines call center called and advised me that I needed to stay in Birmingham for one more night due to the massive storm barreling throughout the Houston, Texas, area. They confirmed me on a flight for the next day. I was grateful for that heads up and the confirmed seat for the next day because I was set to fly up to Seattle, Washington.

I went out for some southern barbeque and some fine sweet tea that night and called it early. I was up bright and early to catch a 6:10 a.m. flight to Houston's George Bush Intercontinental Airport on my way back to San Diego. I arrived back into San Diego at 10:14 a.m. and went home to change out bags and head back to the airport for my Seattle, Washington, trip departing at 2:50 p.m. to go speak at two Naval commands in the Seattle and Bremerton areas. The rest of the travels were uneventful and fairly smooth.

Before arriving into Seattle, my first ever time into the wonderful Seattle-Tacoma area, I was nervous. I was a nervous wreck on the inside because I was about to speak at two Navy Corpsman Command's Birthday Balls. This was my first time to ever do so, and on such a sacred platform. Speaking at a Hospital Corpsman Birthday Ball is something I still hold close to my heart. I was a nervous wreck on the inside because I had been on the other side of the stage and had heard very lengthy Ivy League school classroom-type speeches. Most corpsmen are there to celebrate our beloved Hospital Corps' history, legacy, and future. We all wish for a guest speaker to keep it motivating and to the point.

I wrote no physical speeches for these events or since. I did make mental notes of key talking points when I briefly spoke to the Commanding Officer, Executive Officer, and Command Master Chief. Even when I was still on active duty and asked to be a guest of honor or guest speaker, I would talk to command leadership and ask about key things within the command that they would like to be addressed in a unique way. I then made my own mental speech accordingly.

Before I even spoke, I needed to explore the city of Seattle and do the typical touristy iconic Seattle culture stuff. This was an all-around exciting trip because it was a great reunion with some of my fellow corpsmen brothers, one from our training days together and one of my former junior corpsmen. Both are still doing great things to this day.

Once I gathered what I needed for a good mental speech, for two completely different commands, I made and performed my speeches. I must say that the one thing that made me feel more awkward than going up on stage with no speech written down was the fact that I had long, shoulder-length hair and was in a suit while everyone else was in their dress uniforms. The speeches were well received. I shook so many hands, hugged so many fellow corpsmen, took many pictures, and had many drinks. Just about everyone thanked me for keeping it short, sweet, to the point, and creating more time for celebrating and not mandatory fun.

On June 22, 2015, I arrived back into home base of San Diego to continue training and work on my plan of attack for my upcoming open tryout with the Milwaukee Brewers outside of Appleton, Wisconsin. With a date of July 19th in sight, I was able to ramp up a three-week training cycle. Although three weeks didn't seem like a long time to train for a big event like a tryout with a professional team, it sure was when you have a great set of trainers, coaches, and training buddies.

As per my personal travel plans, I gave myself a day buffer on the front end of my trip again, since traveling through Chicago's O'Hare during the middle of July could always be a bit of a gamble. My foreshadowing actually came to fruition, and I was stuck in Chicago for another night, hoping to get out the next day. I was able to and barely got a rental car due to my reservation being canceled. I was able to snag one of the last two cars in Appleton's airport rental fleet. There I was with my backpack and bat bag in the middle of a muggy mid-July Wisconsin summer day. Luckily, the air conditioner worked wonders in the little Chevy Sonic. I was more concerned that my bat bag may not fit in the tiny car. I was actually truly impressed with that car and its gas mileage. I think I drove a total of eighty miles and spent well under ten dollars to fill it back up at the nearest airport gas station.

I stayed at a hotel near the field that I was to report to the next morning. There were really great folks in the area who were homey and down to earth. I settled in and prepared for the next morning by static and dynamic stretching while mentally preparing. I also had to resist the easy fast food meal and go out of my way to keep my dieting and hydration levels. Especially with the humid heat.

I woke up early the next morning and began dynamic and static stretches while getting some coffee and a healthy light breakfast in me. I had to be as prepared as possible. I say that mainly because in July 2015, I was pushing thirty years old and knew I was old for professional baseball as it was at that point. I figured with those numbers already stacked against me in whatever algorithm scouts used, I didn't need them to see me slacking in any way possible that could have been prevented.

When I arrived, I parked and went to the bleachers for the briefing and signing of consent forms. This tryout was like that of many others: the sixty-yard dash, fielding, and hitting. The sprinting portion was definitely something my strength and conditioning coach had been working on. In the tall-ish dewy grass of right field, I ran an 8.037 second sixty-yard dash. This was not bad for a one-legged first baseman. I felt good about it and went on to the fielding portion. We first basemen did our part helping the other infielders before it was our turn to shine.

When it came our time to field and throw from first to second and then first to third, I felt really confident and was really impressed with the accuracy and pinpoint location of my throws. By this point, I felt really good about my tryout. We then shagged when we weren't due to be up for our batting portion. I did my part and hustled until being called up. When it came to hit, we were not offered any warm-ups and were given a certain amount of pitches. I noticed I was pulling my front shoulder and thus pulling the ball a bit. They asked me to hit opposite field, but I couldn't shake the pulling of my front shoulder. I knew then and there that I was docked points. I own that, as I could have been able to shake that off and hit opposite field.

When the tryout was over, we cleaned up the field and the dugouts and gathered our gear. I overheard someone being fired up and sounding upset about their judging scale. He said they knocked him down for his age, being over twenty-five years old, and some other things. I knew that wouldn't bode well for me being almost thirty. I found out that I was knocked points for my age, not hitting opposite field, and not throwing with more velocity. I didn't even see my final score; I knew it wouldn't be enough just because of age alone.

All of this information made me realize I needed to finish my degree and try to figure out something where me being an amputee and my age wouldn't be held against me. Although no team can outright say that being an amputee was held against me, I felt that it was due to "preexisting medical condition," and I completely understand any team wanting a roster full of fresh, young, healthy, and competitive talent. However, I was the one that just wanted a one-year contract at league minimum to prove the value of someone like me.

I would soon begin to realize it extended beyond any professional sports. As mind boggling as it may seem, I have always tried to see the bigger picture and find the reasoning and silver lining, all the while trying to pave a new path and help those who I know will need the mentorship and a somewhat beaten path. I soon realized that I needed to keep fighting the good fight for all persons with disabilities and veterans alike.

17.

DREAMS TO REALITY

After the rude awakening that the Milwaukee Brewers had dealt to my "aging" self, I had to dig deep inside and try to find another meaningful path for my soul to take. Although this was a major blow to my ego, hard work, and dreams, I knew this couldn't be the ending to the Doc Jacobs story. From June 2015 until the end of October 2015, I doubled down on my education to help pave the way for a smoother transition into a steady life. I finished my last class in October 2015 to finish up the requirements for an associate's degree in general education.

I know that an associate's degree in general education doesn't mean much, but it was a proud moment for me. It was a stab at those who told me I'd never amount to anything in life. This helped fuel my fire to keep pushing and to better myself in all walks. Granted, an associate's degree in general education is basic and not career specific. I figured with eight years of military experience plus an associate's degree, I could get in the door somewhere and prove myself from there. I wanted employers to see my work ethic and not my leg.

Around November 2015, I took and passed the written exam for a local police department. I was then advanced to the next level, the physical agility exam. This looked intimidating but wasn't going to knock me out of the game. I knew I was in great shape from all of my training, and I tackled the obstacle course. It was a pass/fail test, and I passed. The next portion was a pre-investigative questioner, or PIQ. The PIQ immediately followed the obstacle course. I passed and was assigned a backgrounds detective. I began working with this gentleman to cover all aspects of my background, covering a span of ten or more years.

While deciding to go down another path that really intrigued me and that I had a passion for, as well as knowing I could be of great help to the local community, I was still pursuing baseball. I just didn't want to give up on my dream. I had a friend that worked for a professional baseball team and spoke with their assistant general manager, or assistant GM, and got me in on an open tryout. This was what seemed to be a sure thing. I was even texting the assistant GM about the details. Throughout the whole texting chain, I was nothing but respectful and courteous.

I was also in talks with a great friend, the Ranger, who was trying to get me a job utilizing my combat trauma skills. During the timeframe from November 2015 to January 2016, I had three career paths in front of me, and I was training and pursuing all three with full intent in hopes of one working. By this time, I had been out for over three years and had experienced the difficult transition as a combat-wounded warrior. I felt great and special knowing that I had not one, not two, but three options in front of me.

The week of the professional baseball tryout, January 2016, the text messages suddenly stopped from the assistant GM. Was I seriously about to be ghosted by an assistant GM of a *professional* baseball team? I figured this couldn't happen. I kept up with an occasional text message, trying to figure out the location and time of the tryout.

Still no response. I eventually ended up calling to see if I could get a response, but even after leaving a voicemail, there was still nothing. I was really taken aback by the lack of professionalism from this assistant GM. At this point, I knew the tryout was set for January 25, 2016, and I had an offer to start a contracting gig on January 26th. After I reached a certain point of not dealing with this assistant GM's lack of professionalism, I called the CEO of the contracting company back and told him I was good to go to start January 26th. I had a flight within a matter of hours. On January 26, 2016, I set off to start working in the field that the military trained me to do.

My buddy apologized so many times for how the assistant GM treated me. I told him, just as many times, that it's not for him to apologize and I appreciated him, his effort, believing in me, and being a hell of a training partner. I told him that things worked themselves out, and I could never be mad or upset at him for him believing in me. I was just grateful to be with a company that saw me for my abilities and not any "disabilities." It was serious soul booster to have someone see me for what I had done and could do without getting tunnel vision on my leg and any sort of "liabilities."

When I did the official interview with the contracting company, I showed up with long hair and in cargo shorts. I did this because I didn't want to hide my leg from the company and wanted full disclosure. The vice president of the contracting company was a Marine from Vietnam. We instantly connected and got along very well. It turned out that he lived only five minutes from me, and the meeting was at a local coffee shop. After he heard where I served, what unit I served with, and what I did during the deployment, he was instantly on board with bringing me onto the team.

During my first trip overseas, I was working with my backgrounds detective. We emailed back and forth on a few things and tried to make deadlines. This proved difficult as he was partially retired and I was contracting throughout different spots around the world. I figured this wouldn't be a big barrier, and we kept working on my backgrounds stuff.

At some point during this mini-deployment, I found out that I was officially being nominated for at least a Bronze Star with "V" for Valor, regarding the work I did on the day that my unit and I were hit. I felt a great sigh of relief knowing that closure was in the future. This closure was also kind of a big middle finger to those in previous chains of command that refused to help me and threatened my benefits if I sought assistance outside the chain of command while also outright refusing to help me. It was also a great big middle finger to those who told me that if I didn't have any sort of award write up, then I shouldn't talk about it. That made me feel like I wasn't even worthy to share my story and that I was guilty of stolen valor, even though my Marines and I knew what happened. I had a devilish smile and tears in my eyes at the same time.

Meanwhile, I knew I needed to get my knee better, and in March 2016, I went under the knife for another knee scope to see what was going on. It turned out that I tore more cartilage from my left knee. This seemed like another blow to my health and spirit, but I knew this wouldn't stop me, and I had to keep the bad thoughts of self-doubt out of my head, even though I was told the cartilage loss was very significant. I trusted that the orthopedic surgeon cleaned up any frayed and/or loose cartilage. He did so, and this gave me some relief, but once the surgical pain wore off, I knew it was significant and needed further action. I kept at contracting and returned overseas, all the while continuing to train and run half marathons.

I know that running half marathons on an amputation sounds crazy enough, but adding full thickness cartilage loss to the same limb sounds even dumber. I knew this but couldn't fall victim to my injuries and allow myself to be out of shape, which in turn could cause more issues with arthritis, anyway. I saw the road with the lesser of evils and decided to keep beating myself up for the sake of the rest of my body, mind, and spirit.

During this month off from my mini-deployment, I took another course and began my pursuit of my bachelor's degree in criminal justice. I wouldn't be able to take any more classes until the fall/winter of 2016 due to the mini-deployments. September 2016 was the end of my 2016 mini-deployments. I knew I needed my knee fixed and had to get on the schedule for the work-ups and all the post-op and physical therapy appointments.

On October 16, 2016, Bruce and I ran our third consecutive Detroit International Half Marathon. This began our streak for consecutive Detroit International Half Marathons, and to this date, it still continues. We ran our third consecutive Detroit International Half Marathon with our Achilles International and Achilles Freedom Team family coupled with their lovely Detroit local sponsors. Throughout the run, and after, I was in a deep amount of pain. This was paired with pain in my right iliotibial band, or IT Band, from subconsciously compensating with my right side to ease the impact of the left side.

With each mile, I could see the light at the end of the tunnel. I knew that November 7th was my microfracture with PRP (Plasma Rich Platelet) injection surgery for my left knee. We finished the half marathon, and I flew back to San Diego to do workouts while building up to another major surgery, just continuing the rollercoaster of emotions in having to deal with more and more surgeries and more and more recoveries. The cycle seemed to be a merry-go-round in a horror movie. The ride just never seemed to stop.

I kept my mindset and kept seeking the positives in every situation. In October and November 2016, I was taking core classes for my criminal justice degree while assisting in research for the contracting company and dealing with my surgery and physical therapy.

While going through the surgery and rehabilitation, I was able to continue to do contracting but as an assistant researcher. The work was very intriguing, and I thoroughly enjoyed every minute of it. I would be on a treadmill doing my own rehab while reading a book or material for my research. When back in my hotel room, I was working on schoolwork.

When I was back in San Diego, I was working with some excellent physical therapists out of Carlsbad, California. In true Doc

Jacobs fashion, I was working on strengthening my left knee and bettering myself when all went to hell. I was doing a simple twelve-inch step up and felt, and heard, a loud pop in my right knee. It was instantly painful, and I had to stop my therapy session for the day. We immediately put ice on it and compressed it. I knew it wasn't anything too serious like my ACL or PCL, but it was deep in the lateral aspect of my knee joint. I knew it was a meniscal tear.

This was truly a true me moment, and I just laid there and laughed. It seemed like only I could be rehabbing a microfracture surgery and tear my meniscus on my opposing knee. I decided to do what most orthopedic surgeons would make me do before taking me back under the knife: more physical therapy and other conservative methods. I did the whole rest, ice, compress, and elevate (or RICE) method while doing easy physical therapy, stationary bike with stretching, massage therapy, and icing.

After weeks of conservative treatments, I knew it wasn't going to get better. I called my doctor and told him what happened, what I had been doing since, and my current situation. He tried to get as detailed imagery as he could for a knee without an MRI. We did x-rays, a CT scan, and an ultrasound. All of these images were not conclusive enough. I ended up scheduling my right knee to be scoped and cleaned out.

This put my Mount Kilimanjaro trip on hold for at least a year. How was I going to climb Mount Kilimanjaro with two freshly sliced-open knees? This bummed me out pretty hardcore, but I knew it was for the best and gave my word for the following year. In March 2017, I was under the knife again, this time for my right knee. It turned out that I had torn the lateral meniscus.

Having two seemingly bum knees and no real guidance on what to do or where to go, as there is no real protocol for such a life, I ended up stepping away from contracting to focus on my degree and start my own nonprofit, a vision I had since my first professional baseball tryout. This was a bit depressing, but I knew that I couldn't let it eat away at me. I kept pushing forward and trusting in the bigger picture.

During this time, I was receiving ongoing updates on my Silver Star nomination. These updates seemed to bring a great deal of happiness, as I knew closure was soon to happen. I just wanted my military chapter to be closed so I could move on to the bigger and brighter future. Granted, I am extremely grateful for the military and all that happened during my time in and as a result of. It felt like without closing the chapter that I had a file on my computer open and running that I couldn't close out and file away before putting the system to sleep.

On a whim, I applied for a ramp agent job with a domestic airline. To my surprise, I was hired for the position and began training with them. It was a physically demanding job, and I really wasn't fully ready for it yet, but I didn't know when I'd ever get into their system otherwise. I was really hoping to grind it out on the ramp and then become a supervisor or manager of some sort. My knee wasn't fully ready, and my third toe was getting absolutely destroyed. It was so bent that the tip of the toe rubbed the bottom of the shoe and the top of the curve rubbed the top of the shoe. This caused many blisters and bleeding. My knee constantly hurt, but I figured I would have to bite the bullet and do my time in the pit.

I started training with them in May 2017, and had a family event in early August, so I had to decide on being with family at the hospital or going into work. I decided to resign to avoid being fired. I figured that if I resigned on a good, and medical note, I could get my toe fixed and be rehired without many issues. I was so wrong. On September 11, 2017, I had my third toe amputated rather than having it straightened out and dealing with the possibility of losing it anyway while rehabbing it and dealing with intense pain. By chopping it off, I was up and walking, with significant pain, within a day but still way faster of a recovery.

That solved my toe problem, and my knees were better, so I reapplied for my job as a ramp agent again. I didn't even get a phone interview. This really hit me hard. I had two medical supporting documents proving why I had to step away, yet I was being treated like the plague. This was a very difficult pill to swallow because I had built a reputation with that station, and so many people kept saying to use them as references when I reapplied. I even had their veteran's department call and say I should reapply. Yet nothing.

This deflated me even more. Once again, I kept on pushing forward and believing that this couldn't be the end of the Doc Jacobs story. I doubled down on school and focused on my local police department application. While doing so, I began a very lengthy PTSD treatment called "Prolonged Exposure Therapy." This was on a voluntary basis, but I knew it would be tough. I volunteered to go through this treatment to help me process the day that I was hit and how it had impacted me since. The treatment was set for around twelve weeks at one day per week (outpatient), but with the holidays, this added a few sessions.

Just before starting these therapy sessions, I had a tentative academy start date of November 2017. Again, true to the Doc Jacobs tradition, there was another hold up, and it was postponed due to the psych exam. I didn't pass but didn't fail the exam and evaluation with the contracted doctor. I went into the exam in a suit and tie, like everyone else. Prior to taking the exam, we were told that the one-on-one interview could be in casual, relaxed, attire. When I completed the exam, I scheduled my one-on-one interview to review the results and to discuss anything else further.

I wore khaki shorts and a polo shirt. I did this so I wouldn't be withholding anything regarding my leg. I didn't want anyone along the way to be blindsided by the fact that I was an amputee. To this day, I have mixed reviews (in my head) on how that played out. I checked in for my appointment and waited to be called in to the tiny office in the bunch of small offices in the complex. When I was called in, I greeted him with a smile and a handshake. When I sat down, he noticed my leg and immediately had tunnel vision on it. The first thing he said was, "Hmmm, this is interesting!"

The next few things he said were, "You have sacrificed so much. Why would you want to be a patrol officer? You could do anything you want. Why be a beat cop? What is your big plan?" After trying to persuade me from being a patrol officer, he then said, "If you want, I could put you in contact with a buddy of mine with another department and you could do something else with them."

I was really taken aback by what had just happened. We barely discussed the results or any concerns he had about any sections. He said he'd send his recommendation to the department and I'd hear from them. It turned out that I needed a second opinion. I obliged and was willing to pay for the second opinion. Luckily, or so I thought, I didn't have to pay for another one, but I still had to do another exam and evaluation.

The time between waiting to see if I was required to pay for a second opinion or not was a fair amount of time, and I missed my proposed academy start time of November 2017. This pushed me back a few months, but I was training and ready for whenever I was given the green light for a start date.

As the holiday's time frame of 2017 came and went, I waited for word and kept training and going about my usually scheduled activities. In late February 2018, I began my trek to Arusha, Tanzania, in Africa for my attempt to climb Mount Kilimanjaro with some really incredible folks. Our team consisted of a variety of professional athletes, both active roster and retired, and veterans.

This trip was a real eye opener of the struggles of other cultures throughout the world. I had been in third world countries and had experienced their cultures. The whole way over, I kept envisioning those cheesy heartfelt late-night infomercials about the starving kids in Africa. When we arrived and ventured out the next day, we experienced the local culture around Arusha as we traveled to a distant village to check in on a self-sustaining clean water well that other teams had helped fund.

We were welcomed with a warriors' welcome, as the local village recognized us as "water warriors." We learned how just one self-sustaining clean water well impacted the village as a whole. The children didn't have to walk miles every morning to sift through a nearly dried-out creek bed with stagnant water before school. The one well helped ease their morning journey and allowed them more time in class for their daily studies, and all the while, their chore helped bring water to the village for daily consumption and for their crops.

The next day, we visited a school in Arusha that needed a self-sustaining clean water well. Those kids didn't have to venture far, but the water they were bringing to the school for daily consumption was muddy and infested water that came from upstream where there was so much trash, oil, and God knew what else. This was really saddening to experience, and I vowed to help out whenever I could and to whatever abilities I had.

A day or so later, we started our journey up Mount Kilimanjaro. It took a few days to reach Kibo Hut, which sits at about fifteen thousand five hundred feet. That day, I began to get a headache that made me feel like my temporal lobes were caving in. My O2 stats were not bad but not great. The main guide told me to stay focused on hydrating and slowly taking in foods like fruit and trail mix. I did so, but the higher we got in altitude, the more I hurt, and I began dragging my feet (well, foot). I had no idea that I was even doing that until one of the guides took my pack to ease my slow ascent.

When we leveled out at fifteen thousand five hundred feet, I felt absolutely horrible. One of the guys gave me a ginger candy to see if that'd help with the nausea, but it barely touched it. I was three liters of water in and was feeling like a semi truck used my head as a speed bump. When the head guide checked my pulse and O2 stats with the digital pulse oximeter, he looked at it and said, "The batteries must be dying because that can't be right." He left me sitting there and came back with new batteries to just see the same results. My O2 stats were bouncing between sixty-three and eighty-five percent. He told me that I could try to rest and risk ascending more but cautioned against it. I told him I would make the call as the time got closer.

The hours after were miserable. My head hurt so bad that I couldn't sleep or really rest. I kept having to get up and go throw up and just be completely sick. I knew I couldn't go higher and waste resources. I called it but agreed to stay at Kibo Hut and be miserable to make sure everyone else was okay. I laid there feeling horrible but wanted to be useful and awaited the team to summit and begin the decent down. I was ready to assist in any medical standpoint to ensure that everyone was as safe as possible. In doing so, one person did have to descend before summiting, but they seemed to improve as they were at the Kibo Hut level.

When the team summited and started their decent, I had a guide come grab my stuff, and we headed down to the next camp. Throughout the trip down, I felt like a bag of metal bearings was bouncing between my temples. I ate some mangos and drank around one and a half liters of water. After the mangos didn't settle well, I vomited just the mangos. My body was in crisis mode and absorbed the full liter and a half but rejected just the mangos. That was a real interesting feeling. Soon after being at vegetation level, I began to slowly feel better. The next day, we didn't even stop at the camp we were scheduled to stay at and hiked on out of the gate.

I was due to start the March 2018 Academy, but my encounter with my second opinion was not a great one, either. The second opinion that I was granted turned out to be with a doctor, and we knew mutual people and knew of programs that we both worked on or with. I felt like this was a conflict of interest and wasn't an unbiased opinion. The results were the same, and I was told that I needed to pay for a second opinion, but I could pick from the list of city-approved doctors.

The really messed-up part of this was I was never given the list of city-approved doctors to go to in order to pay to have a second opinion. The list was withheld for no real reason, at least that I knew of, until a later date. There I was, finishing my degree in criminal justice administration with eight years of honorable service and a name within the community that I would swear to protect and serve, willing to pay out of pocket to (once again) prove myself worthy, and I was being held up by one email or letter.

I followed up weekly and was told that I was nearing expirations on some of my tests. At that point, I knew what was going on. The list was going to be withheld from me so the problem fixed itself and I'd fall off the map and disappear. Sure as the sunrises in the east and sets in the west, that was what happened. I received an email stating that one of my tests had expired and I was no longer eligible. The email made it sound like they did me a favor, though, and I could reapply right away and not have to wait the standard length of time after being ineligible.

I later found out that one of the decisions behind withholding the list of city-approved doctors was because they felt that I had too much community involvement and wouldn't be fully dedicated to the department. Of course, that was a decision made without even asking me via text message, email, phone call, or even a professional in-person meeting. I had a good laugh, but the laugh was masking my severe disappointment in all of the false motivation and a complete disregard for the hard work and dedication that I brought to the table.

I passed every other test, met every deadline, worked hard to finish my degree by the time I would have been out of the academy, engaged in physical training, and had my overall focus on their department to later find out that I wouldn't be dedicated to the department. Meanwhile, I was led on and fed false motivation and couldn't get a phone call to discuss my dedication levels. I was really shocked but kind of expected it in the back of my brain.

This really was a sad thing to be dealing with as in the summer of 2018, I was literally finishing my degree requirements for a bachelor's degree in criminal justice administration. I kept thinking, *What can I do with this degree and no experience in the field? If I would have known this shit, I could have changed my degree course when I first applied and was only at my associate's degree.*

While dealing with finishing up my degree requirements and having no foreseeable future within my degree field, I did receive some very amazing news that I'd been waiting to hear for nearly thirteen years. This news definitely offset the horrible nonsense I was dealing with because of the actions, or lack thereof, of one or a few people.

18.

THE FINAL CHAPTER

As I sit here and type out "The Final Chapter," it comes with a variety of mixed emotions. Some may use the term "bittersweet." As for me, it is difficult to place one term on these emotions that I am feeling as I sit here in seat 4D on a 767-400 from Berlin to JFK on this July 24, 2019, afternoon.

August 21, 2018 was the day I found out that my backdated award had been approved and signed off by the Secretary of the Navy August 3, 2018. On that very mild summer day in August, I awoke to the news that I would be receiving a Bronze Star with Valor for my actions the day our convoy was hit.

The news hit me with a ton of emotions. I was happy, sad, frustrated, fatigued, but mostly covered with a sense of relief. All of these emotions hit me all at once and with the fury of a category five hurricane, all within reading through the email. The minutes seemed to go on and on as I read the good news, and then I opened and read the award citation. As I opened the attachment and prepared to read it, I felt like I was in the eye of the hurricane and had to brace for the rest of the storm.

As I read the citation, the minutes were filled with a horrific incident. It brought back the sights, sounds, smells, and feelings, all physical, emotional, mental, and spiritual. I ended up rereading it with tears in my eyes, my jaw clenched, and goose bumps covering me from head to toes (all two of them). I put my leg on and went downstairs to work on my ceremony invite list and to call my mentor to discuss our options for the ceremony location and dates.

I did my best to suppress the emotions around others and smiled through knowing that this would finally close out my military chapter and I could actually tell my story without being told that I couldn't have done such actions without an award. I was told by fellow service members that without an award, it didn't happen and that I shouldn't tell my story or it could be considered "Stolen Valor." For so long, I felt ashamed that I couldn't tell my story because I slipped through the cracks and didn't have a piece of paper to show my actions. For years, I doubted whether it happened or not because I didn't have an award for it. I felt as though I would live with the nightmares and night terrors, and I questioned its authenticity.

I damn near wanted to let the anger and frustration rise above my typical level-headed state and wanted to send a screenshot of the email to them and say some horrible things, but I decided that wouldn't be professional and I should let them see my smile with my award pinned on my chest and let that do the talking.

I soon began to feel sad because of so many reasons. One of the biggest was the resurfacing of these suppressed memories and emotions for me and the other families of the fallen and wounded and our brave Marines that were out there with us that late February morning. I pictured the emotions that would take place leading up to the award ceremony and even during. I really wanted to avoid those emotions and just have a quick hole-in-the-wall pinning ceremony but knew that wouldn't be right for my Marines and their loved ones for the healing process.

Another sad emotion that took over me was the fact that I know my career would have been so different if I would have had that award while I was still on active duty, but I was playing a game of "would-a, could-a, should-a." I knew it was a rabbit hole but decided to explore it, anyway.

I knew that my career would have been different in a sense that I would have that award and would have picked up rank faster. I feel like commands would have valued my abilities and utilized me more as a mentor, instructor, and even a poster child. I feel like there is a respect value within the military awards system. When wearing your medals or ribbons, you are assessed based on your stack before you are really sized up. Your medals or ribbons shows where you have been, when you were there, what you did, and sometimes even to what extreme. In a sense, I feel like I would have had more respect and a higher value (in a command's eyes) because of the award.

I knew I had to get out of that rabbit hole fast and ended up telling myself that I couldn't live in the past and to be extremely grateful for those who had worked so hard to help bring this award to fruition and to bring this closure to so many. I burrowed out of the rabbit hole and haven't really gone back, as it doesn't make any sense to.

Did I get frustrated about certain "leaders" in my previous commands that outright refused to help me when I asked them to help me, even after they told me that I couldn't go outside my current chain of command for help? Absolutely I did! Even after reading that email of August 21, 2018. I was frustrated because this closure could have happened up to a decade before August 2018. Granted, it was in 2008, that I received the Page 13, the Navy's formal written warning before a Non-Judicial Punishment (also known as an "NJP," or "Ninja Punched") for going outside the chain of command by contacting the admiral I had an open-door policy with about my return to the fleet. Certain "leaders" within the command held onto this Page 13 and abused the crap out of it. When I would ask for help on bringing closure with my award, they outright refused and then threatened me with NJP and to take away my VA benefits when I got out if I went outside the chain of command.

This further caused frustration for me. Especially when I went back to 1st Marine Division and one of the same "leaders" from a previous command was in the same battalion aid station with me. This same "leader" still had a copy of my Page 13 and, again, kept threatening me. I was frustrated because I felt like my career was, for a lack of better terms, cut short, and there was nothing I could say or do about it. I was frustrated because I fought so hard to return to full active duty and all my work was undermined by certain "leaders." I never knew exactly why they acted the way they did, and none of them ever had the balls to sit down over coffee or a beer and tell me.

I could have been a bitter asshole and done a variety of things. I could have gone off and tried to fight one of them. I could have filed formal complaints. I could have requested a captain's mast, a procedure where it could have been investigated. I could have turned to drugs or alcohol. I could have harmed myself or others. Instead, I used it as a learning tool and have, to this day, used it to be the best leader I can be. I used their failures to help me better my career and learned to be the leader that they weren't. I, in turn, have done everything in my power to help anyone around me that may need even the slightest bit of help. I constantly watch everyone around me, and when I notice them slipping in any way, I am always there with my hand out to offer to help them back up and any bit of advice to keep them from being knocked back down again.

After the many sets of emotions took me on an unimaginable rollercoaster, I began the excitement of planning out the ceremony. This was truly an exciting part. I say that because of this being a true celebration of nearly thirteen years of closure. This would be a ceremony that I would know was coming instead of being at a formation and being called up and surprised by loved ones and being pinned in front of a unit that wouldn't be that of my 3rd Battalion/7th Marines. Not to say that the moment wouldn't have been memorable with them, but it was definitely one I wanted with *my* Marines and fellow docs.

Knowing what I know about the military awards system, I know that the pending award can be approved for one different than the originating award nomination. Being submitted for a Silver Star (the nation's third highest award for valor) meant that it could be a number of awards. It could have been finalized as an award above (without further work and submission of more work, it would be unlikely), it could have been approved as a Silver Star, but more than likely it would be bumped down to a Bronze Star with "V" for Valor. I knew this and tried my best to plan a ceremony for a Silver Star but knew it would be safe to plan for a Bronze Star with Valor.

I had tremendous help with the ceremony and couldn't even begin to describe my gratefulness for them and their love, support, and work to make it all happen. The meetings and planning took the whole time the pending Silver Star nomination was in the system and then some. My incredible friend and mentor, Bob, took the reins and led the way with fighting for the award, guiding me, keeping my patience levels tolerable, and the ceremony. He is truly an incredible angel, and I am blessed beyond words.

We had our sights dead set on the USS *Midway* as the location of the ceremony. We scheduled a meeting with the Admiral of the USS *Midway* well over a year before the award was approved, and he was more than willing to have us. We just had to wait for the approval, and then we'd begin to set up the ceremony details.

While all of this planning was going on, I went over to the Naval Medical Center San Diego to let their public affairs know of the Silver Star nomination and that I would like to have them at the ceremony. Throughout the whole planning and waiting, I visited them three different times. I never once received contact from them regarding this. This really fired me up because it was reminiscent of a Navy group that failed to help me when I reached out to them and their broken promise to my dad when I left National Naval Medical Center Bethesda, that they would look after me even after my time in the Navy. That was, and still remains, a false motivation.

Soon after receiving the news, I reached out to my congressman's office to see if they found out the news yet. I sent them the news and began the scheduling process with them while Bob worked on the USS *Midway* angle. I wanted my Company Commander to pin me, and I began working with his schedule, all while trying to tie in everyone else on my list.

As fate would have it, the best timing for the majority was Veterans Day weekend of 2018. This would be an even more magical weekend for my ceremony due to the history behind that weekend. Not only was I one of the many in my big family to have served our great nation, but the Marine Corps Birthday is same weekend, and my foundation filed for our 501(c)3 status on the Marine Corps' Birthday just a year prior.

I knew this was a weekend many of my military and veteran friends would have off. I knew many folks would have it off and had to work with people's schedules and their financial abilities to make it to the ceremony. There were a lot of moving parts, but I knew it would work out for the best. One key thing that I wanted to do was create some sort of big entertainment for the mass of folks that would be in town for the ceremony.

Bob got the USS *Midway* locked on for November 9, 2018, on the flight deck. I began to reach out to the amazing folks with the San Diego Gulls, an AHL affiliate of the Anaheim Ducks, to get group tickets for a game that weekend. Again, as fate would have it, they had a game on the ninth of November, and they had a bunch of tickets in the same area. These eased my stresses a bit, knowing I could entertain a group for a few hours after my ceremony.

The time between receiving the email and the ceremony seemed to drag on. It felt this way because I knew I would be reliving those moments over and over again as I would be in front of cameras, being pinned, and as many random folks would ask me about the award. I absolutely dreaded the day but knew I needed to get it done and over with, even though there were many times I thought about calling the

Congressman's office and just setting up a quick little pinning ceremony in his office with no one else there. I really wanted that option.

I wanted the quick ceremony for my selfish emotional pride. I didn't want anyone to see the hurt or any other expressions in my heart, in my eyes, or on my face. I wanted to protect myself from expressing any emotions. Although this was what I was feeling deep inside, I kept making up excuses for certain people not being able to make it or I didn't want others to be sad knowing what hell my Marines and I went through and still go through. In a sense, I did want to keep those intimate details of our deployment within our circle. I thought my excuses were to protect everyone else, but I knew deep down I was being an emotional fool and didn't want others to see me in that light and, in turn, protect my emotions.

I ended up realizing that if I kept being an emotional fool, it wouldn't be fair to others who had been awaiting the closure from that day. I owed it to everyone else to stand tall, have tears in my eyes, and honor my fallen Marines. I owed it to my family that had been there for me since taking the ASVAB, shipping off to boot camp, graduating my training commands, shipping off to Ramadi, and especially being there from bedside in Bethesda to every other countless surgery throughout the San Diego region. I owed it to the fine folks of San Diego and all across our great nation to know the kind of troops and veterans within their communities.

The week of the ceremony, folks started to arrive, and I did my best to entertain and see everyone as they got there. I ended up feeling really stretched thin as the week went on and as that Friday approached. Things seemed really good, even though I felt like a madman driving all over San Diego County to entertain everyone and try to spend time with as many folks as possible before the madness of the ceremony kicked off.

The day of the ceremony came about, and I must have checked my uniform items a dozen times that morning and prepared just about everything else. I had the group tickets for the San Diego Gulls game,

I had my uniform ready to rock and roll, and I was heading down to the USS *Midway* to arrive early so I could personally greet everyone as they arrived and so I could introduce everyone to everyone they hadn't already met before.

As I was greeting and introducing everyone, one of the families of a fallen Marine from my incident arrived. I was so emotional seeing them and tried to hold it all together while I hugged them and introduced them to everyone else. We were then ushered up to the flight deck of the USS *Midway* to be seated and so I could handle some pre-ceremony media stuff. Soon after I was introduced to the recently arrived Congressman, we were ushered to our seats so we could begin. Being out of the military and having a congressman at the ceremony, this wasn't your typical military ceremony. This was one of a presentation and celebration opposed to being called up and being pinned as the citation was being read.

As I sat on stage in my Navy dress blues and the cool breeze off the San Diego Harbor made the flags dance behind me, I heard one of my 3/7 buddies, and best friend Mildred, yell at me to take my sunglasses off and be respectful. Instinctively, I snapped to and threw my shades off the stage at him with an immediate, "Aye, Gunny!" Even though we are best friends, I still immediately knew his rank and respected it.

Soon after the ceremony began, I was looking out at all of my family, friends, loved ones, my recruiter, the media, and various tourists on the USS *Midway* on that beautiful Friday November afternoon. I wanted to focus on what that breeze off the Harbor felt like, the sounds of the flags dancing behind me in the breeze, and everyone's faces as the words were being read of things that transpired since the day I was hit and how I had devoted my life since to honor those who hadn't been able to come home to their loved ones. I wanted to feel all of that beautiful San Diego weather and sounds before reliving those horrific moments again.

As the citation was about to be read, I stood up and went to the position of attention while the Bronze Star with Valor was being handed to my Company Commander. As the citation was being read, and I started to relive those memories, I tried to focus on the feel of the breeze on my back as I faced the city line aft of the USS *Midway*, to the east. The award was pinned on the left of my chest, under my previous award in ribbon form, and there were many tears in my eyes. Definitely the best moment with my daughter on my side as I we stood there being pinned.

Luckily, when I turned back to the forward aspect of the ship, the breeze dried out those tears fast. I was called to speak at the podium just before ending the ceremony and heading over to the Cheesecake Factory. As I began thanking everyone for being there and acknowledging their love and support, I got super emotional and thanked the family of my fallen buddy for their sacrifice and their love, all while ensuring that our love for his and their sacrifice would never end. Again, with tears in my eyes, I tried to change topics real quick and get to a more upbeat note.

The ceremony ended, and I was quickly ushered to the eagerly awaiting media. I was excited for this part so I could elaborate more on the award and how much it meant to me. I mainly wanted to share how much the award meant because it added to the notoriety of my platform for my foundation and how great of an impact that could have. I was excited to explain to the media and those watching about the importance of individual awards and achievements but to point out the true importance of teamwork as well.

I hung around and chatted with as many people as I could while taking pictures with my 3/7 Marines. I was, and am, truly grateful for those pictures. They speak volumes and will last a lifetime. Soon after getting some pictures on the flight deck of the ship, I was ushered to an eagerly waiting group of friends and loved ones at the Cheesecake Factory. When I walked in, one of my good friends, Shane, met me near the bar, and we did a shot of his choice and then had a beer to start. I did bring my drinking leg for others to chug a beer, or many, out of. I did not partake in the beer chugging but did enjoy a few drinks with everyone.

I did get fairly tipsy as I drank and socialized with everyone. We ended our Cheesecake Factory adventures and headed to our modes of transportation to take the evening to the San Diego Gulls game. As Bruce and I got to my car so I could change out of my uniform and into regular clothes, it was getting dark, and I was a bit tipsy. With it just being the two of us, I took off my Navy dress blues jumper top and threw it in the car, saying, "I'd rather have them here than this freaking stupid award!"

He said, "I know it, man. I know you have lived the past twelve-plus years in honor of them and we'd rather have them all here with us. The fact is we can't go back and change the past, but we can continue to live every day in honor of them."

I said, "I know, I know. I just hate all this attention on me over what happened that day. They are the true heroes and deserve everything."

We just left my drunk talk and sober thoughts at that and put on some music and headed to the game while I drank a liter of water to sober up a bit so we could go enjoy some hockey and the company of my family, friends, and loved ones. At the game, in the third period, I was honored with a plaque at the Mount Soledad Memorial. The coolness of the evening, the plaque, the great hockey, and the excellent company of my loved ones was truly the icing on the cake to complete a day of closure that I had been awaiting nearly thirteen years for.

Doc's Bronze Star with Valor Citation reads:

"For heroic achievement in connection with combat operations while serving as Corpsman with Company I, 3d Battalion, 7th Marines on 25 February 2006. While conducting a mobile screen mission in support of an Iraqi Army unit, Petty Officer Jacobs' vehicle was destroyed by an improvised

explosive device. Despite being severely wounded, he refused treatment while consistently encouraging all around him and assisting in the treatment of the other wounded. After being moved to the casualty collection point, he requested to be placed against a wall so he could continue assisting with the treatment of the wounded. Despite his grievous injuries, he remained calm and steadfast as he encouraged and verbally guided fellow corpsmen through procedures he could not perform himself. Realizing a wounded Marine required a second tourniquet to stop profuse bleeding, Petty Officer Jacobs self-amputated his mangled left index finger so he could retrieve and apply a tourniquet from his field kit. He then refused any morphine and redirected it for use on the other wounded Marines. By his outstanding professionalism, self-sacrifice, and complete dedication to duty Petty Office Jacobs reflected great credit upon himself and upheld the highest traditions of the United States Naval Service.

The Combat Distinguishing Device is Authorized."

Navy Boot Camp photo.
Taken August-September 2004.

Taken days before
deploying to Ramadi
Iraq. Taken at Aunt
Sheila and Uncle
Tim's house.

3/7 BAS, Camp Ramadi, Ramadi Iraq. 2005-2006.

A bullet meant for my head. Ramadi Iraq 2005-2006.

Taking a knee near Seven Story in Ramadi Iraq. 2005-2006.

Awaiting to head out on another combat patrol. Ramadi Iraq. Pictured: Allen McKerchie.

On patrol in Ramadi Iraq. 2005-2006.

Tim and I heading out for another combat patrol.
Camp Ramadi, Ramadi Iraq. 2005-2006.

Photo taken just before another combat patrol in Ramadi Iraq.
3/7 India Company, 3rd Platoon.

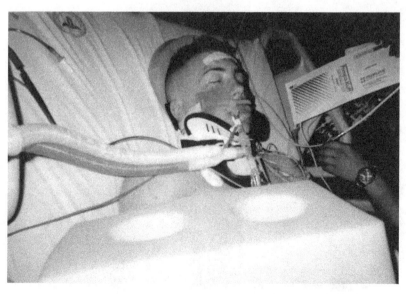

In my coma. Late February - early March 2006. At National Naval
Medical Center Bethesda's ICU. Photo Credit: Grover Jacobs.

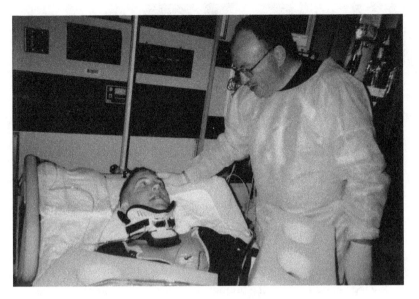

Dad and I in the ICU. National Naval Medical Center Bethesda.
Early 2006.

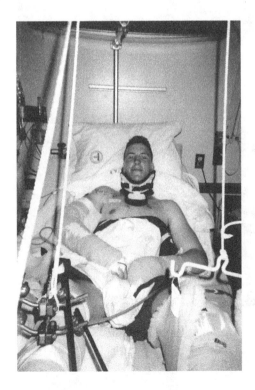

Taken early March 2006
in Bethesda MD, at
National Naval Medical
Center Bethesda. Photo
credit Grover Jacobs.

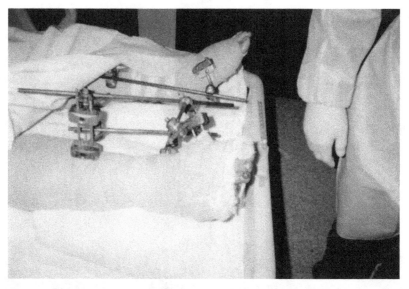

My legs early on. ICU at National Naval Medical Center Bethesda.

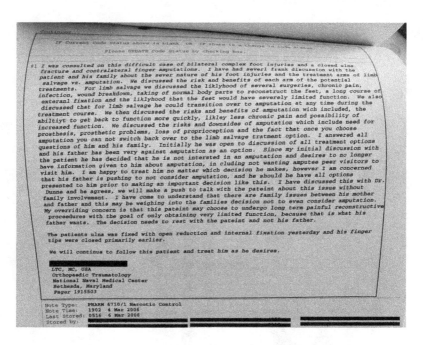

Initial conflict with limb salvage and being pushed for a decision.
Using my family against me and the overall decisions of my future.
March 4, 2006.

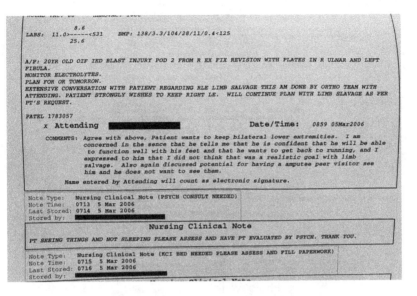

Being pushed for amputee peer visitors early on in my care.
Again, with the doubting my goals. March 5, 2006.

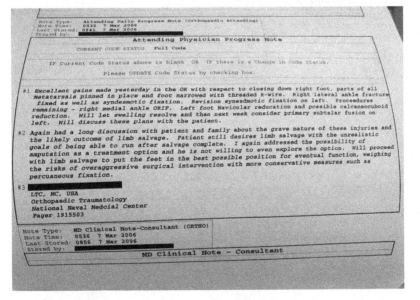

Note in my medical record from orthopedic surgeon pushing
amputation and verbally against limb salvage. March 7, 2006.

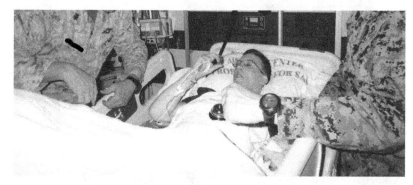

My Modified FMF Board, in the ICU. March 2006.
Photo credit Grover Jacobs.

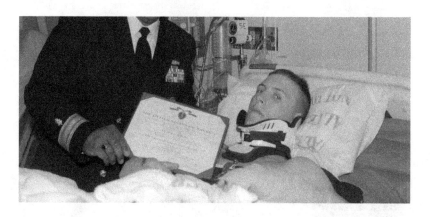

Receiving my Purple Heart. Five East, National Naval Medical Center
Bethesda. March 2006. Photo Credit Grover Jacobs.

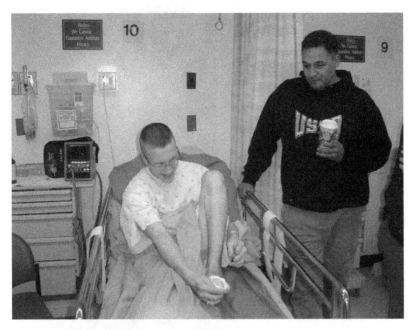

Mario Borrego with me in the surgery waiting area before being taken back to the operating room for amputation of my left leg.
October 20, 2006.

My first time standing after amputation. 3/7 Marine Corps Ball 2006.
Pictured is Allen McKerchie.

Second toe fixed,
on the second attempt.
Excellent surgical work.

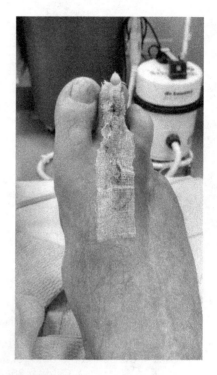

Back in uniform after
my IED injuries.
2007-2008.

Picture taken April 2008 after re-enlistment. At Naval Medical Center San Diego.

Romeo's sweet way of telling me he didn't want me to go to work.

Photo taken on Camp Pendleton December 2010. My Dad was out to pin me to Hospitalman Second Class, HM2.

Dad and I before he pinned me to Hospitalman Second Class, HM2. December 2010. Camp Pendleton CA.

Romeo laying on me after I came home from my first jaw surgery.

Yes	No	N/A	ITEM
			17. For service/family members with underlying medical conditions: (if not applicable, check block and skip to #18)
✓			a. Is there a requirement for special medical supplies, adaptive equipment, assistive technology devices, special accommodations, etc.?
	✓		b. If exposed to a physically or emotionally demanding environment, could the underlying condition become life threatening, pose a risk for dangerous or disruptive behavior, or result in a limited duty or MEDEVAC situation?
✓			c. Can the gaining MTF/operational platform provide the current required medical support?
✓			d. Can the gaining MTF/operational platform provide required medical support (diagnostic and therapeutic) if the underlying condition is exacerbated?
✓			e. Are there any chronic medical or mental health conditions requiring routine or continuing access to care or access to specialized medical care? (document on DD 2807-1)
			f. If required, were potential environmental concerns and possible health effects communicated to each service and family member? (document on appropriate SF 600)
✓			18. For infants and toddlers (birth through 2 years, inclusive) with a disability, is the child receiving or eligible to receive early intervention services as evidenced by an Individualized Family Service Plan (IFSP)?
			19. For preschool and school children (ages 3 through 21, inclusive) with a disability, is the child receiving or eligible to receive special education and related services as evidenced by an Individualized Education Program (IEP) and DD 2792, Addendum B?
			20. Specify other concerns:

IF ANY OF THE ABOVE SHADED BLOCKS ARE CHECKED, QUERY THE GAINING MEDICAL TREATMENT FACILITY OR MEDICAL DEPARTMENT SUPPORTING THE OVERSEAS, REMOTE DUTY OR OPERATIONAL LOCATION CONCERNING LOCAL CAPABILITIES TO PROVIDE REQUIRED SUPPORT. (Attach Reply)

| Yes | No | IS THE SERVICE/FAMILY MEMBER SUITABLE FOR THE OVERSEAS, REMOTE DUTY OR OPERATIONAL ASSIGNMENT? (completed by an MTF medical screener only) |

MTF Medical Screener (Signature)   4/26/11 - see below   Date   Civilian Medical Screener (Signature)   4/15/11   Date

KAREN KLIPPERMAN, MSN, FNP-C

Printed Name, Rank or Grade	Printed Name
	92 ADMC
MTF or Duty Station	Address
	Camp Pendleton, Ca. 92055
Telephone Number (include area/country code)	City, State and ZIP Code
	760-725-7268
DSN Number	Telephone Number (include area/country code)
Telefax Number (include area/country code)	Telefax Number (include area/country code)
E-mail Address	E-mail Address

NAVMED 1300/1 (Rev. 9-2010), Part 1 - Back

*Note pt. is not medically qualified to be assigned to infantry duty due to his physical impairment 4/26/11

The form from my medical screening when I got orders to 1st Marine Division in May 2011. The doctor's changed answer, after being bullied.

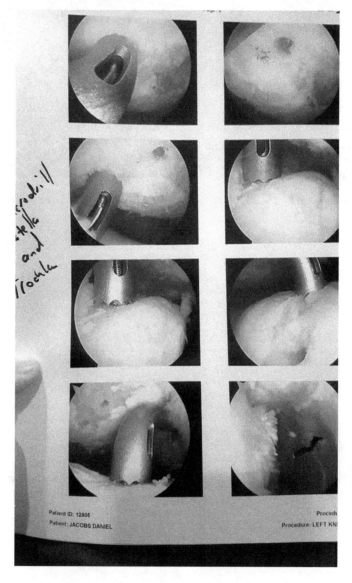

Photos of getting microfracture to my left knee
(amputated side).

Putting in the work.

Getting some training in.

Incredible support after my Dodgers' tryout. February-March 2013.

GOO DODGER BLU!!!!
Unlike · 2 · More · Mar 3, 2013

Danny I am so proud of you for not giving up on your dreams.. You have always wanted to play baseball since you were little... I pray that you make it, but if you dont, you did not give up.. I love you.... I am proud to call you my nephew!!!!
Like · 1 · More · Mar 3, 2013

Go get em!!!!!!!
Like · More · Mar 4, 2013

I love this!
Like · More · Mar 4, 2013

Wow, that will be great to have a 2nd chance in life.
Like · More · Mar 4, 2013

nice form
Like · More · Mar 4, 2013

That is awesome
Like · More · Mar 4, 2013

I hope you get the place you want on the team,[good luck] and thank you for your service.
Like · More · Mar 4, 2013

Snapped prosthetic at Angels Stadium during a baseball game I was playing in. My one and only snapped leg in fourteen years.

The day that I became a dad. The greatest thing ever. August 2013.

Being a dad is the best part of my life. Love snuggle time.

My daughter and I after receiving Doc Jacobs Day (November 17th) by San Diego City Counsel.

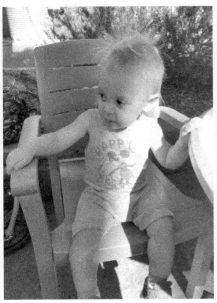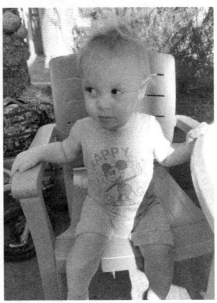

Adam looking at a squirrel. I love every moment with Adam and Aubrielle.

More random smiles from Adam.

White Sox Tryouts ★

Me
1/13/2014, 12:29 PM

Mr. Jacobs,

Thank you for your interest in the Chicago White Sox. Our current plan is to hold our 2014 minor-league tryouts during the summer at our Double-A affiliate in Birmingham, Alabama. Exact details for that tryout aren't yet available, so please contact us closer to that date to confirm the specifics.

All the best,

Coordinator of Baseball Information

Chicago White Sox

Initial response for my invite to my first Chicago White Sox tryout. 2014.

My second invite to tryout with the Chicago White Sox.

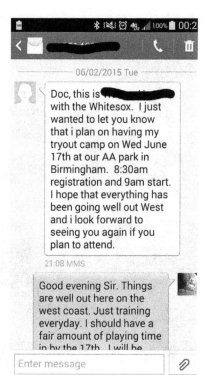

06/02/2015 Tue

Doc, this is _____ with the Whitesox. I just wanted to let you know that i plan on having my tryout camp on Wed June 17th at our AA park in Birmingham. 8:30am registration and 9am start. I hope that everything has been going well out West and i look forward to seeing you again if you plan to attend.

21:08 MMS

Good evening Sir. Things are well out here on the west coast. Just training everyday. I should have a fair amount of playing time in by the 17th. I will be

Enter message

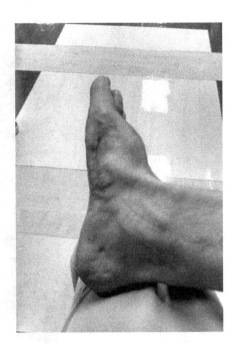

My foot after hitting a fastball off of it. Looks like a baseball in my foot.

My last ever picture with Romeo. Taken just before leaving for one of my best friend's funeral. May 2015.

The highest I climbed on my first attempt to climb Mt. Kilimanjaro. Take in February-March 2018. Trip was with Waterboys.

Completion of the San Diego Half Marathon June 2019. Broke the Three hour mark again.

Being honored for Navy Appreciate day at Petco Park.
May-June 2019. San Diego, California.

Aubrielle and I enjoying an evening of hockey in San Diego.

Hockey time with Aubrielle. I love our hockey time together.
We love our San Diego Gulls.

All smiles from Adam and I.

Funny face from Adam.

My 2nd time up Kilimanjaro with Waterboys. February 2020.

My 2nd time up Kilimanjaro with Waterboys. February 2020.

At the summit of Mt. Kilimanjaro. Love the San Diego Gulls and had to represent. February 29, 2020.

Finally got my certificate for summiting Mt. Kilimanjaro with Waterboys. February 29, 2020.

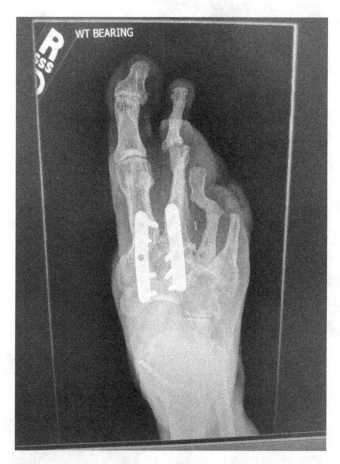

My most recent x-ray. Over 30 surgeries on my foot. I have ran 8 half marathons on this foot, after being told that my goal of running again was "unrealistic".

ACKNOWLEDGEMENTS

There are many folks that I would like to acknowledge and the ones I may miss, I love and appreciate you all just as much. A very special thank you to: G-Ma, Dad, Bob, Mom, Brother, Sister, Chaz, Rachelle, Nina, Romeo, Juliet, Mildred, Kerch, Jamie, BamBam, Huff, Tino, RyRy, LT. I, Major Hickman, Bruce, Aunt Sheila, Uncle Tim, Uncle Mike, Aunt Charity, Papa, Grandpa Mick, Ron, Mario, JB, The Thompson family, Kevin, Dr. Girard, Dr. Gould, Dr. Hanling, Dr. Sigmon, Baskee, Fig, Stark, and all of my fellow Doc friends. Special thanks are in order to many organizations that have helped me throughout my fourteen years of being a combat wounded veteran. Thank you to: Doc Jacobs Foundation, Gary Sinise Foundation, Achilles International and Achilles Freedom Team, Semper Fi Fund and America's Fund, Waterboys, MVP, History Flight, Los Angeles Dodgers, Chicago White Sox, Detroit Tigers, Milwaukee Brewers, San Diego Gulls, Upper Deck, General Motors, Cigna, Navy Medicine, Navy Orthopedic Surgery, US Navy and US Marine Corps.

ABOUT THE AUTHOR

After Doc was pinned his Bronze Star with Valor on Veteran's Day weekend in 2018, he has gone on to accomplish even more and literally reached new heights. Doc and his foundation, the Doc Jacobs Foundation, has been around for three years and will continue to make an impact fueling the dreams of the youth of our nation's heroes. Doc has completed three more half marathons, all in 2019. Those being a half marathon in Orlando, San Diego and Detroit. Putting a total of eight half marathons completed on one leg and a prosthetic. Soon after Doc's completion of his eighth half marathon, he altruistically donated his left kidney to a stranger in hopes to save a life, or many lives, while advocating for living and deceased donor programs. Not even three months after donating his left kidney, Doc summited Mount Kilimanjaro with Chris Long's Waterboys group. Upon his arrival back into the states, Doc underwent his eightieth combat related surgery. Doc has been busy typing away at another book, a fictional piece called MaCoven, that he hopes to have ready and available soon after There and Back Again: Stories from a Combat Navy Corpsman is published. Doc is authoring another amputee's story and has concepts for two more books beyond that. Stay tuned as Doc has so much more life to live and share with you all. I am honestly so grateful for your love and support.

CPSIA information can be obtained
at www.ICGtesting.com
Printed in the USA
LVHW040054131120
671604LV00006B/128